VARIETIES of SOUTHERN RELIGIOUS EXPERIENCE

VARIETIES of SOUTHERN RELIGIOUS EXPERIENCE

Edited by
Samuel S. Hill

LOUISIANA STATE UNIVERSITY PRESS
Baton Rouge and London

Copyright © 1988 by Louisiana State University Press
All rights reserved
Manufactured in the United States of America

Designer: Sylvia Loftin
Typeface: ITC Garamond Book
Typesetter: G & S Typesetters, Inc.
Printer: Thomson-Shore, Inc.
Binder: John H. Dekker & Sons, Inc.

10   9   8   7   6   5   4   3   2   1

Library of Congress Cataloging-in-Publication Data

Varieties of Southern religious experience.
  Bibliography: p.
  Includes index.
    1. Southern States—Religion—Congresses.   2. Southern
States—Church history—Congresses.   I. Hill, Samuel S.
BR535.V37   1987   277.5   87-3327
ISBN 0-8071-1372-7

CONTENTS

Contents

PREFACE AND ACKNOWLEDGMENTS

It is a mark of an academic field's fertility that conferences and symposia are arranged around it. Dormant for a long season, the field of southern religion has lately germinated a number of such occasions involving both scholars and the lay public. Among the sponsors of those occasions have been Auburn University, the University of Alabama at Birmingham, and the University of Mississippi.

The essays in this volume were presented originally at Florida State University in Tallahassee in April, 1981. The authors gratefully acknowledge the assistance of that university and its Center for the Study of Southern Culture and Religion. We also appreciate the support of the National Endowment for the Humanities, which largely funded the conference.

Some of the material presented in this book has appeared in other publications, and we are grateful for permission to reproduce it. Clarence C. Goen's essay is part of his book-length study *Broken Churches, Broken Nation,* published by Mercer University Press in 1985. Richard L. Rubenstein's essay first appeared in the Fall, 1981, issue of the *Michigan Quarterly Review.*

Other scholars contributed to the sessions in Tallahassee. Among them were Gwen Kennedy Neville of Southwestern University, Donald G. Mathews of the University of North Carolina at Chapel Hill, and E. Brooks Holifield of Emory University. Several professors from the two local universities, Florida State and Florida A and M, also helped make the conference a success.

Much credit is due Karen L. Bickley, conference coordinator, and Richard L. Rubenstein, director of the Center for the Study of Southern Culture and Religion. The longest term of service was provided by Katherine L. Dvorak of the Department of Religion at Franklin and Marshall College. In her untiring work on these essays, she raised significant questions and made many worthwhile suggestions. Her large role in the transmission of the material from papers given orally to essays suitable for publication places all of the authors in great debt to her.

As editor I note that some time has elapsed between the conference and the appearance of these essays in print. But I am convinced the wait was worth it, and I thank my fellow contributors for their patience and, even more, for the excellence of their work.

Varieties of Southern Religious Experience

INTRODUCTION: THE STUDY OF SOUTHERN RELIGION COMES OF AGE
Samuel S. Hill

The study of the religious dimension in southern society and culture has come an impressive distance in the past twenty years. Once largely unattended except in denominational histories, the subject is now a major area for research and analysis. Today historians, sociologists, anthropologists, folklorists, theologians, and specialists in religious studies devote major portions of their professional efforts to the study of religion in the South.

As gratifying as the achievement itself is the motivation behind it. Today the South's religion is no longer viewed as a curiosity, as something quaint and charming that once held power over premodern peoples only to slip into obsolescence. Instead it is seen as a vital force in southerners' lives and culture—sometimes for ill or with mixed results, to be sure, but also often for good, and always as an essential ingredient. The main point is that it is there as an element that the people have taken very seriously. Observers of those people, in treating all periods from colonial times to the present, can do no less than acknowledge the reality of religion and its formative influence.

At least three major factors have contributed to the dramatic increase in the number, scope, and quality of studies done on southern religion over the past two decades. The first is the visibility of religion and the plausibility of approaching it as a force in culture, a relatively recent condition that has resulted partly from the emergence of religious studies as a serious and maturing academic field. Scholars working from "secular"—actually comparative or phenomenological—perspectives are now quite open to treatment of the religious dimension of people's lives, both personally and collectively.

Second, religion—its claims and its practice—is now acknowledged to be bound up with other basic dimensions of living. In order to know southerners, their family life, personal responses to human existence, convictions, values, attitudes, tastes, and styles, as well as their public structures such as their politics and economics, we need to investigate the ways in which they interact. Religion is one of

1

those ways; more accurately, it is a dynamic force existing as part of a whole, with no forces isolable from the others. It is a language, an idiom, a form of popular discourse that has had nearly universal utility in many cultures, emphatically including the American South. The argument against studying religion as a factor in culture used to pivot about the issue of whether religion is an independent variable or merely a function of something else more "real," more basic. The new idea that has challenged that older formulation is that religion is an integral factor in a complex whole in somewhat the same way that politics or family patterns are. In summary, the religious dimension in the lives of both persons and societies is treated with more respect today than in the past. It has come to be regarded as integral in the complex of dimensions in which each particular dimension must be seen in relation to all the others.

A third cause for the emergence of southern religion as a field of inquiry has to do with the new status of the South. Today the region is rarely treated as something alien and inferior. A vital and progressive part of the larger national society, it attracts in-migration and business investments from capitalists and commercial centers elsewhere. Still known to have a distinctive tradition and personality, it is an entity to be taken seriously for exactly that reason. And what is true of outsiders' views of the South has its counterpart among southerners themselves. They take pride in their regional homeland, though far less ethnocentrically than they used to. These attitudes are reinforced by the visibility of the southern style of evangelical Christianity, which now finds expression in other sections of the country. Being a southerner is no longer a liability, and its religion is no longer seen as the charming eccentricity or the grotesque aberration it was earlier taken to be. Sophisticates, secularists, and "modern" people of one kind or another may be puzzled by southern ways and by the intensity of evangelicalism, but those features of regional culture have come to be taken for granted—indeed treated with respect—as a prominent part of American life.

The lingering but revised fascination with the southern region is evident in these essays. All of them make the case for regional studies, specifically for examining the religious history and patterns of the South and religion's role as a language or an idiom in common currency. The mode chosen is usually that of incarnating the plausibility or illustrating the necessity by actually doing it. The peculiarity of the South during the first 175 years of the American republic invites and warrants research into its history. But since the distinctiveness of southern culture has diminished over the past 30 years and the South as a region has become incorporated into the national culture, the question emerges of why there is a continuing commitment to southern regional studies, especially those of the contemporary or recent era. Merely acknowledging the query creates more incentive for coming to terms with the religious heritage and patterns of the South.

Perhaps many of us are informed by a quiet, persistent, partly unrecognized curiosity over the South's continuing religiosity. The persistence of religious dedication in the region is striking. The hold of an "outmoded" world view on an increasingly "modernized" culture is noteworthy. The imperviousness of the South to the erosion of traditional orthodox religion is apparent and does not seem so bad. This fact is made the more powerful by the very incorporation of southern into wider American, and universal, culture. In the same era when the South is shaking off its provincialism, its religion flourishes—and its general style of intense faith grounded on certain authority is enjoying a renewed and enlarged acceptance in the rest of the nation.

These developments are stunning in themselves. But they take on added significance when contrasted with the conventional wisdom on what happens to traditional religion once the modernization process breaks upon a culture. The South, so such cultural analysis runs, might be expected to abandon its evangelical faith. Secularization should be coming into a prominence that is phasing into dominance. To be sure, secularization has grown in the recent South. Yet, it has scarcely made a dent in the fabled religiosity of the southern people—though it has perhaps made more of a dent in the black community than in the white.

Some of the contributors to this volume (not least its editor) were forecasting the decline of religion as the onslaught of fundamental social change took its toll during the 1960s.[1] Some of the literature on religion in the South during those tumultuous years called for change, aiming to be prophetic. Its message was that the South had best mend its ways—set out in new directions—or else lose out and become a throwback to an irrecoverable and not very healthy past. Although that general line of thought could still do with some elaboration, it is far from unexceptionable. More important, health and new possibility were present in the allegedly diseased religion of older southern forms to degrees that were not acknowledged because they were not foreseen. At any rate, the scholarship reflected in these essays, and throughout a much expanded field of research, does not aim to be normative. They investigate, describe, and interpret after the academic manner. They do not pronounce negative judgments on some religious forms while extolling the virtues of others.

The numerous books and articles produced over the past dozen years have been far less involved with prophetic or critical concerns than in the preceding years. An underlying incentive may be the fact that the sharp change that was predicted did not occur, is not likely to occur, and probably should not. It is just possible, though, that the 1960s and the prophetic perspective of those years served to help call attention to and generate the more conventionally academic work undertaken since.

But the impression must be avoided that "conventional" work has been mindlessly that. Far from it. It has been taking into rigorous account the history and social roles of blacks, plain folk, intellectuals, Roman Catholics, Jews, women, Fundamentalists; in other words, the "high" and "low," the real and complex diversity of southern society, are being acknowledged. Rosemary Magee's bibliographical essay of 1980 highlights the increasing methodological sophistication and widening scope that have characterized analyses of religion in southern culture from 1964 forward.[2]

Another trend that has had an impact on the study of religion in the South is the emergence of social history. Whether its methodology has been traditional and straightforward or innovative and highly self-conscious, social history has altered the field. Earlier work tended toward institutional religious history—histories of churches or denominations at the state or local level. Only rarely did scholars treat the theological beliefs and practices of the group under examination. These scholars typically showed little awareness of the interaction of religion with the political, economic, and social aspects of the culture. But in recent years a whole school of social historians has begun to do high-level, important work. Among them are Rhys

Isaac, Donald Mathews, Anne Loveland, Scott Strickland, and Robert Calhoon. They have focused upon religion not because they are "church historians" but because they find religion a vital, integral element in southern society. These scholars do not take a condescending attitude toward the church, church historians, or religious beliefs. Neither do they show any disposition to treat religion as merely a factor, much less a dependent variable. They write about religion because they are studying the South, and in that culture religion has been basic to popular discourse. The only "language" or idiom that included everyone was the religious.

To date most of the attention of this new social history has focused on the late colonial and antebellum periods (though the coverage is in the process of expanding). But its accomplishments are signal and promise to apply to later periods as well. With reference to the antebellum South, the basic question dealt with by this school of social historians is, What was the social significance of evangelical Christianity? Their work has suggested several answers: It produced "marks of civility" and gave structure, form, and coherence to people's lives. It helped provide the social organization of the Old South. Calhoon has said that religion contributed to the "moral economy" of that society. Other studies have said that it helped lead to the decentralization of the society and that it defined personal slothfulness as an enemy, for fear of disorder. Loveland has maintained that religious leaders saw themselves as "guardians of the religious and moral purity of the southern people." These assessments may be summarized this way: in the South religion has made for good people and a good society—both. Challenging most older interpretations of the role of religion for pre–Civil War southerners, which took the position that it wielded muscular personal effect but had anemic social impact, the new social historians have found the place of religion to be basic, influential to the point of being formative, and inextricably bound up with the other fundamental elements in the life of the people.[3]

Analysis from another angle, the theological, has recently come to be viewed as an essential undertaking. For a long time, anyone interested in studying the history of religious thought in America would hardly have been attracted to the southern church scene. It is true that the South has contributed theology and theologians in smaller quantity and of lesser substance than the colonial New England tradition, the New Divinity School, the social gospel tradition, twentieth-century neoorthodoxy, or even northern evangelical thought.

But three firm points about the South's theology must be made. The first is that there has been some tradition of sophisticated theologizing going on in the South. Brooks Holifield's *The Gentlemen Theologians* reveals that a network of well-educated, highly reflective pastor-theologians served southern cities and towns in the antebellum period. The fruits of their intellectual labors were impressive even if their creative achievements were not dominant or long-lived in regional religiosity.[4] After the Civil War there was less theologizing, but some notable work has been done all along, through teaching in Presbyterian, Methodist, and Baptist seminaries and through some publications. Today some of the best American seminaries are to be found in the South, and scholarship, in biblical studies especially, is outstanding.

The second and most telling point about theology in the South is the high level of its social significance. When judged by the standards of classical theological activity, the South's accomplishments are not very impressive, admittedly. Hardly any constructive theology produced by southern thinkers has been exported; even less has made its way into any nonsouthern mainstream, though the work of William Porcher DuBose of Sewanee in incarnational theology did enjoy fairly widespread reference. In evangelical circles Baptist E. Y. Mullins' experiential theology has been read beyond southern confines. (DuBose died in 1918, and Mullins in 1928.) And of course the theological ethics of Martin Luther King, Jr., is known throughout Christendom.

In recent decades, apart from King's work, the social significance of southern theology outside the region has been negligible. But inside the South it has been enormous—and that is enough to command attention to it. To any who would say that southern theology is not interesting, that it is not "going anywhere," that it is not part of an accruing tradition, one can only reply by asking what the criteria are for reaching such conclusions. Its vast importance is suggested by the recognition that it has shaped and continues to shape, in considerable measure, a whole culture. It has gone far toward engendering the outlook of southern people with notions of what is true, good, valuable, and responsible; with a basic world view and ideas of hu-

man destiny; and with a sense of the high road in family life, inter-
personal relationships, and personal integrity. That is hardly to be
taken lightly, notwithstanding the facts that its capacity for breaking
new ground has been limited and that its propensity for perversity
led to decades of support for slavery and segregation.

It is also important to remember that the major fronts of southern
church activity have not been formulative or theological; rather, they
have been practical, most notably the conversion of the lost and the
building of the institutional church. Yet, as Ernest Sandeen and George
Marsden have established, conservative Protestantism may well live
by a rather fully developed and elaborated theology. Their work has
introduced us to Fundamentalism, which is by nature rationalistic
and heavily doctrinal, and is admittedly quite different from the
South's evangelicalism, which has a greater concern with experience
than with systematic thought. Nevertheless, students of religious
movements need to recognize that the "simple, plain-folk" traditions,
southern evangelicalism included, live by systems of thought, too.[5]

Brief mention will have to suffice for the third point about southern theology. It is that a stronger and more pervasive strain of rationalism may exist in the South than has been usually recognized. So
argues David Edwin Harrell, Jr., against the mainstream scholarship
typified by Donald Mathews, John B. Boles, myself, and many others.
We must wait to hear Harrell's claims, and when we do, we must dis-
criminate between southern rationalism and northern expressions in
the same tradition. But the region's popular rationalism has been
neglected and may be demonstrable as a substantial and even sophisticated stream in southern religious life. It has certainly had currency
in the sizable Churches of Christ movement, in which discrete scriptural texts are accorded definitive status, though without being
blended and developed into any kind of philosophic whole. Another
form has been a Fundamentalism more noted for its elevation of certain concerns, biblical authority and inerrancy especially, than for
any comprehensive, systematic elaboration. In addition to these
manifestations, rationalism of the Princeton school from Hodge to
Warfield to Machen has had its exemplars in the South, more often
among conservative Presbyterians and independent seminaries and
Bible schools from Dallas to Chattanooga to Columbia.

The organization of the essays that comprise this book reflects the subtleties of the subject matter. Two studies of origins launch us. The first, by Clarence C. Goen, is on the origins of the regional (sectional) denominations during the years preceding the Civil War. The second, by David Edwin Harrell, Jr., traces the beginnings, around the turn of the twentieth century, of several bodies of "plain folks" such as the Churches of Christ, the Pentecostal movement, and the Holiness movement. Harrell's essay occasions our recalling that millions of southern Christians stand in that heritage and also that many of them are no longer plain folks.

Several of these essays treat continuities, which appear in a number of areas, some of them unexpected. Few are stronger than the persistent fiber and direction of black people in the region. From 1800 and even earlier, faith has been a vital force in the public and private lives of Afro-American southerners. C. Eric Lincoln takes us to many points on this long journey. In a completely different vein Richard Rubenstein interprets William Styron, Tidewater Virginian that he ineluctably is, as using the enslavement of human beings as the basic motif of *Sophie's Choice*, which seeks to establish continuity between the Old South's system of slavery and Nazi Germany's reduction of humanity to systematic extermination.

Other essays concern anomalies in southern religious life. Proceeding chronologically, the first is found in John Boles's description of blacks and whites together, sometimes relatively equally, in the churches of the antebellum society characterized by white over black. Randall M. Miller then presents us with the curiosity of an alien people, Roman Catholics, acquiring a southern style in condoning slavery while belonging to a church that condemned it. Although the popular churches adopted individual conversion as the hallmark of their evangelical faith, some pastors and members were inventive and vigorous in their advocacy of a kind of "social gospel" found in several places between 1890 and 1920, a development described by Wayne Flynt. In the same period William Porcher DuBose, Episcopal seminary educator, formulated a "liberal" theology, one based on the doctrine of the Incarnation (rather than on atonement theology). Ralph E. Luker affords us insight into the emergence and growth of that tradition from its beginnings in antebellum South Carolina.

On the recent and current scene, according to William Martin, southern evangelicalism has been outdone at its own evangelical game through a rational (and only sometime and partially southern) crusade by television evangelists to link right-wing politics with conservative religion. Finally, Wade Clark Roof exhibits the drawing together of the South and the rest of the country by showing that the unchurched patterns of the two regional cultures are in statistical terms nearly indistinguishable. Irreligion coexists with piety in the anomalous southern culture and is not notably weaker in the very religious South than elsewhere in the nation.

In sum, several points impress themselves on those who observe the study of the South's religion. They are all manifestations of the field's coming of age: 1) Much work is being done in various areas of scholarship. 2) An agenda for additional work has been formulated and is constantly being enlarged. 3) The region and regional religion are being viewed more and more in the context of the nation and of studies of national history and culture. From a scarcity of solid scholarship and a series of provincial perspectives only three decades ago, the study of religion in the South has come a long way indeed.

NOTES

1. See Samuel S. Hill, *Southern Churches in Crisis* (New York, 1966).

2. Rosemary Magee, "Recent Trends in the Study of Southern Religion," *Religious Studies Review,* VI (January, 1980), 35–39.

3. Robert M. Calhoon, "Faith and Consciousness in Early Southern Culture" (Unpublished paper read at the Algie Newlyn–Rembert W. Patrick Symposium on Southern History, Guilford College, March 28, 1980); Anne C. Loveland, *Southern Evangelicals and the Social Order, 1800–1860* (Baton Rouge, 1980); Donald G. Mathews, *Religion in the Old South* (Chicago, 1977).

4. E. Brooks Holifield, *The Gentlemen Theologians: American Theology in Southern Culture, 1795–1860* (Durham, N.C., 1978).

5. Ernest R. Sandeen, *The Roots of Fundamentalism: British and American Millenarianism, 1800–1930* (Chicago, 1970); George M. Marsden, *Fundamentalism and American Culture* (New York, 1980).

SCENARIO FOR SECESSION:
DENOMINATIONAL SCHISMS AND THE
COMING OF THE CIVIL WAR
Clarence C. Goen

Politicians, secular and religious journals, pamphleteers, men in all classes of society, freely lay the blame of this Rebellion, in great measure, or wholly, at the door of the Church; charging the ministry, more especially, with having caused it. This is a very prevalent sentiment, if we may judge from what has been said and written."[1] These words came in 1864 from Robert Livingston Stanton, professor of practical theology in the Theological Seminary of the (Old School) Presbyterian Church at Danville, Kentucky. The case against the churches, which Stanton prosecuted in a book of 562 pages, had been building for more than a quarter of a century. Confronted with the paradox of human bondage in a professedly free society—even a Christian republic, as many claimed—the churches for the most part had equivocated, first stumbling uncertainly between stern pronouncements and ambiguous enforcement, then reacting defensively to strident abolitionism and proslavery apologetics. When they proved themselves incapable of dealing intramurally with the question of slavery in terms of their own moral discipline and some sundered over the issue, fears grew that the open fracturing of religious institutions presaged the rupture of the nation.

An early prognostication came from William Lloyd Garrison. On July 4, 1837, he scored the recent Presbyterian schism, and prophesied: "Our doom as a nation is sealed. . . . *The downfall of the republic seems inevitable.* . . . The corruptions of the CHURCH, so called . . . are obviously more deep and incurable than those of the STATE, and therefore, the CHURCH, in spite of every precaution and

---

This essay summarizes a thesis developed at book length in *Broken Churches, Broken Nation: Denominational Schisms and the Coming of the American Civil War,* published by Mercer University Press in 1985. See also C. C. Goen, "Broken Churches, Broken Nation: Regional Religion and North-South Alienation in Antebellum America," *Church History,* LII (March, 1983), 21–35.

safeguard, is first to be dashed to pieces. . . . *The political dismember-ment of our Union is ultimately to follow.*"[2]

Whatever allowances one makes for Garrison's characteristically extremist rhetoric, his words still seem uncannily prescient, render-ing a solemn judgment, as it were, before the event. When Lincoln's election in 1860 brought Garrison's prophecy near to fulfillment, a Louisville newspaper observed: "The very worst omen of the times is the fact that the religious men of the country stand apart to so great an extent in this hour of trial. Most of the Churches have split on the very rock upon which the State is foundering. In fact their divisions have prepared the way and laid the foundation for the political divi-sions which now exist."[3] As national disruption loomed, many Ameri-cans spoke of a connection between the denominational schisms and political breakdown.

The connection has rated mention in most of the standard text-books of American religious history. Robert T. Handy's recent *History of the Churches in the United States and Canada* is typical. "The reli-gious ties that had been shaped during the Great Awakening and that had helped to bring a nation together, ties that had been strength-ened in the Second Awakening to the point that the Kingdom seemed close, were now rudely broken," Handy declared. "The separations not only foreshadowed the political division but prepared the argu-ments by which each section would claim its cause as God's cause."[4]

Neither have secular historians been oblivious to the point. For ex-ample, Avery Craven, who wrestled persistently with the problem of why the nation broke apart in 1861, observed that the church splits marked the moment when the slavery controversy "had passed out of the realm of abstract discussion and had begun to influence the everyday affairs of men and institutions. When churches divided, how long could political parties withstand the disrupting force?"[5] But though comments and rhetorical questions of this sort are fre-quent, no investigator has yet pulled together sufficient evidence to permit an assessment of the churches' influence in breaking the Union and provoking the war.

My own research on the question has led to four theses. 1) Evan-gelical Protestantism was a major bond of unity for the United States during the first third of the nineteenth century. 2) The chief institu-tional forms of evangelical Protestantism were the large popular denominations (that is, churches of the people)—namely Methodist, Baptist, and Presbyterian—each with nationwide constituencies.[6] 3) The popular denominations, increasingly agitated by disputes over slavery, found the problem ultimately unmanageable in terms of ecclesiastical discipline and divided their national organizations into northern and southern factions long before political rupture, thus marking the first major cleavage between slaveholding and non-slaveholding sections. 4) The denominational schisms presaged and to some extent provoked the crisis of the Union in 1861: they broke a primary bond of national unity, set before the nation a persuasive example of sectional independence, encouraged the myth of "peaceable secession," reinforced alienation between North and South, and heightened the moral outrage that each section felt against the other.[7]

THE EVANGELICAL BOND

Evangelical Protestantism as a force for cultural cohesion stems from the Great Awakening of the 1740s, which H. Richard Niebuhr has called "our national conversion."[8] He meant, of course, not that the whole population converted to evangelical Christianity but that the Awakening, by transcending local and particular allegiances, stimulated and reinforced a rising national self-consciousness. To be sure, the process of molding the separate colonies into a united nation was long and complex, but the Awakening encouraged a *consensus cordum* that would shape a scattered and diverse people into one common sense of nationhood.

A second wave of revivals, beginning about 1795 and peaking in the 1830s, carried forward the social processes set in motion by the first, further displacing traditional standards of social participation based on ancestry, learning, and wealth, and strengthening new ones based on common experiences. The revivals stimulated an associative impulse that multiplied local congregations and overflowed into a veritable phalanx of evangelical organizations. This "united front," as Lois Banner noted, became a way of "insuring that democracy would actually function within the republican framework, of bringing together in harmony people of the various competing classes and sections, and of providing stable organizations and a sense of community within a society in continual flux."[9]

Table 1   States in Which Baptists and Methodists Both
Outnumbered Every Other Denomination
Number of Churches in 1850

STATE	METH-ODIST	BAP-TIST	PRESBY-TERIAN	LARGEST OTHER DENOMINATION	
Maine	199	326	7*	Congregational	180
New York	1231	781	671	Dutch Reformed	233
Virginia	1025	649	240	Episcopal	173
North Carolina	784	615	151	Episcopal	50
South Carolina	484	413	136	Episcopal	72
Georgia	795	879	97	Episcopal	20
Florida	87	56	16	Episcopal	10
Alabama	577	579	162	Episcopal	17
Mississippi	454	385	143	Episcopal	13
Louisiana	125	77	18*	Roman Catholic	55
Texas	176	82	45	Roman Catholic	13
Arkansas	168	114	52	Roman Catholic	7
Tennessee	861	646	363	Episcopal	17
Kentucky	530	803	224	Roman Catholic	48
Missouri	250	300	125	Roman Catholic	65
Illinois	405	282	206	Roman Catholic	59
Indiana	778	428	282	Quaker	89

*States in which Presbyterians were not in third place behind Methodists and Baptists

The evangelical impulse found its most visible institutional expression in the popular denominations. Before the Revolution, Methodists and Baptists had been among the smaller sects on the fringe of American Christianity. By 1820 they were the largest religious bodies in the United States, with Presbyterians not far behind. These three denominations embraced constituencies widely distributed from Maine to Georgia and from the Atlantic seaboard to the Mississippi River and beyond. At midcentury, the United States consisted of thirty-one states and the District of Columbia. Table 1 shows that in seventeen states the Methodists and the Baptists both reported more churches than any other denomination; in fifteen of these states the Presbyterians were in third place.

In ten states and the District of Columbia, as Table 2 demonstrates, either the Baptists or the Methodists had more churches than any other denomination. In six of these eleven jurisdictions the Presbyterians were in second place, and in four of those six the Baptists were in third place.

In three New England states, as Table 3 shows, none of the nationwide denominations could claim a plurality, but the combined total of Methodist and Baptist churches was greater than the number of churches reported by any other body.

In only one state were evangelicals in a minority—California, where Roman Catholics outnumbered all other religious groups combined. Thus the picture of evangelical dominance, particularly in that part of the United States most affected by the Civil War, seems clear. In the eleven states that seceded from the Union in 1861, the Methodists owned 45 percent of the total number of churches, the Baptists 37 percent, and the Presbyterians 12 percent—a stunning 94 percent of the churches in the Confederacy (see Table 4).

Even though the total enrolled church membership was still a small percentage of the entire population—about one in seven—this statistic should not mask the fact that nearly every minister preached

Table 2   States in Which Either Baptists or Methodists
Outnumbered Every Other Denomination
Number of Churches in 1850

STATE	METH-ODIST	BAP-TIST	PRESBY-TERIAN	LARGEST OTHER DENOMINATION	
New Hampshire	103	193	13	Congregational	176
Rhode Island	23	106	0	Episcopal	26
New Jersey	312	108†	149*	Dutch Reformed	66
Pennsylvania	889	320	775*	Lutheran	498
Delaware	106	12	26*	Episcopal	21
Maryland	497	45	56	Episcopal	133
Dist. of Col.	16	6	6	Episcopal	8
Ohio	1529	551†	663*	Lutheran	260
Michigan	119	66†	72*	Roman Catholic	44
Wisconsin	110	49	40	Roman Catholic	64
Iowa	71	20†	38*	Roman Catholic	18

* Presbyterians in second place
† Baptists in third place

15

Table 3   States in Which Baptists and Methodists Combined
Outnumbered Every Other Denomination
Number of Churches in 1850

STATE	METHODIST	BAPTIST	COMBINED TOTAL	CONGRE-GATIONAL
Vermont	140	102	242	175
Massachusetts	262	266	528	448
Connecticut	185	114	299	252

Table 4   Churches in the Eleven States of the Future
Confederacy, 1850

	METHODIST	BAPTIST	PRESBY-TERIAN	ALL OTHERS
Number of Churches	5,536	4,495	1,423	762
Percentage of Total	45.3%	36.8%	11.7%	6.2%

regularly to congregations three or four times the size of his church's membership. On the eve of national disruption, "the country had one church for every 580 people, [and] the churches had facilities for seating three-fifths of the population at one time." [10] Such data add up to more than a generally pervading influence; they document a massive social reality.

No other organization in the country was in direct touch with more people than were the churches. In fact, the Methodist Episcopal Church was probably the most extensive national institution besides the federal government. Its traveling ministry helped to give the Methodists not only what some scholars have called "a common world of experience" but also a national outlook, as itinerant preachers circulated news among their charges and disseminated information garnered at regional and national conferences.[11] Baptists, their congregational polity notwithstanding, also exerted broad influence by coordinating their far-flung missionary work through three national societies. Presbyterians functioned as a graduated hierarchy of ecclesiastical judicatories equally vested with nationwide influence. What a Cincinnati newspaper declared of the Presbyterian General Assembly as it gathered in Philadelphia in 1837 could apply to the national convocations of the other denominations as well: "The Assembly is composed of religious teachers, who from the desk [pulpit] and in pastoral intercourse and supervision, have access to, and authoritative influence over a vast multitude of minds. The Assembly is held, not in a remote corner, but in a great and central city, and the eyes of the American people are upon it, and its voice goes into all the land. . . . For good or evil, it is indeed a body of immense power."[12]

There was, in short, no more pervasive presence that touched the lives of more Americans at more points than the popular denominations. That is why the involvement of the churches in the increasingly acrimonious debate over slavery was significant on a national scale. Whatever happened in the churches' inner civil war inevitably would be reflected in the wider community of the nation.

FROM DENOMINATIONAL SCHISMS TO NATIONAL RUPTURE

The conflict that eventually sundered the Union was focused earliest and most sharply in the churches. Presbyterians divided in 1837 after a series of quarrels in which conflicting views of slavery figured significantly if not decisively. The Methodist Episcopal Church split in 1844 and the national Baptist societies in 1845, explicitly because of sharp internal disputes about slavery. Throughout each controversy many of the arguments rehearsed in ecclesiastical context the same exacerbating conflict that would soon rend the Union.

The Presbyterian schism was the first open break in a national body. Although the line of division was not drawn strictly between the North and the South, the schism evoked dire predictions of political consequences. William S. Plumer, pastor of the First Presbyterian Church in Richmond, cast the issue in apocalyptic terms: "Our church is rent asunder. . . . Nothing is left . . . except to . . . rend the star-spangled banner in twain. . . . Soon the hostile forces will be marshalled against each other, and the Potomac will be dyed with blood. . . . Can it be that the righteous Judge of all the earth has so dreadful a controversy with the Presbyterian Church of the United States as to give her up to the folly and madness of being the first to hoist the gate and let the flood of desolation roll in?"[13]

As Methodists approached their own schism in 1844, similar forebodings were frequently voiced. Thomas Crowder of Virginia warned that if a slaveholding bishop could not retain both his slaves and his episcopacy, "the division of our Church may follow—a civil division of this great confederacy may follow that, and then hearts will be torn apart, master and slave arrayed against each other, brother in the Church against brother, and the north against the south—and when thus arrayed, with the fiercest passions and energies of our nature brought into action against each other, civil war and far-reaching desolation must be the final results. My dear brethren, are you prepared for this?"[14] But such dire predictions did not dissuade even those who voiced them from voting to divide the church.

Baptists acted out Scene 3 of the scenario when southerners withdrew from their national societies in 1845. Shortly after the Methodists decided to split, a southerner in New England wrote to a Richmond paper: "A separation of the churches of the North from the churches of the South must act as an entering wedge to a dissolution of our political bonds. . . . If the Baptists, unmindful of their duty to Christ and their country, shall bite and devour one another, and array themselves into two great parties, the Northern and the Southern, what conservative principles, what salt of the earth, will be left to restrain and moderate the madness of political strife and ambition and save from ruin our Republic?" One week before southern Baptists gathered in Augusta, Georgia, to organize their separatist convention, a Baptist editor in Louisville noted the Methodist rupture about to be consummated in his own city as well as continuing strife among Presbyterians. The editor warned, "Let the three great denominations of christians be divided, by State lines, upon the subject of abolitionism, and who does not see that all social intercourse between parties will be sundered, and the parts continually recede?" A Philadelphia Presbyterian wrote somberly that in the denominational schisms "the die has been cast" for a disunited country and asked, "If a union cemented by all the finer influences of the gospel could not last, what can?"[15]

The apprehensions of church leaders found resonance in the secular press. There were some 1,200 newspapers in the United States in the 1840s, and they covered the church divisions closely, quoting copiously from each other in order to pass along the disquieting news. In Philadelphia on May 27, 1844, the *Public Ledger* gave half of its front-page news coverage to the Methodist debates over the slaveholding bishop—at the same time the Democratic national convention was in session selecting its presidential candidate! After the separations became *faits accomplis,* the New York *Journal of Commerce* spoke ominously of the "line of demarcation" that had been drawn "between almost the entire body of Northern and Southern Christians," breaking the strongest bond of national union.[16] The Charleston *Mercury* editorialized grimly: "In this contest of religions, we have an entire and remediless severance of the Union—a division that henceforth creates in the two most numerous denominations of the country *a Northern and a Southern religion*—and this separation brought about by no accident nor heat of the moment, but after much deliberation and unwearied efforts to reconcile the dissension—efforts that yielded only to a settled conviction that reconciliation was impossible."[17] In 1848 a Louisville editor, John Lightfoot Waller, expressed the continuing apprehensions of the western border states: "Who can expect that our country will remain united when the bonds of religious concord are broken? If the ties of Christian love are sundered, what bands can unite this nation together?"[18]

Thoughtful people continued to ponder the possible consequences of the denominational schisms. By the end of the decade other portents of sectional rift—the Wilmot Proviso, disputes over slavery in newly acquired territories, changes in tariff policy, the weakening of the Democratic party, and the increasing stridency of the abolitionists—had deepened the sense of crisis. As debates over the Compromise of 1850 brought national controversy to fever pitch once again, the denominational schisms were recalled with the same forebodings as in 1845. The most famous and articulate statement came in the United States Senate on March 4, 1850, from John C. Calhoun, who made a compelling analysis of the bonds of national union and how, one by one, they were snapping: "The ties which had held each denomination together formed a strong cord to hold the whole Union together; but, powerful as they were, they have not been able to resist the explosive effect of slavery agitation. . . . If the agitation goes on, the same force, acting with increased intensity . . . will finally snap every cord, when nothing will be left to hold the States together except force."[19] Calhoun—who certainly did his part to pave the road to secession—seems to have recognized with somber finality that the example of the churches in going their separate ways had established a persuasive precedent for the final breach of the Union.

Henry Clay, whose last years were devoted to efforts of pacification and compromise, brooded frequently over the political impact of the church schisms. A few weeks before his death in 1852, he described how the splintering of the churches had weakened the Union: "I tell you this sundering of the religious ties which have hitherto bound our people together, I consider the greatest source of danger to our country. If our religious men cannot live together in peace, what can be expected of us politicians, very few of whom profess to be governed by the great principles of love?"[20]

Following the example of the churches, the Union finally broke on December 20, 1860, when the South Carolina legislature met in the First Baptist Church in Columbia and passed without dissent an ordinance of secession. The next day the Cleveland *Daily Plain Dealer* sadly reminded its readers of the whole process leading to breakdown: "For years the Union has, in fact, been dissolving. . . . The churches North and South divided. Then our Bible, Tract, and Missionary Societies, and finally the social relations [deteriorated] to an alarming extent. . . . The Secession of South Carolina, yesterday, was but the culmination of events which had been progressing for years."[21] If there was one condition *sine qua non* for the final disruption, according to many, many witnesses, it was the severing of ecclesiastical ties. As the Civil War began, a southern Presbyterian voiced the common opinion: "Much as is due to many of our sagacious and gifted politicians, they could *effect nothing* until the religious union of the North and South was dissolved."[22] There was a great deal of truth in his claim. The popular churches had scripted a scenario for secession almost a quarter of a century before Sumter.

In May, 1845, a correspondent for the Charleston *Mercury* dispatched from Augusta, Georgia, his final report on the organization of the Southern Baptist Convention. His closing comment stands as something of an epigram for the dissolving nation: "how little is to be expected from any other *Union*, if the union of Christians fail."[23]

How prescient, we can see now, were the warnings of so many within the churches and outside them who had predicted that if the national church bodies should divide, the Union would be fatally weakened. But their warnings went unheeded, and even after six hundred thousand American men had died by their brothers' hands, in the stillness at Appomattox there was little contrition in the broken churches that had prefigured the broken nation.

NOTES

1. Robert Livingston Stanton, *The Church and the Rebellion: A Consideration of the Rebellion Against the Government of the United States, and the Agency of the Church, North and South, in Relation Thereto* (New York, 1864), vi.

2. *Liberator,* VII (July 28, 1837), in Truman Nelson (ed.), *Documents of Upheaval: Selections from William Lloyd Garrison's "The Liberator," 1831–1865* (New York, 1966), 123.

3. *Presbyterian Herald* (Louisville), November 22, 1860.

4. Robert T. Handy, *A History of the Churches in the United States and Canada* (New York, 1977), 194.

5. Avery O. Craven, *The Coming of the Civil War* (2nd ed.; Chicago, 1957), 201.

6. The so-called voluntary societies, of course, represented another important institutional form of evangelicalism. Many of these enlisted national memberships, and several suffered sectional losses on account of the slavery controversy. But they are not the primary objects of this study, because they did not break cleanly into ongoing sectional organizations. See n. 21 below.

7. Here I can do no more than sample the evidence that supports these theses. For every quotation cited here, there are many additional ones, along with much more interpretative comment, in *Broken Churches, Broken Nation.*

8. H. Richard Niebuhr, *The Kingdom of God in America* (New York, 1937), 126.

9. Lois W. Banner, "Religious Benevolence as Social Control: A Critique of an Interpretation," *Journal of American History,* LX (1973), 40.

10. Allan Nevins, *Ordeal of the Union* (2 vols.; New York, 1947), I, 58n.

11. Robert Cooley Angell, *The Integration of American Society* (New York, 1941), 8. See also Donald G. Mathews, "The Second Great Awakening as an Organizing Process, 1780–1830: An Hypothesis," *American Quarterly,* XXI (1969), 23–43.

12. *Journal and Luminary* (Cincinnati), June 15, 1837.

13. *Southern Religious Telegraph* (Richmond), August 8, 1837, p. 124, quoted in Ernest T. Thompson, *Presbyterians in the South,* Vol. I: *1607–1861* (Richmond, 1963), 393–94.

14. Robert A. West (ed.), *Report of Debates in the General Conference of the Methodist Episcopal Church* (New York, 1855), 95.

15. *Religious Herald* (Richmond), October 24, 1844, quoted in Mary B. Putnam, *The Baptists and Slavery, 1840–1845* (Ann Arbor, 1913), 45; *Baptist Banner and Pioneer* (Louisville), May 1, 1845; *Christian Observer* (Philadelphia), May 23, 1845. The latter paper was edited by Amasa Converse, who copied the quoted piece from the Charleston *Courier.*

16. The comment was also printed in the *Baptist Banner* (Louisville), June 5, 1845.

17. The editorial was also printed in *Niles' National Register*, May 24, 1845. The widespread copying of such exchange items greatly increased their circulation and thus their impact.'

18. In Andrew T. Foss and Edward Mathews (comps.), *Facts for Baptist Churches* (Utica, N.Y., 1850), 342.

19. Richard K. Crallé (ed.), *Speeches of John C. Calhoun, Delivered in the House of Representatives, and in the Senate of the United States* (1868; repr. New York, 1968), 556–58. Sigma, a writer in the New York *Daily Tribune* of June 6, 1850, charged Calhoun with deploring schisms he "did all he could to bring about." Rumors in several places nurtured the suspicion that the withdrawal of the southern churches had been planned as a prelude to political secession. See John Nelson Norwood, *The Schism in the Methodist Episcopal Church, 1844: A Study of Slavery and Ecclesiastical Politics* (New York, 1923), 194.

20. *Presbyterian Herald* (Louisville), January 5, 1860. Editor W. W. Hill reported this on the basis of an interview with Clay in 1852.

21. Howard C. Perkins (ed.), *Northern Editorials on Secession* (New York, 1942), 695–96. The slavery controversy in the national benevolent societies did not produce sectional separations as clear-cut as in the popular denominations. Abolitionists provoked several defections from regional Bible societies, installed sympathetic officers in the American Home Missionary Society, and organized a separatist antislavery tract society—all in the late 1850s. See Clifford S. Griffin, *Their Brothers' Keepers: Moral Stewardship in the United States, 1800–1865,* (New Brunswick, N.J., 1960), 177–97.

22. Abner A. Porter, editorial in the *Southern Presbyterian*, April 20, 1861, copied in Stanton, *The Church and the Rebellion*, 198.

23. Charleston *Mercury*, May 9, 1845.

THE EVOLUTION OF PLAIN-FOLK RELIGION IN THE SOUTH, 1835–1920
David Edwin Harrell, Jr.

For three decades at the turn of the nineteenth century Lorenzo Dow was the scourge of Calvinists, Jesuits, and other spokesmen for the Devil in the South and West, and a somewhat erratic friend of Methodism and God. But by 1830 he had become thoroughly disenchanted by the growing sophistication of the Methodists. He wrote: "A preacher being asked in the solitary days of Methodism, during the time of their simplicity; why the *Methodists* did not have 'doctors of divinity?' boldly replied, our Divinity is not sick! But now matters are reversed; and the *doctors* are to be found at the helm of affairs, to keep pace with other societies, and be like all nations round about." Most modern historians agree that Dow knew what he was talking about. "By the 1830s," confirms Anne Loveland, "Baptists and Methodists had gained respectability by virtue of their increasing wealth and higher educational level. . . . To become a Baptist no longer obliged one to 'lose standing or influence in society.'" Donald G. Mathews described southern evangelicals of the same period: "They had come a long way from their origins as sturdy religious folk who had attacked the pretensions of a previous aristocracy." [1]

The changes in the Baptist and Methodist churches—the two great people's churches of the frontier—were widely visible. After several decades of rapid expansion and growth, both churches began to solidify their gains and to build more adequate organizations. American Baptists established their first missionary society in 1814; the Methodists followed in 1820. By 1830 both churches bristled with the beginnings of denominational apparatus. In addition to countless benevolent and missionary societies, the Baptists founded many "theological institutes" in the 1830s and 1840s, climaxing with the permanent establishment of Southern Baptist Theological Seminary in Greenville, South Carolina, in 1859. Although the Methodists did not build a seminary in the South before the Civil War, increasingly they did "emphasize the need for self-education on the part of candidates and ministers." [2]

A new generation of leaders also appeared in each denomination. Early Baptist and Methodist preachers had been earthy men of the people. Methodist pioneer Jesse Lee "abhorred all . . . religious pomp"; in fact, wrote a contemporary, he "carried his aversion to an inexcusable extreme." All through the antebellum period the minutes of the Methodist conferences recorded the passing of that generation of ministers—men like Peyton Pierce Smith of Franklin County, Georgia, who began riding a circuit with a horse and saddle, "a five dollar watch," and five dollars in money." When he had finished his course thirty-one years later, he had "preached 4,414 sermons, baptized 1,529 persons, made 5,979 visits, written 4,941 letters, and traveled . . . 103,623 miles." Crude and cantankerous as he was, the astonishing commitment of Lorenzo Dow is apparent enough to the casual reader of his diary. In an 1804 entry, he noted, without complaint or comment, that he had preached to an audience of 1,500 in Rockingham, North Carolina, for about two hours and that his listeners were "solemn and well behaved, considering the inconvenience of standing in the freezing air and falling snow." Dow then rode twelve miles to speak again in the evening.[3]

Although all of the old breed were not gone by 1835, the Baptists and Methodists had self-consciously developed a new kind of leadership. Among the Baptists were Richard Furman, Richard Fuller, and Jesse Mercer, men who, in the words of Baptist historian Albert Henry Newman, were "better educated and abler than those of the past," men destined to "lead the denomination to still nobler achievements." Among the Methodists were William Capers, Henry Bascom, and Martin Ruter, who, in the words of an early Methodist historian, had attained a "higher intellectual culture," had "the commanding attractions of genius," and were destined to receive "a sort of national rather than denominational recognition." Such men did much to raise the self-image and aspirations of their churches; new buildings began to replace the old log houses of the frontier period, some of them being "an honor to the cause."[4] They also worked to improve the quality of ministers and to raise the level of support for ministry. The result was a growing disparity between the salaries of urban and rural ministers, particularly among the Baptists, where such matters were left entirely to the local churches.[5]

To some extent, the appearance of a new visible class of respectable planters, town dwellers, and urban ministers in the Baptist and

Methodist churches left them open to flanking movements by competitors for the loyalty of the plain people. The early successes of the Disciples of Christ and the Cumberland Presbyterians were gained partly at the expense of, or at least in competition with, the Baptists and Methodists. Especially during his early, iconoclastic days, when he edited the *Christian Baptist* from 1823 to 1830, Alexander Campbell played on western and lower-class prejudices. In the first issue of the *Christian Baptist* in 1823, the Disciples leader published his famous "Third Epistle of Peter," which cuttingly instructed clergymen how to live sumptuously, assume titles, and generally abuse the people.[6] Campbell repeatedly scored "hireling" clergymen and in his early days seemed to be opposed to all salaried ministers. Although anti-aristocratic prejudices became less marked in Campbell's own writings in the 1840s and 1850s (he was a reasonably wealthy man), many of his frontier-style followers continued to preach an anti-institutional and anti-aristocratic message that reaped a large harvest among the independent farmers of the Midwest and Upper South. In the decade of the 1830s the Disciples drained off "hundreds of Baptist churches," as well as many discontented Presbyterians.[7]

The Cumberland Presbyterian church also began amid the prejudices of the small farmers of the West and South. The issues that led to the founding of the independent Cumberland Presbytery included objections to extreme Calvinistic fatalism, protests against what some believed to be abusive centralization of authority, and opposition to excessive educational requirements for the clergy. Although it is hardly true, as their early critics charged, that the Cumberland Presbyterian leaders were "illiterate exhorters with Arminian sentiments," it is clear that the movement embodied many of the prejudices of the common people. As late as 1827, Finis Ewing, one of the founders of the church, objected to the convening of a general assembly because he feared centralization and had a "great aversion to pride and vain glory." The Cumberland church remained almost entirely rural; as late as 1840, urban congregations were still exceptional.[8]

Generally, both the Disciples of Christ and the Cumberland Presbyterians can be described best as partners (or competitors) with the Baptists and Methodists in the religious conversion of the plain people of the South in the nineteenth century. Both groups were orthodox, they drew the same types of supporters as the larger evangelical churches, and both showed signs of the same upward mobility as the major churches. The Cumberland Presbyterians organized their first missionary society in 1836; the Disciples, coming on the scene slightly later with strong anti-institutional biases, organized a missionary society in 1849. Both churches attracted a smattering of urban and sophisticated followers, and the leadership increasingly fell into the hands of abler and better-trained ministers. In both churches most local congregations remained rural and lower class, however, and by the 1860s each was showing clear signs of class tension.

The most singular example of religious class tension in the antebellum South was the Baptist antimission movement, a rebellion of which the Disciples were the most separatist wing. Throughout the South in the 1830s and 1840s, rival Baptist associations mushroomed; the movement, according to Bertram Wyatt-Brown, "exhibited deep-seated class antagonisms." By 1844 there were 900 antimission preachers, 1,622 churches, and at least 68,000 members, mostly in the South. The "effect of the antimission movement," writes a modern Baptist historian, "was devastating." According to Robert Torbet, because of the antimission movement "Baptist missionary societies were dwarfed."[9]

It is clear that the antimission protest was both southern and lower class. The patronizing "religious dandies" who toured the South with the support of missionary societies were regarded by the older Baptist leaders as both foreign and decadent. Elder Joshua Lawrence of Tar River, North Carolina, protested against the "tyranny of an unconverted, men-made, money-making . . . factoried priesthood." As Wyatt-Brown points out, this gospel sold best among "people who lived in districts far from centers of trade and refinement."[10]

The most famous, and probably the most important, of the early antimission preachers was Daniel Parker; he was the embodiment of the powerful prejudices behind the success of the movement. According to an early Baptist historian, Parker was "raised on the frontier of Georgia, without education, uncouth in manners, slovenly in dress, diminutive in person, unprepossessing in appearance, with shriveled features and a small piercing eye." Yet, "few men, for a series of years, have exerted wider influence on the lower and less educated class of frontier people. [He worked] with a zeal and enthusiasm bordering on insanity, firmness that amounted to obstinacy, and perseverance that would have done honor to a good cause." Parker objected to "all institutions of modern times as incompatible with the simplicity and spiritual nature of the kingdom of Christ" and was particularly opposed to the "money qualifications for memberships in the B. Triennial Convention." He believed that "ministers of the gospel should go forth without appointment from the organizations of men, and without any stipulated compensations for their services." Parker's views expressed the antimission protest. It had two main planks, sometimes preached together and sometimes separately: first, a biblical, primitivist belief that all church-related organizations were unscriptural, and second, a lower-class prejudice against the financial base and outside control of the Baptist missionary convention.[11]

The most visible impact of the antimission movement was the formation of Primitive Baptist associations and the appearance of countless "hard-shell," "hard-rind," "square-toed," and "broad-brimmed" independent Baptist churches in the rural South. Generally strongly predestinarian, the Primitives were an obstinate resistance movement among the poor whites against the condescending leadership of their betters. It was natural that predestination became the test issue. Here was a symbol of loyalty to the beliefs of the fathers, a rationale for opposition to education and soft-headed modern ideas; in addition, the harshness of Calvinism still seemed an adequate explanation of life to the poor farmers of the South. Furthermore, Calvinism proved a means for testing the orthodoxy of moderate preachers who shunned controversy. Sermons were searched for proper code words that defined one's broader loyalties. In the mid-1830s, the Georgia Association felt compelled to justify its fellowship with the Central Association after the latter had been charged with Arminianism: "We admit that the Central ministers are more practical in their preaching than some of our brethren; they do not in a formal manner discuss election, predestination, and covenant in every sermon, though they have again and again avowed their belief in them. . . . They urge the church to awake to the solemn command of Christ, 'go ye into all the world, and preach the gospel to every creature.' If this is Arminianism, then are the central ministers Arminian, then is the Georgia Association Arminian, then were Christ, Paul, and all the Apostles, the greatest Arminians that ever lived." The antimission division was not simply doctrinal, however; class prejudice was never far beneath the surface. In 1848 Baptist historian David Benedict wrote:

> It has been my settled opinion, for a long time past, that the cause of missions has had but little to do in this business, so very slender is its hold on the minds of the great mass of our community in most parts of the country, however they are distinguished. This is shown by their doings for benevolent objects. The fact is, that personal altercations, rivalships, and jealousies, and local contests for influence and control have done much to set brethren at variance with each other. The mission question is the ostensible, rather than the real cause of the trouble, in many places. New men and new measures have run faster than the old travelers were accustomed to go, and they have been disturbed at being left behind.[12]

Probably equally important as the formation of Primitive Baptist associations in the 1830s and 1840s was the pressure the conservatives put on Baptists in general. The antimission movement pushed the entire Baptist community in the South to the right and, in the words of Torbet, "delayed the development of stronger leadership." When the Southern Baptist Convention was formed in 1845, many of the churches identified with it shared the prejudices of the antimission Baptists and had little respect for the new clerical elite in the church. Many congregations hovered on the fringes of the cooperative movement. In 1840 the West Tennessee Association included the following statement in its articles of belief: "We believe, from experience, the Missionary, Bible, Temperance, Tract, and Masonic Societies, S. S. Unions and Theological Seminaries to make preachers for the Lord, are destructive to the peace and fellowship of the baptist church; therefore, we will not tolerate any member of our churches in any of the above named societies. But all almsdeeds any member is at liberty to perform; *Provided* he does not let his *left hand* know what his *right* doeth."[13]

The persistence of this conservative turn of mind was reemphasized in the 1850s with the eruption of Baptist Landmarkism. The Landmark movement was most clearly associated with the career of James R. Graves, longtime editor of the *Tennessee Baptist* and an influential Tennessee minister, but the ideas he promoted were present before the 1850s, and they outlived Graves's influence. The movement was almost entirely southern and constituted a renewed effort to save Baptist churches from "liberalism." Based on an ecclesiology that claimed a historical continuity of Baptist local churches from biblical times and, consequently, identified the Baptist church as the true church of Christ, the movement was a reaction both to external sectarian assaults and to the growing, intense influence of sophisticated urban ministers. The Landmarkers reasserted the equalitarian Baptist emphasis on the independence of the local church and restated old antimission prejudices against "priestism" and missionary societies. The vigor of the Landmark movement in the South in the 1850s confirmed that the Southern Baptist church, even after shedding the Disciples and the Primitives, continued to be a predominantly rural and conservative fellowship.[14]

In summary, most of the plain people's churches of the antebellum South were both economically diverse and traditionally evangelical. By 1860 all of the churches that had followed the people West—the Methodists, Baptists, Cumberland Presbyterians, and Disciples of Christ—boasted new leaders and new denominational efficiency, but all were also only one generation removed from the log churches of the frontier and were still composed primarily of the small farmers of the South. Only the Methodists seriously tried to build churches in towns and cities, a development that partly explains their rapid advance in the latter half of the nineteenth century. After 1835 the Baptist denomination was the only one in the South to experience sufficient class tension to trigger a major division. That division, when it came, was reactionary rather than reformist; it was, as Bertram Wyatt-Brown has written, "crabbed and backward."[15] While the North and West witnessed three decades of vigorous religious experimentation and revolution after 1830, much of it related to class feeling, the plain people of the South remained intensely orthodox, more orthodox than the conservative leaders of southern evangelicalism who were visible in the wider world. Essentially, antebellum southern poor farmers did not bolt their churches because they still controlled them. Rural Baptists and Methodists—and some Disciples of Christ—felt mildly threatened by the 1840s because of changes within their denominations, but the new urban leaders in their churches were both more conservative theologically and less powerful than their northern counterparts. Congregational independence remained strong in the South; rural Methodists still shouted when the Spirit moved; Primitives, Landmarkers, and Cumberland Presbyterians still guarded their local independence and doctrinal purity; and southern Disciples still stood firm on apostolic patterns. The plain folk of the Old South still felt at home in their local churches on the eve of the Civil War, even though they sometimes detected signs of drifting among their city brethren.

The Civil War and Reconstruction blurred the slight class divisions that had emerged and delayed for another generation serious schisms in the southern churches of the plain people. The camaraderie born of war, defeat, and the economic destruction wrought by both the fighting and its aftermath had a powerful impact on the churches, including the churches of the poor. In 1925 Edwin Mims noted that for a generation after the war the churches of the South had been "scarcely touched" by the intellectual and cultural changes revolutionizing the North because they were "so engrossed . . . in the reordering of a broken life." Noting the almost monolithic religious conservatism of the South during the Fundamentalist controversy of the 1920s, historian George Marsden wrote: "In the South generally, religious conservatism was directly tied to cultural conservatism in ways that differed from the North. . . . Their Northern counterparts had experienced the secularization of a society once dominated by evangelical thought. In the South, however, evangelicalism was still a virtually unchallenged establishment." [16]

For a generation after the Civil War, southern white churches were characterized by a real, if temporary, equalitarianism. Katherine Du Pre Lumpkin, a well-bred southern lady and Episcopalian who was reared in genteel deprivation during the difficult years around the turn of the century, later remembered that her family always attended the yearly summer revival "at the little Baptist church on a hill about two miles distant from our home." Presided over by a "taciturn, withdrawn man" who was "section boss on the railroad," the little country church was attended by the entire community—rich and poor—"save a few special sinners, and everyone knew why they did not come. . . . Moreover," concluded Miss Lumpkin, "it was seemly. People would not have understood" if her family had failed to attend. Southern society became elementary; one's religious choices were limited. "In many localities," wrote another cultured southerner in 1897, "there is practically nothing but the church and its affiliated societies to dispute with the bar-room the laborer's leisure hours;

and in such a contest the friend of culture cannot but side with the meeting-house, in spite of the apprehensions to which revivals, camp-meetings, and other paraphernalia of emotional Christianity of a low type must give rise." Other southerners remembered the experience warmly. Brooks Hays, looking back on his youth in a rural Baptist church, wrote: "In Western Arkansas at the turn of the century, the typical congregation covered the whole spectrum of community life. There was an admirable reflection of it in the emphasis on equality. My first Sunday School teacher was a blacksmith. Later I was instructed by a coal miner, whose gnarled hands symbolized for me the hardships of the period's life. There sat on the same pew with my parents the woman who did my mother's washing . . . and her presence on the third pew with them remains with me an authentic symbol of Baptist democracy." The Civil War and Reconstruction had disrupted the growing class consciousness and thus spawned in the South an abnormal period of religious accord. The Baptist Landmark movement virtually disappeared during the 1860s and 1870s because the whole church was "engulfed in the general impoverishment and paralysis of Southern life and culture." [17]

It is clear that southern religion began to experience some serious strains about 1885. These tensions opened a new chapter in plain-folk religion in the region. First, Baptist and Methodist leadership attached itself firmly to the middle-class aspirations of the New South. Both groups suffered major defections to the Holiness and Landmark movements. Second, both the Disciples of Christ and the Cumberland Presbyterians divided along sectional and rural-urban lines. Third, the South became a breeding ground for the new Holiness and Pentecostal sects, which were fed by a steady stream of poor migrants from both the southern Methodists and Baptists. After sixty years of relative denominational stability—a stability nurtured by slavery, war, defeat, poverty, and isolation—years in which the major religious revolutions of the poor had passed the South by, the South in the early twentieth century became the incubator for the fastest-growing and most innovative new religions of the common people.

Evidence was everywhere apparent by the 1890s that the Baptists and Methodists of the South were developing a mature new leadership. "One who travels about in the South," wrote Edwin Mims in 1925, "finds in newspapers, in conversations, in public addresses,

evidences that there are circles here and there, institutions of learning . . . that are as enlightened and as free as any in the country." [18]
This new cultural respectability was represented by such religious institutions as Duke and Vanderbilt and such Baptist leaders as William L.
Poteat and Ashby Jones. "Emotional religion is to be expected of [the
lower and middle classes] and the whole mass of the negroes," wrote
a southern intellectual in 1897, but among the "upper classes" in the
traditional churches such excesses were no longer tolerated. "It
would be almost as strange," he continued, "to hear a 'fire and brimstone' sermon in a fashionable church in the South as it would be to
hear a similar deliverance in New York itself." [19]

The Methodists and Baptists were at the center of the instability in
southern religion at the turn of the century. In the last quarter of the
nineteenth century the changes in southern Methodism, in both belief and practice, were rapid and far-reaching. The doctrine of holiness was deemphasized, interest in social Christianity grew, the old
rigorous standards of dress and restrictions on amusements were relaxed, and a "more adequately trained ministry" appeared. In 1891
Jeremiah Jeter looked back over his long ministry in the Southern
Baptist ranks and summarized the changes he had witnessed. On
the positive side Jeter listed a growth in the "construction of good
meetinghouses," an increase in the support of ministers, a "striking
improvement in the order of religious assemblies," and a greater emphasis on "practical piety." At the same time, Jeter saw changes for
the worse. Although Baptist ministers were more learned and refined
in the 1890s, they were lacking in "unction and pathos." Worship,
especially in the "city churches," was more orderly but less fervent;
Baptists had become more knowledgeable about "religious subjects
generally" but were "less carefully indoctrinated than their fathers."
The veteran preacher concluded: "We have now much talk on topics
more or less closely connected with religion. We hear of plans for
usefulness, the doings of conventions, the merit of preachers, the
qualities of books, the progress of churches, and the like, but we
rarely hear a conversation on personal piety. That was the almost universal topic among our fathers. Wherever and whenever they met
they conversed of their experiences—the dealings of God with their
souls." Times were changing, and they continued to change. In the
1920s a Baptist and Methodist church building boom gripped the

South; millions of dollars were invested and church buildings were started at a rate of one a day. Typical of this new generation of facilities was an $850,000 sanctuary constructed by the First Methodist Episcopal Church, South, of Dallas and the $500,000 First Baptist Church of Shreveport, which included a gymnasium, broadcasting station, banquet hall, nursery, and roof garden.[20]

Of course, the movement of southern Baptists and Methodists to middle-class respectability was by no means uniform or complete. Beneath the increasingly visible layer of moderate leadership in southern churches remained a huge conservative evangelical base. Both the Baptist and Methodist churches remained predominantly rural and small-town in the early twentieth century. Both were still overwhelmingly churches of the plain people. The 1916 religious census confirmed the relative poverty and rurality of both bodies. The Bureau of the Census in 1916 reported 92.4 percent of the Southern Baptist membership and 89.8 percent of the Methodist membership "outside the principal cities." Baptist historians have noted that at the turn of the century most southern Baptist preachers were still "country-bred [and] preferred to live on their farms and preach within reach of their homes rather than attempt to plant churches in the towns and cities."[21]

The continued presence of lower-class prejudices in the Southern Baptist church was evidenced by a resurgence of Landmarkism in the 1880s and 1890s. The revival was so powerful that in the 1880s James R. Graves asserted that fifteen of the sixteen Baptist papers published in the South agreed with his positions. By the 1890s the movement once again challenged more moderate Baptist leaders for control of the convention, though it remained largely "a virile grass-roots, people's movement." In a series of battles in the eighties and nineties, the Landmarkers once again attacked the organized mission work of the Southern Baptist Convention, forced the resignation of Professor William H. Whitsitt from Southern Baptist Seminary because he challenged their ecclesiology, and kept constant pressure on such moderate Convention leaders as Edgar T. Mullins.[22]

Signaling a growing resentment and insecurity among rural and lower-class Baptists, the Landmark agitation at the turn of the century had two effects on the Baptists. First, as Primitives had earlier, the movement once again slowed the moderating drift in the church.

"In the first half of this century," writes a recent historian, "Landmarkism continued to exert a marked influence, especially in church practice and Baptist isolation." According to another modern historian, not until the 1950s did Southern Baptist leadership seriously challenge Landmark doctrines. Although the Landmarkers did not control the church's institutions, they powerfully influenced them. They won some important battles, particularly the Whitsitt controversy; all except the most disgruntled believed that their church was not beyond rescue.[23] Most poor and rural Baptists still felt at home in the Southern Baptist Convention in 1920, secure in their independence and isolation; they were suspicious of the professors in Louisville and the leaders of the city churches but heartened by periodic assurances of Baptist orthodoxy and a common commitment to evangelization.

A minority of the Landmarkers decided at the turn of the century that they could no longer tolerate the encroachments of liberalism in the church. Led by Ben M. Bogard of Arkansas, nearly 1,500 Baptist churches in the Southwest bolted the Convention in 1905 and formed a new movement which came to be called the American Baptist Association. Bogard's paper, *The Baptist and Commoner,* printed in Little Rock, was powerful in the historic "Landmark belt," and by 1926 the association numbered 117,585 members. In Arkansas the new association captured 39.4 percent of the Baptist churches in the state, including 41.2 percent of the rural churches.[24]

Parallel to Landmarkism among the Baptists was the Holiness movement among the Methodists. The Holiness associations that blossomed in the late nineteenth century served as safety valves for poor and rural Methodists who were increasingly isolated from the sources of power within their denomination. The early roots of the Holiness movement were in the North: the National Association for the Promotion of Holiness was established in 1867 in New Jersey, and the North had been swept by waves of Holiness revivalism just prior to the Civil War.[25] As Holiness associations and campgrounds proliferated in the 1870s and 1880s, northern Methodist leaders increasingly resisted the movement. A profane observer wrote: "As the Methodists grew in worldly wealth and wisdom, the suspicion dawned among their sophisticates that orgies which notoriously led to female and lay exhortation, trances and holy turmoil at the altar, were tending to discredit all socially aspiring members of the denomination with their Episcopalian acquaintances and bankers. Consequently in the last three decades of the century, their bishops launched a subtle but determined campaign to put the Holiness movement under restraint."[26] The result of such pressure was a growth of "come-outism" in the northern Holiness movement and the formation of a number of new sects—the Church of the Nazarene, the Christian and Missionary Alliance, and the Church of God (Anderson, Indiana) being the most important. These new churches were all moderate within the Holiness context; they were predominantly urban (providing way stations in the cities for the rural Methodists moving into lower-middle-class jobs) and were not particularly strong in the South. In 1916 the largest of the Holiness bodies, the Church of the Nazarene, reported less than 25 percent of its membership in former Confederate states.[27]

The southern Methodist experience, like the southern Baptist, was influenced by the cultural solidarity of the South after the Civil War and the continued prominence of conservative rural influences within the church. In the 1870s southern Methodist bishops encouraged the Holiness movement, calling for "a general and powerful revival of Scriptural holiness." At the heart of the Holiness crusade in the 1870s and 1880s in the South were local Methodist ministers. Vinson Synan reports that in the 1880s "200 of the 240 ministers of the North Georgia conference professed to have received the experience of sanctification as a 'second blessing.'"[28] But in the 1890s southern Methodist leaders moved to quell the growing movement, fearing its potential to encourage doctrinal extremism and separation. Led by Bishop Atticus Haygood, in 1894 the bishops condemned the movement and moved to control its most outspoken promoters.

In short, the Holiness–southern Methodist experience roughly paralleled the Landmark–southern Baptist experience. In each case the conservative movements won wide support among the poor and farmers and retarded the growth of liberalism. "The Methodist preachers are the preservers of every old idea," wrote a disgruntled liberal Methodist at the turn of the century, "timid to the point of cowardice." In the South a large number of the Holiness campgrounds continued to operate under Methodist control. At the same time, the Holiness splinters in the South tended to attract only the most radical and doctrinally extreme Methodists. Although the moderate Holiness churches did grow in the South in the late 1890s, establishing colleges in four states, the southern "come-outers" were strongly influenced by the "fire-baptized" movement led by B. H. Irwin, which urged the sanctified to press on to additional baptisms—including "dynamite, lyddite, and oxidite." The small, exclusively southern, splinter Holiness sects that began to appear in the census by 1916 were strikingly poor and rural.[29]

The two historic southern churches of the plain people experienced class tension at the turn of the century, but there were clear class divisions in the two smaller people's churches, the Disciples of Christ and the Cumberland Presbyterians. Both churches suffered major divisions officially dated in 1906. Both divisions were partly sectional. A small majority of the Cumberland Presbyterians voted to unite with the Presbyterian Church of the United States of America after that body diluted its Calvinistic creed in 1903, but a majority of the southern churches refused to accept the union agreement. At the same time, a majority of the southern Disciples of Christ separated themselves in the 1906 religious census into the Churches of Christ. Theological issues aside, both divisions were sectional and economic. In the case of the Cumberland Presbyterians, sectional prejudices and racial fears played a part in the rejection of the merger by many southern churches. The 1916 census reveals that the uniting churches were also larger and wealthier. While just over 50 percent of the Cumberland Presbyterian churches joined the northern church, they carried with them two-thirds of the value of church buildings and over three-quarters of the value of the parsonages in the denomination. The churches that remained Cumberland Presbyterian had contributed less than 20 percent of the church's domestic missions budget in 1906. One promerger leader charged that his opponents were "anti-church-erection, anti-mission, anti-education and anti-everything." After the merger the Cumberland Presbyterian church became even more rural than before; in 1916 less than 5 percent of its membership attended churches in towns with a population of over twenty-five thousand. The church also remained poor. Only about one-fourth of its ministers in 1916 were seminary graduates; about 40 percent were farmers, and those reporting to the census as "full-time pastors" earned annual wages of $607.[30]

Even clearer is the sectional and urban-rural character of the division in Disciples of Christ.[31] In 1916 the Church of Christ (the name taken by the conservative wing of the movement) claimed 196,835 members in the former states of the Confederacy (61.9 percent of its total membership) as opposed to 185,144 for the Disciples of Christ in the same states (15.1 percent of its national membership). The schism followed clear class as well as sectional lines. The Church of Christ outnumbered the Disciples in the mid-South and Southwest, but the Disciples outnumbered it both in the coastal states and in the cities everywhere. In Memphis each group had four churches but the Disciples led in membership 1,688 to 368; in Birmingham there were two Churches of Christ with 250 members and the three Disciples of Christ congregations with 645 members; in Little Rock there was one Church of Christ with 65 members and three Disciples of Christ churches with 1,139 members; in Dallas the eight Churches of Christ had 997 members and eleven Disciples churches had 3,122. In southern towns with populations of over 25,000 in 1916 only Nashville, the center of the Church of Christ influence, reported more Churches of Christ than Disciples. The Church of Christ was the most rural major religious group listed in the census of 1916, reporting 95.5 percent of its membership "outside of principal cities."[32]

The economic statistics collected by the census confirm this pattern. The average value of church edifices reported by Churches of Christ in 1916 was $1,101.30; for the Disciples of Christ it was $4,803.14. In Alabama the figures were Disciples of Christ $3,188.14, Churches of Christ $863.65; in Arkansas, Disciples of Christ $2,363.00, Churches of Christ $606.98. The average value of a Disciples church in the South was $3,516.73; that of a Church of Christ, $962.32. The average membership of Disciples congregation was 146; that of a Church of Christ, 57. Nor were the crusty farmer-preachers who led the Church of Christ division unaware of what was happening. In 1897 one editor explained the schism: "As time advanced such of those churches as assembled in large towns and cities gradually became proud, or, at least, sufficiently worldly-minded to desire popularity, and in order to attain that unscriptural end they adopted certain popular arrangements such as the hired pastor, the church choir, instrumental music, man-made societies to advance the gospel and human devices to raise money to support previously mentioned devices of similar origin. In so doing they divided the brotherhood of disciples."[33]

For the most part, all of this religious turmoil had to do with the resentments of small farmers and, particularly in the case of the Holiness movement, small-town artisans and laborers. A nineteenth-century Church of Christ preacher described his church as the "industrious, sober and comparatively moral poor." But by the 1920s it was clear that another white social class had emerged in the South. Writing in 1925, Mims reported that the South had an educated elite who were much like their peers in the North, a second class of "half-educated, who have very little intellectual curiosity or independence of judgment" (a group that might well include the morally upright Landmarkers, the Church of Christ, the Holiness movement, Cumberland Presbyterians, and Primitives), and a third class composed of "a great mass of uneducated people—sensitive, passionate, prejudiced." It was among this group—the abjectly poor, the tenants, and the mill workers—that Pentecostalism flourished in the early twentieth century. By the 1920s the South had become, and for a generation remained, the nation's best neighborhood in which to peddle the gospel of poverty. This teeming layer of southern religion seldom came into public view; rural southern Methodists and Baptists were curious enough to baffle most urban Americans in the 1920s. H. L. Mencken, at the peak of his career of ridiculing Baptists, Methodists, and southerners, was utterly stunned to witness Brother Joe Furdew preaching to an outdoors "holy roller" meeting in the hills outside Dayton during the Scopes trial. As he returned from the meeting late in the evening, Mencken surveyed the scene in Dayton: "There was the friar wearing a sandwich sign announcing that he was the Bible Champion of the world. There was a Seventh Day Adventist arguing that Clarence Darrow was the beast with seven heads and ten horns described in Revelation XIII, and that the end of the world was at hand. There was an evangelist made up like Andy Gump, with the news that atheists in Cincinnati were preparing to descend upon Dayton, hang the eminent Judge Raulston, and burn the town. There was the ancient who maintained that no Catholic could be a Christian. There was the eloquent Dr. T. T. Martin, of Blue Mountain, Mississippi, come to town with a truck-load of torches and hymnbooks to put Darwin in his place." But as the crowd dispersed to Robinson's

Drug Store for a Coke, Mencken mused that the air of true devotion was missing. "The real religion was not present," he wrote; "it began at the bridge over the town creek, where the road makes off for the hills."[34] What Mencken had learned was that Dayton was to Rhea County what Atlanta was to Georgia and Paris was to France. If the God-fearing people of Dayton, southern Fundamentalists all, were an embarrassment to urban southern Baptists and Methodists, they seemed shamelessly decadent to the Pentecostals in the hills.

By the 1920s the three largest Pentecostal churches in the South were the Assemblies of God, with headquarters in Springfield, Missouri; the Pentecostal Holiness church, headquartered in Franklin Springs, Georgia; and the Church of God, with headquarters in Cleveland, Tennessee. All three of the churches had direct connections to the Holiness movement. When the Pentecostal experience of speaking in tongues rushed through the American Holiness movement after the Azusa Street meeting in Los Angeles in 1906, it found its readiest reception in the South. As southern Pentecostalism developed in the early twentieth century, it tended to be doctrinally more radical, less interested in cooperation with the organized Fundamentalist movement, and more rural than its northern counterpart. The first major split in the movement involved the question of whether the baptism of the Holy Spirit was the second or third work of grace, and a majority of southern Pentecostals (the Pentecostal Holiness church and the Church of God) took the more radical third-work view. This doctrinal stance clearly indicated the influence of Methodism in southern Pentecostalism.[35] There was a sprinkling of southern Baptists among early southern Pentecostals, and some minor Baptist groups—particularly the Free Will Baptists—became wholehearted participants in the Pentecostal revival. But generally, poor Baptists felt more at home in their churches than did poor Methodists by the turn of the century. At least, southern Methodism was less able or willing to accommodate radicalism and independence than were the southern Baptists.

Although the theological roots of southern Pentecostalism are somewhat diverse, the movement was uniformly successful among the lower class. In 1916 the Assemblies of God reported 118 congregations, including 47 in the South. Only 30 of the southern churches owned church buildings; they averaged $734.26 in value. This small denomination of 6,703 members reported 600 ministers, a ratio of 1 minister to 11 members. Only 27 of these ministers received salaries; the average was $578 per year. The Church of God reported 202 congregations and 7,784 members, almost all in the South. The average value of a church building in the sect was $586.26. The Church of God claimed 477 ministers, and 81 reported wages averaging $232 per year.[36]

By 1920 a bewildering array of Pentecostal sects were competing with one another, reflecting endless nuances in their hostility to the alien culture around them. Most were rigidly puritanical; the "frivolities" of the rich were condemned, including "moving picture shows, baseball games, picnics, circuses, dancing halls, county and state fairs," and other activities "calculated to destroy spirituality." Members were required to avoid "oath-bound secret societies, social clubs, and corrupt partisan politics." In 1928 a bewildered outsider caricatured Pentecostal beliefs: "In all their sects the Holy Rollers are against the vices of infidelity, evolutionism, sexual recreation, the use of gin, and fallen Methodism. They are against plain prayer without orgies as much as they are against dancing, liquor, and tobacco. They are against faith without a personal Devil as much as they are against jewelry, tea and coffee, transparent female garments, polygamy and theological liberalism."[37]

There were significant variations within this religious fringe. The moderate Church of the Nazarene attributed speaking in tongues to the "power of the devil" and in 1919 removed the word *Pentecostal* from its name "to dissociate themselves from what seemed to them fanaticism."[38] At the same time, many Pentecostals were disgusted by the Nazarene emphasis on education, despite the fact that one Nazarene college adopted "Hallelujah" as its school yell. But even the more rigid Pentecostal churches were plagued by divisions because of small accommodations to the world. In the 1930s the Pentecostal Holiness church relaxed an earlier law and allowed its members to belong to labor unions "consistent . . . with the legal effort of the part of labor, to prevent oppression and injustice from capitalism." Members were required not to use, sell, or grow tobacco, but in a concession to the poor of the tobacco-farming belt, the church's *Discipline* added an exception in the 1930s: "The word 'growth' in regard to tobacco shall not apply to hired help, or wives, and children who are required to work for tenants and landlords." As early as 1917 the Pentecostal Holiness church established standards for ordination that required a candidate to "recite in consecutive order the Books of the Bible," to "read the Bible through twice, and in addition to read at least 1,000 pages of other suggested books in harmony with the doctrines of the Pentecostal Holiness Church." The Church of God was criticized by other Pentecostals when in the mid-1920s it allowed its members to wear "wedding rings costing less than five dollars . . . in communities where their absence would cause scandal." On the fringe, the Church of God with Signs Following, founded in 1909, scorned all other Pentecostals who refused to handle serpents.[39]

In summary, the 1890s were a watershed in southern religious history as well as in southern political history. Most visible was the growing identification of the old churches of the people with the new southern elite. Wrote historian Frederick Bode, "Southern white Protestantism (unwittingly or not) became one of the mechanisms of the ruling-class hegemony."[40] The point, however, is not so much whether the Baptists and Methodists either wittingly or unwittingly were captured (or bribed) by the business elite to legitimize the New South, but that the leaders in those churches increasingly came to believe in the vision themselves. They were a part of the new elite. "Religion," wrote Methodist Bishop Raymond Brown of Arkansas, "grabbed hold of the coat-tails of secular prosperity and growth."[41]

As always, the upward mobility of the old churches of the plain people was only a part of the story. Although not directly related to Populism, the sectarian religious revolt at the turn of the century was clearly a parallel movement. The new southern middle class captured only one segment of southern evangelicalism. Many southern churches continued to be dominated by sturdy and moral farmers and laborers. Perhaps for the first time in southern history, the region experienced a grass-roots rebellion by the truly economically and religiously dispossessed.[42] For some southerners the religious crisis meant a continued though increasingly loose connection with their old churches, but for others conscience demanded secession. This new religious class consciousness turned the South into a caldron of sectarianism for half a century. As a region that had endured for three-quarters of a century without the introduction of a significant new religious group and in which the old churches of the people had seemed to be classless, the South suddenly became a maze of class consciousness in which Liston Pope found Presbyterians looking down on Baptists and Methodists who in turn spurned the Wesleyan Methodists, who regarded members of the Church of God as fanatics.[43]

The story of the plain people's churches of the South raises important questions about the reasons for their success and about the role they played in the lives of poor southerners. One appeal of the sectarian gospel, perhaps the element most visible to outsiders, was a message combining rejection of this world and the centering of man's hopes in the next. The new middle class may well enough rivet its attention on the construction of $500,000 buildings and other earthly causes, but the poor know that religion concerns that which lies beyond this vale of pain and tears. "This House of Clay is but a Prison," reminded a familiar hymn. A poor saint testified, "I just pray for God to take me out of the world; there is nothing here for me." "The mountain hymns," wrote James McBride Dabbs of the mournful but powerful song of the hill farmers, "are Protestantism gone to seed—beautiful seed, but, like thistledown, ethereal, floating on vague currents of air. That is what happens when the individual pursues himself too far."[44] But it was also a real world, a world that Pentecostal historian Robert M. Anderson vividly described: "The world of early Pentecostals was one of share-cropping and tenant farming, of backwoods cabins and ghetto tenements, of poverty and unemployment, of crime and vice, of racism and discrimination, of grinding, monotonous labor and fatigue, of material squalor and spiritual despair. . . . Rejected by the world, the Pentecostals in turn rejected the world."[45]

In such escapism there was also something for this world: there was the security that came from knowing that one was standing on the solid rock and living in the presence of God, of knowing that one day the last would be the first. It was with some dismay that a northern newsman awakened to the spiritual security enjoyed by Pentecostals.

Yet within their own sphere the Holy Rollers obviously live a life of tension as deliciously and sensuously gratifying as that of campus agnostics and cow town sophisticates. Ladies who meet the Lord God Sabaoth socially in their boudoirs before breakfast and gentlemen who may at any moment break out with soul-saving words in White Russian naturally have no thrills to ask of Earl Carrol. They know, too, that the thrills of the sort they like best will never end: that in Heaven the sanctified will be nearest

Jesus and have the best seats for watching the fallen Methodists, the cocktail drinking Episcopalians, and the Devil-serving Papists jump through the fiery hoops.[46]

Probably more important was the social significance of the sects and their place at the center of the poor's communities. Misled by the simplistic theologies of the sects, their disinterest in politics and social reform, their opposition to organized social Christianity, and their intense individualism, mainstream Christians often overlook the social significance of the religious communities of the plain people. Some sociologists have noted the cohesion of the sectarian congregation. In 1957 Russell R. Dynes wrote: "In the life style of the sectarian the religious group appears to be his most meaningful association and source of friendship. . . . Sectarian groups with their organizational simplicity and congregational similarity produce a type of loyalty, satisfaction, and religious intensity that complex religious organizations do not reproduce." A more recent study of the churches in a lower-class southern urban community concluded: "For some persons, involvement in their church's program is the core of their existence. Meaning and purpose of life, values to live by, encouragement in the face of constant adversity, are given through their church associations. Real joy and integrity in the lives of these individuals seems traceable to their commitment to a religious community." Donald Mathews has written persuasively of antebellum evangelicals' obsession with "replacing the disorder of the world with the order of 'Christian society.'"[47]

In the poor farming communities of the nineteenth-century South and in the growing mill towns at the turn of the century, the poor person's church was the heart of his or her community. It was in many cases the only institution that related to one's social class. The antimission Baptist emphasis on the church rested on social as well as theological assumptions: "We, as an Association, declare a nonfellowship with Masonry, Missionary, Bible, and Tract Societies, Campbellism, State Conventions, Theological Seminaries, and all other new institutions that have the appearance of a speculation on the gospel; we know of but two societies, viz: *Civil* and *Religious.*" In such simple societies the church was central, in a sense identifying everyone in the community—brothers, sisters, and outsiders. When H. L. Mencken encountered a pasty-faced youth who was the first person he had not met in Dayton to admit he was not a practicing Christian, the young man said: "I don't belong to no church. . . . I'm a sinner."[48]

It has often been assumed that poor people's churches rejected "anything approaching the notion that 'being saved' might involve concern for the plight of one's fellow man." Such assertions, of course, reflect the prejudices of the institutionally oriented middle class; it was their perception of the anti-institutional religion of the poor. In fact, the churches of the poor were important social institutions; members were related by close personal, familial ties. A recent writer described a rural Baptist congregation at the turn of the twentieth century: "The Old Regular Baptist Church was once the center of Appalachian community life. Stressing the need to establish unity and cooperation among its members and to act as a working example of harmony, its influence extended into the broader community. . . . To me, this church, which embodied the spirit of unity, cooperation, harmony, and fellowship, is the very essence of Christianity." Such Christians were brothers and sisters; the local church records of the nineteenth century teem with entries such as the following from the Bethel Baptist Church in Missouri: "Resolved, that the church take Sister Elizabeth Poe under their care and maintain her." A North Carolina Church of Christ preacher wrote in 1876: "The Church of God keeps the Lord's treasury filled. She takes care of her own poor. She feeds her own hungry, and clothes her own naked. She feeds and clothes her own Widows and Orphans." In their own individualistic and limited way, the poor people's churches extended their concern to others. Church of Christ editor David Lipscomb wrote in the midst of the Tennessee depression in 1875: "We daily see numbers of people, especially negroes in and around the highways of this city whose countenances but too plainly tell of the cold and starvation they are enduring. . . . The only way to prevent further suffering is for each one to do what he can for the poor of his immediate neighborhood."[49]

Finally, the churches of the plain people arose and survived in the South precisely because they were of the people. Francis Simkins, in an incredibly condescending assessment of the "primitive" churches in the twentieth-century South, stumbled onto some plain truth: "The poor whites do not have the clothes or the manners to make them feel at ease in church; they are not sophisticated enough to understand the King James Bible or the 'seminary language' of a clergy among whom 'educational standards' are rising."[50] It is true that the churches of the poor succeeded because they insisted on being religious in their own way, in their own places, and with their own preachers.

No information gathered by the twentieth-century religious censuses throws more light on the people's churches of the South than the statistics on ministers. Of the 15,946 ministers reported by the Southern Baptist Convention in 1916, only 2,411 reported regular salaries. These averaged $1,072 per year. Over a thousand reported their occupation as farmers.[51] The Primitive Baptists reported 976 ministers; only 57 received salaries, which averaged $338 per year. Over two-thirds of the Primitive Baptist ministers listed their occupations as farmers. The Old Regular Baptist Church, which had 21,521 members in the South, had 494 preachers; 35 reported receiving wages, which averaged $120 per year. A visitor to the Appalachians at the turn of the century found that "the backwoodsmen did not like the preacher to be a preacher only."[52] When one visited a poor man's church in the early-twentieth-century South, whether a rural Baptist congregation or Church of Christ or a mill-town Pentecostal church, the preacher would likely be one of the people— probably a farmer, a barber, or a factory worker. For most of the poor such an arrangement was not only necessary; it was fitting.[53]

Perhaps the surest sign that a major class chasm has developed between religious classes appears when upwardly mobile churches become consciously concerned about the plight of the poor. Nothing irritated the pioneer Methodist and Baptist preachers in the South and West more than eastern anxiety about ignorant frontiersmen whose only light was viewed as "a feeble glimmering from UNEDU-CATED men." Just as ominous was the awakened interest of the Federal Council of Churches in "revitalizing the rural church" in the early twentieth century. In 1912 George Frederick Wells, assistant to the executive secretary of the Federal Council of Churches, called for a concerned effort to establish a church in "every country community" and outlined how each of these congregations was to work for the "moral and religious welfare and betterment of society." The rural churches must be "systematic," he urged, in promoting "visitation, evangelism, temperance and other moral reforms, religious education and missions," and of course, they were urged to consolidate under the reform leaders of American religion. Shortly after the turn of the century the Southern Baptist Convention identified the three million inhabitants of Appalachia as the nation's most pressing mission concern.[54] Such efforts probably always tell more about the planners than about what is going to happen to the objects of their solicitude.

What happened was that the religious poor took care of themselves, as they always have. Much of the effort of early-nineteenth-century southern evangelicals had been aimed at dismantling "mediating elites." Donald Mathews described antebellum evangelicalism as "a volatile social movement providing a value system to raise converts in their own esteem, giving them confidence in themselves and their comrades, and create the moral courage to reject as authoritative for themselves the life-style and values of traditional elites." Bertram Wyatt-Brown argued that the Primitive Baptist protest was simply a "persistent southern struggle to preserve old values in an alien, changing, and often self-righteous world."[55] When the Methodists and Baptists moved up the class ladder in the nineteenth century, they created a religious vacuum at the bottom of southern society. It is no surprise that the vacuum was filled not from the top but from the bottom. Writing in the late nineteenth century, veteran Texas preacher Thomas W. Caskey summed up the sectarian view of the changes that had occurred in southern religion:

> We never heard religious people talking about "how to reach the masses" fifty years ago. In fact we had not so much as heard whether there be any masses then. Such talk in these later days shows that some churches and church folk are anxious to have it understood that the gulf between them and the masses is so wide that it is a problem which puzzles the wisest of heads among them as to how they can reach the masses. Now, if Christ were here on earth today, He would be one among the masses . . . and all the talk of professed Christians about "how to reach the masses" is but so much talk about how to reach Christ.[56]

NOTES

1. Lorenzo Dow, *The Dealings of God, Man and the Devil; as Exemplified in the Life, Experience and Travels of Lorenzo Dow . . .* (2 vols.; New York, 1851), II, 165–66; Anne C. Loveland, *Southern Evangelicals and the Social Order, 1800–1860* (Baton Rouge, 1980), 33; Donald G. Mathews, *Religion in the Old South* (Chicago, 1977), xvii.

2. Mathews, *Religion in the Old South,* 27.

3. Minton Thrift, *Memoir of the Rev. Jesse Lee with Extracts from His Journals* (1928; rpr. New York, 1969), 348–49; *Minutes of the Annual Conference of the Methodist Episcopal Church, South, for the Year 1863* (Nashville, 1870), 467; Dow, *Dealings of God, Man and the Devil,* I, 89.

4. Albert Henry Newman, *A History of the Baptist Churches in the United States* (6th ed.; Philadelphia, 1915), 320; Abel Stevens, *A Compendious History of American Methodism* (New York, 1867), 552; David Benedict, *A General History of the Baptist Denomination in America and Other Parts of the World* (New York, 1849), 754.

5. Loveland, *Southern Evangelicals and the Social Order,* 59–62. For a thorough discussion of this point see the entire chapter, "The Ministry," 30–64.

6. Nathan O. Hatch, "The Christian Movement and the Demand for a Theology of the People," *Journal of American History,* LXVII (December, 1980), 553. For a general discussion of this lower-class emphasis, see Hatch's entire article and David Edwin Harrell, Jr., *Quest for a Christian America* (Nashville, 1966), 647.

7. Robert A. Baker, *The Southern Baptist Convention and Its People, 1607–1972* (Nashville, 1974), 150.

8. Benn Barrus, Milton L. Baughn, and Thomas H. Campbell, *A People Called Cumberland Presbyterians* (Memphis, 1972), 86, 116, 127. See also 50–104.

9. Bertram Wyatt-Brown, "The Antimission Movement in the Jacksonian South: A Study in Regional Folk Culture," *Journal of Southern History,* XXXVI (November, 1970), 502; Baker, *Southern Baptist Convention,* 152; Robert G. Torbet, *A History of the Baptists* (Rev. ed.; Valley Forge, Pa., 1969), 273. See also Newman, *History of the Baptist Churches,* 437, 440.

10. Wyatt-Brown, "The Antimission Movement," 515–16.

11. Benedict, *General History of the Baptist Denomination,* 787; Wyatt-Brown, "The Antimission Movement," 503.

12. Benedict, *General History of the Baptist Denomination,* 733, 935.

13. Torbet, *History of the Baptists,* 276; Benedict, *General History of the Baptist Denomination,* 773, 808.

14. See Baker, *Southern Baptist Convention,* 208–19; William Wright Barnes, *The Southern Baptist Convention, 1845–1853* (Nashville, 1954), 103–17; James E. Tull, "A Study of Southern Baptist Landmarkism in the Light of Historical Baptist Ecclesiology" (Ph.D. dissertation, Columbia Univer-

sity, 1960); Hugh Wamble, "Landmarkism: Doctrinaire Ecclesiology Among Baptists," *Church History,* XXXIII (December, 1964), 429–44.

15. Wyatt-Brown, "The Antimission Movement," 525.

16. Edwin Mims, "Why the South Is Anti-Evolution," *World's Work,* L (September, 1925), 552; George Marsden, *Fundamentalism and American Culture: The Shaping of Twentieth-Century Evangelicalism, 1870–1925* (New York, 1980), 179.

17. Katherine Du Pre Lumpkin, *The Making of a Southerner* (New York, 1947), 162–63; W. P. Trent, "Tendencies of Higher Life in the South," *Atlantic Monthly,* LXXIX (June, 1897), 777; Brooks Hays, "Reflections on the Role of Baptists in Politics and the Future of America," *Baptist History and Heritage,* XI (July, 1976), 170; Baker, *Southern Baptist Convention,* 277.

18. Mims, "Why the South is Anti-Evolution," 549. See also Gerald W. Johnson, "The Battling South," *Scribner's Magazine,* LXXVII (March, 1925), 307.

19. Trent, "Tendencies of Higher Life in the South," 777–78.

20. Ralph E. Morrow, Introduction to Part IV of Emory Stevens Bucke (ed.), *The History of American Methodism* (3 vols.; New York, 1964), II, 592–93; Jeremiah Bell Jeter, *The Recollections of a Long Life* (Richmond, 1981), 310–19; "Epidemic of Church Building in the South," *Literary Digest,* LXXIII (June 24, 1922), 30–31.

21. U.S. Bureau of the Census, *Religious Bodies: 1916* . . . (2 vols.; Washington, D.C., 1919), I, 121; Newman, *History of the Baptist Churches,* 383.

22. W. Morgan Patterson, "The Influence of Landmarkism Among Baptists," *Baptist History and Heritage,* XI (January, 1976), 44–45; Baker, *Southern Baptist Convention,* 278; Wamble, "Landmarkism," 444; William E. Ellis, "The Fundamentalist-Modernist Schism over Evolution in the 1920s," *Register of the Kentucky Historical Society,* LXXIV (April, 1976), 114–16.

23. Patterson, "Influence of Landmarkism Among Baptists," 54; Wamble, "Landmarkism," 444; Baker, *Southern Baptist Convention,* 284.

24. U.S. Bureau of the Census, *Religious Bodies: 1926* . . . (2 vols.; Washington, D.C., 1930), II, 224–27, 104.

25. Timothy L. Smith, *Revivalism and Social Reform in Mid-Nineteenth Century America* (New York, 1957), 135–47.

26. Duncan Aikman, "The Holy Rollers," *American Mercury,* XV (1928), 183. For general information on the Holiness movement see Timothy L. Smith, *Called unto Holiness: The Story of the Nazarenes* (Kansas City, 1962); Robert Mapes Anderson, *Vision of the Disinherited: The Making of American Pentecostalism* (New York, 1979); and Timothy L. Smith, "Holiness Crusade," in Bucke (ed.), *History of American Methodism,* II, 608–27.

27. Contrary to the general denominational pattern, most of the Nazarene churches in the South were rural. Bureau of the Census, *Religious Bodies: 1926* . . . , II, 383–85. See Charles Edwin Jones, "Disinherited or Rural? A Historical Case Study in Urban Holiness Religion," *Missouri Historical Review,* LXVI (April, 1972), 395–412; Vinson Synan, *The Holiness-Pentecostal Movement in the United States* (Grand Rapids, 1971), 75.

28. Smith, "The Holiness Crusade," 615; Synan, *Holiness-Pentecostal Movement,* 39.

29. Frederick A. Bode, *Protestantism and the New South* (Charlottesville,

David Edwin Harrell, Jr.

1975), 150; Anderson, *Vision of the Disinherited,* 35; Raymond O. Corvin, "History of Education by the Pentecostal Holiness Church in South Carolina and Georgia" (M.A. thesis, University of South Carolina, 1942), 204; Bureau of the Census, *Religious Bodies: 1916. . . ,* II, 633–37, 989.

30. Barrus, *A People Called Cumberland Presbyterians,* 341, 332, 275, 376; Bureau of the Census, *Religious Bodies: 1916. . . ,* I, 348, II, 572.

31. David Edwin Harrell, Jr., "The Sectional Origins of the Churches of Christ," *Journal of Southern History,* XXX (August, 1964), 261–77.

32. Bureau of the Census, *Religious Bodies: 1916 . . . ,* I, 365–66, 386, 428, 443–44, 121.

33. Bureau of the Census, *Religious Bodies: 1916. . . ,* I, 209, 249; Daniel Sommer, "The Signs of the Times," *Octographic Review,* XL (October, 1897), 1; David Edwin Harrell, Jr., *The Social Sources of Division in the Disciples of Christ, 1865–1900* (Atlanta, 1973), 323–50.

34. "The Church as God Ordained It," *Gospel Advocate,* XXXVIII (July 9, 1896), 436; Mims, "Why the Church Is Anti-Evolution," 551; H. L. Mencken, *A Mencken Chrestomathy* (New York, 1974), 8.

35. The southern Pentecostal churches were unquestionably predominantly Methodist in origin and doctrine. On the other hand, the Assemblies of God, which was a less southern denomination, revealed clear Baptist influence in its early beliefs and practices. For discussions of this interesting point, see Anderson, *Visions of the Disinherited,* 153–75; Marsden, *Fundamentalism and American Culture,* 94; Edith Lydia Waldvogel, "The 'Overcoming' Life: A Study in the Reformed Evangelical Origins of Pentecostalism" (Ph.D. dissertation, Harvard University, 1977); Synan, *Holiness-Pentecostal Movement,* 147–53.

36. Bureau of the Census, *Religious Bodies: 1916. . . ,* II, 40–42, 210–13.

37. *Discipline of the Pentecostal Holiness Church, 1937* (Franklin Springs, Ga., 1937), 12–43; Aikman, "The Holy Rollers," 191.

38. Jones, "Disinherited or Rural?" 400; Corvin, "History of Education by the Pentecostal Holiness Church," 195, 251, 285–90.

39. *Discipline of the Pentecostal Holiness Church, 1937,* p. 42; Corvin, "History of Education by the Pentecostal Holiness Church," 275; Aikman, "Holy Rollers," 191; Synan, *Holiness-Pentecostal Movement,* 187.

40. Bode, *Protestantism and the New South,* 7. See also Frederick Bode, "Religions and Class Hegemony: A Populist Critique in North Carolina," *Journal of Southern History,* XXXVII (August, 1971), 417–38.

41. Francis Butler Simkins, *The Everlasting South* (Baton Rouge, 1963), 82.

42. It is entirely proper, as Donald Mathews noted, to view the early-nineteenth-century poor of the South as only relatively underprivileged. Most owned farms, and many owned a few slaves. They were "poor" largely in the sense of being independent and anti-aristocratic. See Mathews, *Religion in the Old South,* 36–38.

43. Liston Pope, *Millhands and Preachers* (New Haven, 1942), 138.

44. Harry Lefever, "The Church and Poor Whites," *New South,* XXV (Spring, 1970), 1–32; James McBride Dabbs, *Haunted by God,* (Richmond, 1972), 17.

45. Anderson, *Vision of the Disinherited,* 240. For a discussion of the

same spirit among early Methodists, see Loveland, *Southern Evangelicals and the Social Order,* 93.

46. Aikman, "The Holy Rollers," 191. Also see Dickson D. Bruce, Jr., "Religion, Society and Culture in the Old South: A Comparative View," *American Quarterly,* XXVI (October, 1974), 399–416.

47. Russell R. Dynes, "The Consequences of Sectarianism for Social Participation," *Social Forces,* XXXV (May, 1957), 331–34; Harry Lefever, "The Church and Poor Whites," *New South,* XXV (Spring, 1970), 32; Mathews, *Religion in the Old South,* 40.

48. Benedict, *General History of the Baptist Denomination,* 2; William Manchester, *Disturber of the Peace* (New York, 1950), 168.

49. Louis D. Rubin, Jr., Introduction to Rubin (ed.), *The American South* (Baton Rouge, 1980), 10; Ron Short, "We Believe in the Family and the Old Regular Baptist Church," *Southern Exposure* (Fall, 1976), 61–62; "Minutes of the Bethel Church . . ." (Mimeographed copy made by St. Louis, Missouri, Historical Record Survey Division of Professional and Service Projects, Works Progress Administration, 1940, in Mullins Library, University of Arkansas, Fayetteville), 16; "The Law of Love," *Watch Tower,* IV (September, 1876), 107; David Lipscomb, "Destitution: Its Cause," *Gospel Advocate,* XVII (March, 1875), 227.

50. Simkins, *The Everlasting South,* 88.

51. Bureau of the Census, *Religious Bodies: 1916 . . . ,* I, 71. See also Newman, *History of the Baptist Church,* 463.

52. Bureau of the Census, *Religious Bodies: 1916 . . . ,* II, 136–47, 128–31; John Fox, Jr., "The Southern Mountaineer," *Scribner's Magazine,* XXIX (May, 1901), 468.

53. For an exploration of this general theme, see David Edwin Harrell, Jr., *White Sects and Black Men in the Recent South* (Nashville, 1971).

54. Dow, *Dealings of God, Man and the Devil,* II, 161; C. Luther Fry, "Change in Religious Organizations," in *Recent Social Trends in the United States* (1-vol. ed.; New York, 1933), 1052; "The Rural Church," *Annals of the American Academy of Political and Social Science,* XL (March, 1912), 459. In 1944 the Southern Baptist denomination initiated a "rural missions" program. Concern about the decline of rural Baptist churches was a persistent theme of the editors of Baptist state newspapers. See *Encyclopedia of Southern Baptists* (20 vols.; Nashville, 1958), II, 1176–77.

55. Hatch, "Theology of the People," 551; Mathews, *Religion in the Old South,* xvii; Wyatt-Brown, "The Antimission Movement," 529.

56. Fletcher D. Srygley, *Seventy Years in Dixie* (Nashville, 1891), 3.

THE BLACK CHURCH IN THE CONTEXT OF AMERICAN RELIGION
C. Eric Lincoln

The peculiar circumstances out of which the black church developed in America were not regionally discrete. Black religion is not so much a response to a spiritual *modus vivendi* peculiar to the South as it is a response to a cultural syndrome in which the South and the North were common participants. The Puritans of New England were hardly more avid in their zest to Christianize the blacks among them than were their Anglican counterparts in the plantation South. Their preferred belief that blacks were of another order was sufficient to modify the notion of Christian responsibility so that South and North were united in a kind of spiritual obliviousness toward blacks. Curiously, religion was the area of both greatest consistency and greatest confusion between North and South. How else could the black church have been born of segregation in the North, yet practically nurtured in the spiritual bosom of the South?

The establishment of the black church as an independent institution was a dramatic registration of blacks' capacity for Christian liberty and of their determination to achieve it. That the independent black church came hard on the heels of the American thrust for political independence probably was assigned no significance at the time; perhaps we have still to learn that Christian liberty and personal freedom cannot be strangers to each other. But the black Christians knew then, even as they know now. Henry Highland Garnett, a black preacher and abolitionist, assured his listeners that "the humblest peasant is as free in the sight of God as the proudest monarch" and that God would smile "upon every effort they might make to disenthrall themselves."

Nathaniel Paul in his perplexity was moved to address God himself: "And oh Thou, immaculate God, be not angry with us while we come into thy sanctuary and make bold inquiry . . . why it was that thou didst look with calm indifference . . . when thy whole law is violated, thy divine authority despised, and a portion of thine creatures reduced to a mere state of vassalage and misery."[1]

But Thomas Fortune labeled the white man's religion "a living

lie . . . fit only to be cast to the dogs." And David Walker in his cele-
brated appeal to revolution assured his brothers in bondage that God
would deliver them if they would but strike for their freedom:
"When the hour arrives and you move, be not afraid or dismayed; for
be assured that Jesus Christ and the King of heaven and of earth, who
is the God of justice will surely go before you. And those enemies
who have stolen our rights and kept us ignorant of Him, He will remove. . . . Put everything before us to death in order to gain our
freedom which God has given us."[2] Such sentiments spoke the sup-
pressed rage and sense of injury every black Christian had to endure,
and life on the white man's terms grew more onerous as time passed.

Once the precedent of independent congregations had been established, black churches sprang up wherever they were permitted, and
by the end of the Civil War, to belong to an "African" church was
an irreducible statement of how one felt about one's place in the
scheme of things in America.

THE BIRTH OF THE AFRICAN CHURCHES

In 1778 Andrew Bryan became pastor of the First African Baptist
Church in Savannah, succeeding George Liele as leader of what was
probably the first of the independent African churches. Liele had
founded the church around 1771 at Silver Bluff, South Carolina,
and had escaped to Jamaica with the British during the Revolution. Bryan's church was under constant surveillance by the hated
"pattyrollers" (slave patrols). His meetings were repeatedly broken
up, and he and members of his congregation were whipped and
thrown into prison. Finally, through the efforts of his master, he was
released and permitted to continue his ministry in a barn set aside
for his use on the plantation. He became well known throughout
the area for his ministry. When he died in 1812, the white Baptist
Association of Savannah issued a memorial statement noting his
good works.[3]

Further north, on a fateful Sunday in November, 1787, a small
group of black church members were pulled from their knees while
praying in what they did not realize was a "white" section of a segregated gallery in Saint George's Methodist Church in Philadelphia.
Among the offenders were Richard Allen and Absalom Jones, both

free blacks known widely for their industry and Christian deportment. Their request to be allowed to finish their prayers was denied, and after a brief consultation among themselves, "all went out of the church in a body and [the whites] were no more plagued with [blacks] in the church."[4]

Because they considered the moral and family interests of their followers to be endangered in the absence of a full and regular church life, Allen and Jones soon moved to found an organization they hoped would at least partially fill the void created by their departure from Saint George's. On April 12, 1787, they led in the establishment of the Free African Society, "a self-improvement association which was designed to provide mutual aid in times of misfortune, and to exercise a kind of moral oversight over its membership by visitation and prayer." It was not a church, but in its organization and vision the Society showed remarkable insight into the peculiar construct of needs common to the black condition. Gayraud Wilmore finds that:

> The suitability of The Free African Society pattern for meeting multiple needs in the Black community is amply demonstrated by the rapidity and the enthusiasm by which it spread from Philadelphia to other cities. Wherever the Societies were organized, they began as protests against white prejudice and neglect, and with the objective of providing not only for religious needs, but for social service, mutual aid and solidarity among "people of African descent.". . . The African Societies did not only express the need for cultural unity and solidarity, but the protest and resistance of a persecuted people.

Wilmore concludes: "It created, therefore, the classic pattern for the Black Church in the United States. A pattern of religious commitment that has a double focus . . . the free and autonomous worship of God in the way Black people want to worship him, and the unity and social welfare of the Black community."[5]

The Free African Society was not intended to be a church, but it turned out to be the practical preparation for the black church that was to come. By 1790, no less busy in the abolition enterprise than in the care of widows and orphans and the moral uplift of its membership, the Society decided to sponsor regular religious services. On January 1, 1791, the decision was reached to organize a church. The prevailing sentiment was for affiliation with the Church of England, and on July 17, 1794, the African Protestant Episcopal Church of Saint Thomas was dedicated, with Absalom Jones as pastor. Less than two weeks later, on July 29, 1794, Bethel African Methodist Episcopal Church, under the leadership of Richard Allen, also was dedicated. Both churches were spawned by the Free African Society. Saint Thomas remained a black church within the Episcopal communion. Bethel became "mother" to the first venture in African Methodism and was the spark that ignited the independent black church movement. Soon after its dedication Bethel issued a public statement with a preamble that said in part, "Whereas, from time to time many inconveniences have arisen from white people and people of color mixing together in public assemblies, more particularly places of worship, we have thought it necessary to provide for ourselves a convenient house to assemble in, separate from our white brethren." The statement went on to list in detail the reasons for the act of separation. They included: "First, to prevent any offense being given to whites by their presence and their mingling with them in public worship; second, to prevent any of the colored people from taking offense at religion itself because of the partiality which was shown white worshippers on account of color . . . and third, that they might 'build each other up.'"[6]

After a protracted legal struggle with Saint George's, which claimed oversight of Bethel and title to its property as well, the church eventually gained informal independence. Allen was ordained deacon in 1799 and later became an elder. In the meantime African Methodist churches were being organized along the Atlantic coast as far south as Baltimore. In 1816 several African Methodist churches met in conference in Philadelphia, and a national denomination—the African Methodist Episcopal Church—was formed. Allen became its first bishop. Thereafter African Methodism spread rapidly with churches in Massachusetts, New York, Pennsylvania, and South Carolina. In Charleston the Reverend Morris Brown pastored a congregation numbering three thousand in 1812.[7]

The second of the African churches reached denominational status when the African Methodist Episcopal Zion Church elected James Varick to be its first bishop in 1822.[8] The Zionites, as they were called, had their origins in circumstances similar to Richard Allen's Bethelites. In 1796 a group of black Christians led by Varick and Abraham Thompson withdrew from the John Street Methodist Church in New York to arrange for separate worship for black members of that church. There were no violent incidents, as there had been at Saint George's. Indeed, it has been argued that:

> [The] Methodist Episcopal Church at the time Varick and his followers withdrew from it was a victim of circumstances. African slavery had produced its sickening effects all over the country, in Church and State. The Methodist Episcopal Church, like all other churches at the time, had been influenced by it. They did not persecute their colored brethren, however, they simply denied them their rightful privileges. . . . But this the colored brethren did not think they could stand and at the same time work out for themselves the high destiny which God holds out to all men who serve Him aright.[9]

The issue again was segregation and the demeaning treatment segregation implied. But it was more than the matter of inconvenience and injured pride: the notion that people, perhaps in particular Christians who perceive themselves to be in the image of God, simply are not to be manipulated runs deep in the spiritual understanding of black religion. The white Christians' posturing and arrogant gestures of superiority were not only offensive to blacks, but they were also seen as offensive to the whole spirit of Christianity and therefore to God himself. To submit willingly to such racial idolatry was to become an accessory to it. To what degree whites were victims of circumstances or whether morally and ethically they simply were remiss in the choices they made is not to be judged here. However, it is certainly true that what went on at Saint George's and at John Street was not in any sense unusual. It represented the prevailing spirit in the American churches in regard to black Christians, and the felt need of the blacks to come out from among them soon became a fever. Bishop William J. Walls, a historian of the African Methodist Episcopal Zion Church, described the situation from which black Christians felt compelled to escape.

> [The Negro] was wanted in the church for the support he gave it, for the numbers he enabled sectarians to claim in exhibiting their strength, and with the minority, who were truly pious, he was wanted there for the good of his soul. For these and other reasons he was not kept entirely out of the church. But in the church he was hampered and regulated. His privileges were proscribed and limited; every possible effort was made to impress him with a sense of inferiority. Preachers were selected who delighted in discoursing upon such texts as *"Servants, obey your masters,"* and who were adept at impressing the Negro with inferiority in the most ingenious and least offensive way. . . . This state of things was not confined to any one particular branch of the American Church, but it was

found in every denomination in every community in which there was any considerable number of the black race.[10]

Several denominations owe their origin to the movement for an independent black church symbolized in the breakaway of the African Methodist churches. In time the African Methodist Episcopal (AME) and the African Methodist Episcopal Zion (AMEZ) churches would be joined by yet another black Methodist church, three major Baptist conventions, one major Pentecostal body (the Church of God in Christ), and a number of splinter sects and cults.[11] Together the black Methodist churches, the three major Baptist conventions and the Church of God in Christ make up the main body of black religion in America. They represent about 95 percent of black Christians in the country today, with the remainder scattered among the major white Protestant denominations and the Catholic church.

A NEW CULTURE FOR THE NEWLY CHOSEN

One of the peculiar advantages available in Christianity was that it provided a ready-made culture and a ready-made tradition for a people who had been separated brutally from their own. The Christian God was active in history. He involved himself in human affairs. He delivered Israel from bondage. Were the slaves themselves not in the hands of the western pharaohs, and would not God deliver them? If God was just and if God was merciful, if God was on the side of the oppressed, then must not they be the chosen people of God? Who else could better qualify! Such was the genesis of an idea destined for extended theological examination in the apologia of black religion when black theology emerged as a discipline a hundred years after slavery had ended. But a tradition was not what the black church was in need of. The black church invented its own tradition. Although the deliverance of Israel from bondage was a useful illustration of the power and justice of God, the black church in America never confused itself with biblical Israel. Black Christians knew themselves to be God's *black* chosen—a recognition and an affirmation of the illimitability of divine love and concern. If God could choose once, God could choose again.

Like the Jews, blacks chose God, and conceived themselves as chosen by God, because of their understanding of the nature of his all-encompassing love and the character of his righteous justice. Although there are black cults that have found the appropriation of a synthetic Jewish culture less anxiety-producing than the search for and the interpretation of the legitimate black experience, mainstream black religion has pursued an authentic heritage that, for the most part, has been able to avoid both the fantasies of escapism and the stigma of being contrived. The Jewish heritage has remained with the Jews, and American religion with the white Americans. Black religion had its own reason for being, its own experience to draw upon, and its own counsel to be kept.

Since religion and culture are inseparable, black Americans had no need to have a culture thrust upon them, noblesse oblige, as it were. But precisely because nobility self-perceived needs a sense of obligation to survive, the blacks in America have been the shoals of consternation and despair for legions of social scientists, government planners, academics, concerned Christians, and countless others in the business of racial social engineering. The African diaspora, however, are not in America in search of a culture, despite the fact that they involuntarily were separated from their own. Tragic as that separation was, it has come to pass that out of the ancient treasuries of the African heritage and out of the survival learnings of the black experience in America, a new culture has evolved. That culture is the black Americans' own creation out of their own experience. All cultures are syncretistic—the sure sign of human commonality—just as all cultures are innovative—the evidence of human genius. Black American subculture is inevitably modified and restricted, benefited and inspired, by the prevailing culture that surrounds it. But it is rooted in the singularities of the black experience, and its characteristic refraction is through the black church, the source of its nurture and of its creative potential.

The black church, the cultus of black religion, was characterized by a crucial social interest from the beginning. It was for much of its history an invisible system of relationships, a nexus of otherwise ungathered power. It was not a particular place, and often it had no place except the bayous and the swamps. There the search for a more suitable truth than a segregated church provided gathered the black faithful in furtive, clandestine assemblage. It was the black church that organized the energies and systematized the beliefs and practices of the slaves in such a way as to transcend the cultural deficit caused by their estrangement from Africa. But more than that, the black church was the unifying agent that made of a scattered confusion of slaves a free people, a *Blackamerican* people.

The black church began as a religious society, but it was more than that. It was the black Christian's government, social club, secret order, espionage system, political party, and impetus to revolution. It provided the counterpart of the important social institutions blacks had known and participated in in the African culture from which they had been separated. Under its aegis were the rites of passage from puberty to adulthood, from singleness to marriage, from life to death. The church sponsored the communal meal, the ritual of sacrificial togetherness. When freedom came and the invisible church could be made manifest in wood and glass and stone, wherever black people were gathered and by whatever exigencies of fortune, there they built a church—a symbol of their faith in God's continuing deliverance and of their common bond in the black experience.

The church house was funded and raised as a community effort. The church building was the community forum, the public school, the conservatory of music; it was the place where the elocutionary arts, the graphic arts, the literary arts, and the domestic arts were ultimately put on prideful display. It was lyceum and gymnasium as well as sanctum sanctorum. It was the prime developer of black leadership, a fact that is critical to the quality of freedom every Blackamerican enjoys today. Bishop William J. Walls wrote of his own church: "The African Methodist Episcopal Zion Church naturally . . . became to the Afro-American race what Faneuil Hall was to the Anglo-American—their cradle of liberty."[12] What Bishop Walls said of the AMEZ Church is generally true throughout the black church. It was indeed a cradle of liberty. It produced Nat Turner, and it produced Martin Luther King, Jr. Ranged between their respective conceptualizations of the nature of Christian responsibility, the black church has been womb and mother to a whole spectrum of black leadership for every generation of its existence.

The black church is the most authentic representation of whatever it means to be black in America. It is the one institution in which is crystallized the whole range of credits and debits, genius and emotion, hope and fear, projection and recoil that characterizes the scattered people of West Africa who became one people in America. During the slave era the black churches were monitored by white men and not infrequently closed or destroyed if considered a threat to white interests or well-being. But such behavior could not destroy the church itself: It was flesh of the masters' flesh; it was the counterpart of the masters' faith. But it was never substance of the masters' substance. It was a witness and a judgment against the distortions of the prevailing religion, and what its detractors could not effectively smother, they eventually learned to let alone. Amused by its style, confused by its meaning, sometimes a patron to its indigence, but always aloof from its fellowship, the white Christians kept counsel with their own spiritual kin, and the black church was able to become itself in spite of the constraints. Like the living faith it represents, it survived its obstructionists, within and without, to become both the hope and the symbol of the black estate in America.

Over the long history of their pilgrimage in America, the blacks were at times their own chief antagonists, and the whites had to do little to keep control except to catalyze black divisiveness, for black solidarity was impossible under slavery. Even when slavery was ended, the legacy of universal white dominion and universal black subservience was difficult to escape. The white man was in power, and all available evidence suggested that he always had been in power and always would be in power. It followed that the best a black man could hope for was to be as approximately "white" as he could manage.

The felt need to be white—or like white—was the reef on which the first options for black togetherness ran aground. Slavery was the common grist to which all Africans were reduced. But at the same time they were being leveled into one dimension of caste, the stage was being set for intracaste antagonisms that would keep them divided. There were four principal categories of differentiation: civil status, role assignment, skin color, and denomination. Civil status distinguished between blacks who were free and those who were slaves. The distinction was not marked, and life for slave and for free was of essentially the same order. All shared the same restrictions of movement, social exclusion, economic contingency, nakedness before the bar, and, above all, the absence of participation in power. Despite these common disabilities, a few free blacks did manage to distinguish themselves, but then, so did some slaves. The clue to such extraordinary accomplishment therefore was obviously not in the system, slave or free, but in the individuals. There are always some who are born to fly, and fly they will whatever their impediments. But the slave-free dichotomy, while being the most obvious fracture of the black community, was not the most devastating. Thousands of free blacks bought and freed their wives and children; others were reliable agents of the Underground Railroad. Free status was hardly a serious issue in black social relations, for free blacks were generally despised by whites as indigents and troublemakers, and a well-thought-of slave of respectable ownership not infrequently commanded more respect and more leverage than any free black around. In the final analysis, the issue was rendered of no consequence by white response to black expectations. In 1857 that response was documented in the Supreme Court decision *Dred Scott* v. *Sanford,* when Chief Justice Roger B. Taney ruled that no blacks, slave or free, were possessed of any rights a white man was bound to respect. Far from being a moral disclosure, Justice Taney's ruling was merely the ratification of conventional attitudes and practices: South and North, slave or free, being black was all the same.

A more serious source of community fracture was role assignment. During slavery, primary ingroup status derived from being more or less intimately associated with the master or members of his family living in the big house or manor. Valets, maids, cooks, body servants, coachmen, and so on made up a big-house elite with privileges and opportunities not available to the field hands. The field hands seldom had any contacts with the whites other than the poor-white overseer, who was not of the planter class. But the house slaves not only had unique opportunities for acculturation; they were also unusually skilled artisans or professionals: chefs, nurses, wagonmakers, bricklayers, barbers, seamstresses, gardeners, grooms, and so on. Thus, they sometimes identified with the source of their unusual privileges, precipitating agonizing conflicts of loyalty. Once slavery was ended, the slaves who had been associated with the big house were far better equipped for freedom than their counterparts trained only to the plow and the hoe. This difference was to be an inevitable factor in the creation of social and economic distance in the newly emergent subculture of Blackamericans.

The third agent of division was the most pernicious and the most tragic of all. It was skin color. Since masters were white and slaves were black with no exceptions of consequence, within the black caste skin color became an important and contradictory index of worth and status. Like role assignments at the big house, light skin was presumed to be indisputable evidence of the association with power, but at the same time, the quality of that association was necessarily dubious. On many plantations there was a strong correlation between color and role assignment at the big house, light-skinned or mulatto slaves being frequently preferred for the more intimate services required by the slave master. However, there was no corresponding correlation of power or privilege favoring any slave solely on the evidence of white blood. The slavocracy provided a disclaimer for the potential problems of white paternity quite early with the convenient dictum "The father of a slave is unknown." It thereby obviated in one fell swoop the moral question implicit in the breakup and sale of slave families, as well as the troublesome implications of the "rights" of black children sired by the master or his sons.

These were problems of critical significance to the black church, not only because the church assumed the job of reconstructing the black community but because the black church itself was at times seriously threatened by the divisiveness of color and class within the black caste. There were churches in which only light-skinned blacks of the big-house tradition were welcomed, and these were not uncommon as late as the mid-twentieth century. There were other black churches designed for the masses. Whereas the black congregations affiliated with white denominations often tended to move toward exclusiveness and selectivity, the problem was also endemic to the black church. The black church had borrowed its polity, its structure, and its ritual from the white church *intact,* except for those few emendations necessary to make clear a black proprietorship, but the black church brought to the white church's polity and ritual its own interpretation and style. It was inevitable that points of incongruity would arise, forcing the church to determine again and again what was quiddity and what was dispensable. Such decisions often were made on the basis of developing class interests rooted in the slave heritage. It was not until the black revolution after World

War II that a sudden wave of black ethnic feeling apparently outflanked this problem.

RELIGION AS A FACTOR IN BLACK DISUNITY

It is religion that provides the prime cohesiveness for the black community, and it is in religion that the fracture of the black community is most prominently institutionalized. For the first hundred years of the black experience in America, religion was more an index of separation than a factor of integration. When Richard Allen and his followers detached themselves from Saint George's Methodist Church in Philadelphia because of the racial discrimination that was the condition of their membership there, the Free African Society they founded provided them with a period of reflection about the direction their commitment should take next. When it was decided finally that, under the circumstances, the faithfulness and dignity of black people could best be preserved in a black church, what kind of black church—save that it would be "African"—was not an immediate issue. However, it was to become an issue of the most critical importance as the movement for a black church gathered momentum and the dream of religious independence began to take on the substance of reality. However anomalous it may seem that a people who were so recently and so tentatively permitted to share the faith and who had been so grievously and so persistently demeaned in their efforts to experience its fellowship, and however innocent they must have been of the minutiae of theological distinctions, internal schism was to stalk the black church from its founding. It is to the credit of the founders of the Free African Society that they anticipated the problem and sought to avoid it, at least initially. Dr. Benjamin Rush, the Quaker who befriended them, described the exiles as "the scattered appendages" of the churches of Philadelphia. He also noted that the emergent African church had "drawn up articles and a plan of government so general as to embrace all, and yet so orthodox in cardinal points as to offend none." Nevertheless, when in 1791 the sponsors of the African church met to adopt a plan of government, both Richard Allen and Absalom Jones wanted a Methodist polity, while the majority of other members voted for the Church of England. As we have seen, Jones relinquished his sectarian preference and went on to lead the majority in the founding of the African Prot-estant Episcopal Church of Saint Thomas. Richard Allen, on the other hand, made it clear that he "could go no further with them" and would "leave them in peace." [13] The rest is familiar history.

Through the years there have been several important sources of black sectarianism, but for the most part these have not been the same as the sources of white sectarianism. Religion derives from spe-cific human needs and experiences, and it functions in the interest of helping people to cope with the more traumatic aspects of human existence. In consequence we may expect to find a discernible rela-tionship between the expression of religion and the cultural matrix from which it derives and the social cosmos of which it is a mani-festation. This should mean that in a free society religious prolifera-tion may be expected to reflect not only the intensiveness of human trauma (by which is meant those experiences, realized or antici-pated, which are the most challenging to human endurance and understanding), but also the capacity for cultural invention to shape or modify the religious instrument to make it more effective. The Pu-ritan separatists who settled New England, the Baptists who came to Rhode Island, the Quakers in Pennsylvania, the Methodists on the frontier, the Anglicans along the South Atlantic seaboard, the Catho-lics in Maryland all alike responded to the peculiar cultural impinge-ments and understandings that seemed to dictate their distinctive creedal, ritual, and in some cases geographical predilections. Yet, none of these were prominent factors in the fragmentation of the black church. Why, then, did the black church permit itself to be divided at its inception rather than take advantage of its political and theological innocence to unite all black Christians in a single communion?

The blacks were singularly free of the theological and political en-crustations that predetermined most American sectarianism, but they were not all free of the human and psychological factors that also influence religious preference. At the same time, one notes that though there are a variety of black sectarian expressions, they fall mainly under but three distinctive traditions: Methodist, Baptist, and Pentecostal.

Despite its demonstrated weakness in the face of the prevailing proslavery sentiment, the Methodist church from time to time did evidence unusual solicitude toward blacks. This tradition of concern became a significant part of the black experience. Its importance is reflected vividly in Richard Allen's passionate confession of his own preference for Methodism and even more dramatically in Nat Turner's command that *only* Methodists were to be spared in his determined slaughter of the slave masters who tormented his people with bondage. The Baptists were somewhat less pronounced in their humanitarian concern for blacks, but they did share the tradition. The very first church built for blacks in America was a Baptist church. It was built in violation of the law by a white slaveholder who was subsequently converted by the slave preacher who pastored it. The Quakers, who were the most solicitous of all for the life and liberty of black people, made no special efforts to convert the blacks; nor did they maintain the kind of organizational visibility conducive to replication once the blacks could establish their own churches.

In brief, the Methodist and Baptist traditions became the primary forms of the black religious investment because those denominations were, on the whole, more accessible, and their rituals and worship patterns more familiar. The black Pentecostals, like the black cults, were a later development, with different sources of derivation. The fragmentation within both the black Methodist and Baptist traditions does not reflect substantive differences in ritual, creed, or policy. As a matter of fact, movement across denominational lines within the Methodist connections and the Baptist conventions always has been frequent and unimpeded, as indeed are transitions among most American churches, with the notable exception of certain sects whose barriers to membership tend to define their reason for being.

If the factors that make for fragmentation within the black religious community do not result in the first instance from tradition and are not substantially creedal or theological, then what are their sources? Their causes are to be found in the peculiar nature of the American social structure, which is responsible for a variety of distortions in the black experience in religion. There are four especially significant causes.

1. The confusion of values and the subsequent desire to replicate the white experience. In other words, there is a feeling that if white people have many denominations, so should blacks.

---

2. The rejection of the leveling and homogenization implicit in the caste arrangement. All blacks are not the same. Blacks are capable of (and need) a variety of religious expressions.

3. The dearth of leadership opportunities elsewhere in the society. Leadership is a sign of status, and status is a scarce commodity. There has long been a direct correlation between the number of discrete religious organizations and the available status positions in the black subculture. Closely related is the oversupply of potential black leaders. In the struggle for self-realization and in the absence of more and wider opportunities, this pool of potential leaders is attracted by the church, the largest and most viable black institution.

4. The pervasive longing to be rid of the inordinate stresses of living in a world dominated by whites. The cult syndrome so evident in contemporary religion is peculiarly cosmocentric—that is, escapist—among blacks. It represents an understandable impatience that the coming of the Kingdom of God has been too long delayed for those wracked and broken here on earth.

Standing off a bit and surveying the black religious experience in perspective, one sees a sort of double funnel—an hour-glass-shaped phenomenon into which went a variety of religious traditions as the involuntary African expatriates were led, pushed, enticed, and permitted through the Western matrix to emerge on the other side as black Christians. What was anomalous about the whole experience was that though they took in with them no traditions of Christian sectarianism, in the process of the limited acculturation that went on in the narrow neck of the double funnel, either they acquired traditions vicariously or, in substituting their own more mundane value projections, they found themselves, however inadvertently, in consonance with one or another established American religious tradition. They emerged from the funnel one in faith but divided in the expression of that faith.

Religions are that precipitate of cultural learning that is addressed to what is thought to transcend human experience and that characteristically is crystallized in formal creeds, moral requirements, and ritual practices. The ultimate nature of religious concern often leads the believer to be preoccupied with spiritual or theological details. As a result there arise those various patterns of belief and practice we recognize as churches or denominations. This phenomenon is exaggerated in a free society, in which there is neither establishment nor proscription of religion and in which religious experimentation short of blasphemy or violation of public policy stirs little attention. In consequence, sectarian proliferation is institutionalized in American life and was so long before the advent of the black church.

From the perspective of the prevailing tradition, there could be nothing anomalous about Richard Allen's allegiance to Methodism. On the other hand, from the perspective of black needs and interests it probably could be argued that the advantages in, or even the felt need of, founding a black *Methodist* church in the face of Allen's experience with white Methodists is difficult to understand. The sources of white sectarianism are historic. But the emergent black church, for one fleeting moment in the late eighteenth century, held the advantage of a theological and creedal tabula rasa, had it determined to recognize and make use of that advantage.

Some consciousness of the value of a unified communion was apparent from the first, though the primary impetus for independence appeared to be separation from the white churches rather than creation of a monolithic black church. Blacks were not yet fully conscious of the sociopolitical power inherent in church organization, but from the beginning they were sensitive to their need to control their own spiritual affairs. Allen did attempt to persuade the John Street Methodist separatists to affiliate with his fledgling AME Church. However, the New Yorkers, for reasons of their own, elected to pursue a different vision. They founded the AMEZ Church, a separate communion. Even if Allen had been successful in accomplishing a merger, the problem at best would have been delayed, not resolved. Both the Bethelites and the Zionists were Methodists, and there was still that growing company of black Baptists to consider.

The ultimate question was not whether to be AME or AMEZ, or Methodist or Baptist, for both those choices reflected an obvious commitment to the prevailing tradition from which they had so lately withdrawn. The ultimate question was whether to employ a distinctively new spiritual insight reflecting more precisely the peculiar needs and interests of the African diaspora. Apparently, Allen never gave such an option serious thought, and in his argument for a Methodist church he explained why: "I was confident . . . no religious sect . . . would suit the capacity of the colored people as well as the Methodist, for the plain and simple gospel suits best . . . for the unlearned can understand, and the learned are sure to understand and the reason the Methodists are so successful in the awakening and conversion of the colored people is the plain doctrine and having a good discipline." [14] Although he deplored and rejected the harsh treatment he had received at the hands of the white Methodists at Saint George's, he was unwilling to move beyond the familiar grounds of the faith as he knew it, and what he knew best, he chose for his people. For Allen, a church totally independent of his people's experience was not a realistic option. Still, it is intriguing to speculate on what possibilities might have been available in a fresh start with a less familiar communion, such as the Quakers, for example.

In the Caribbean and in South America, the African diaspora was successful in the eclectic blending of certain African religious traditions with selected Christian motifs. But this blending was not a real option in America, because the practice of slave dispersal and the general suppression of all African religions left relatively little in the way of African traditions available to eclecticism, even if there had been an interest in it. Another possibility might have been the total abandonment of Christianity in favor of some other religions considered more responsive to the needs and aspirations of the black estate. After all, the black affiliation to the established church was always qualified by racial considerations, and any occasion for withdrawal from that church might well have been considered an opportunity to be rid of a religion identified with oppression. But abandoning Christianity was the least probable response. Although movement across sect or denominational lines may be relatively fluid, an en masse, voluntary abandonment of a religious tradition for rational considerations would probably be unprecedented. Mass conversion from one religion to another has sometimes been accomplished by decree, and mass renunciation may have on occasion been a condition of liberty or even life itself. But in the absence of compulsion, the motivations that impel believers to separate themselves from one religion in favor of another are likely to be highly personal, particularistic, and unpredictable. Reason alone is hardly capable of exciting a mass reversal of religious sentiment.

There were other obstacles even more formidable. The blacks in

America were a captive people. Shut off from the rest of the world by the peculiar demands of slavery, Christianity was the only visible religious tradition available (if the remote profile of a mysterious and nonproselytizing Judaism is discounted). Islam, which had been very much a part of the Afro-Hispanic experience in America during the fifteenth and sixteenth centuries, had followed the conquistadors into oblivion, and the spiritual traditions brought from western Africa had been shattered deliberately in the process of estrangement and alienation. Only Christianity was available to fill the void. It was all they knew, these fathers of the black church. It was their peculiar, perhaps their most fortuitous heritage. And it came to them divided.

The early years of the African churches were years of tumultuous competition. Both the AME and AMEZ denominations were aggressive (and sometimes uniquely resourceful) in devising ways to win individuals and established congregations to their respective connections. Following in the wake of the Union armies were powerful black preachers and church organizers gathering in the bewildered hordes, who found themselves suddenly free to make some decisions about themselves for the first time in their experience in America. For the most part, those blacks gathered as appendages to white churches welcomed the "jubilee" that released them at last to their own churches. The Southern Methodists—split away from the main Methodist body over the issue of slavery—were particularly vulnerable to the crusading African churches. Their black membership was perhaps larger than that of any other white church, and in the uncertainty and disorganization brought by the Civil War, they could only welcome a petition from their rapidly eroding black membership to allow them to form an independent black communion. Thus was born in 1870 at Jackson, Tennessee, the Colored Methodist Episcopal Church—the third African Methodist communion. In the meantime blacks were withdrawing from the Baptist churches in ever increasing numbers and uniting in their own black conventions. The Presbyterians, Episcopalians, Congregationalists, and others, having few black members to begin with, were less affected by the black crusade to "bring our people home."

By the turn of the century the black denominational patterns were well set. But the scars of denominational conflict were deep, and the several denominations of the black church were most often inclined to go their separate ways. The new century brought wars, floods, crop failures, and immense shifts in population. As hundreds of thousands of blacks left the agrarian life of the southern plantations for the uncertain existence of the urban ghetto, the black churches were forced to moderate the crusading zeal that had made the competition for members so exciting in times past. The leadership of the people was largely in the hands of the clergy, and the future of the black estate was troubled and uncertain. America's expressed intent to bind its wounds and get on with its destiny seemed to begin with the intent to eclipse history somehow and blot the troubling reality of the black presence from its consciousness. There were difficult times ahead. The Ku Klux Klan once again was unleashed, the dislocations of the First World War fell ultimately on the poor and the black, and there were race riots and counterriots. In the "Red Summer" of 1919 alone hundreds of people were killed or injured in twenty-five white-black confrontations. The Great Depression lay in the offing, and new waves of white immigrants from war-battered Europe got the jobs and the attention that Blackamericans felt belonged to them, the people whose blood and sweat had helped protect and sustain the nation for three hundred years.

The black church was the institution most blacks relied upon to meet the crises of what was to be labeled "the American Dilemma"— the painful gap between American ideals and American performance in race relations. The struggle for real freedom was still ahead. There were schools and colleges to found and develop, political leaders to prepare and support, and millions of disillusioned black "citizens" whose rights evaporated wherever they were in conflict with white interests and who had to be taught to endure. There were civil rights organizations to sponsor, to staff, and to provide with meeting facilities. There were social services to provide for all those blacks forgotten or overlooked by the civil agencies. Above all, hope had to be kept alive, and a continuing vision of God's love for all humanity was crucial for black survival and for public peace. In the meantime, of course, the ordinary spiritual care of the church community had to go on. It did. And it does—in the continuing response to a continuing dilemma.

BLACK ETHNICITY AND BLACK NATIONALISM

The most crucial development for blacks during the World War II era was their growing awareness of black ethnicity, and among the institutions most critically affected was the black church. It was not that the church needed the war experience to find value in accepting blackness, for it was the black church that first awakened the dispersed and demoralized African diaspora to the possibilities inherent in unity and self-affirmation. The church had some success, as is attested by its own growth, but the odds were formidable. For three hundred years the transplanted Africans had lived in isolation in a social and physical environment carefully contrived to promote in them an enduring self-hatred and a belief in their own inadequacy. This notion was reinforced by every public and private institution and by all the conventions according to which the society was ordered. World War I provided the first tentative glimpse "outside," but those blacks who were so reluctantly sent overseas "to fight for democracy" returned home under an ominous pall of suspicion. Those who dared talk about their experiences elsewhere in the world were silenced by violence. A prompt return to the old ways and the conventional insights was the price of a job, the price of being left alone, in some cases even the price of staying alive.

The post–World War II return to normalcy was not so easily managed. Far more blacks were involved in the fighting around the globe. They stayed longer, and they experienced more. And they were better prepared to evaluate those experiences and to make judgments about what they saw and what they heard. When they came home this time, they had firm new concepts about themselves in relation to other people of whatever race, and they were not prepared to resign those concepts and resume the pace and the place America had always reserved for them. For strength they turned inward, toward each other. The core of their internal fortitude was the black church.

Valuing black ethnicity brings the consolidation of the black ego— the affirmation that to be one of God's *black* children is good. It does not confuse blackness with supreme value, but it inculcates a conviction that among competing values of the same order, black is as good as any other—no better, but no worse either. Cultivating ethnic feeling is a survival technique common to practically all cultures; it calls on people of like identity to recognize themselves as centers of value and to respond to one another and to the world at large in terms of that recognition.

A sense of identity is critical if appeals to ethnicity are to have power. In most ethnic groups it is taken for granted or is established through the body of myths and traditions with which a culture is buttressed. However, the peculiar circumstances conditioning the black experience in America produced a body of myth and conventional wisdom designed deliberately to confuse and obscure black identity rather than establish or support it. In consequence, an awareness of black ethnicity was such a late development of the black subculture as to seem both extraordinary and threatening, despite the fact that for generations every immigrant group in America has relied on affirming its ethnicity as a vital part of the process of assimilation. Only blacks had been forced to look to others for definition and identity. The issue was far more critical than a mere name to go by. For how you are styled says a great deal about how you are perceived, and perception is vital to the equation of who you are and how you will be treated. The fundamental issue was how the black experience was to be read and interpreted. That issue persists, and America is still in the process of making this determination despite a hundred years of black citizenship and three hundred years of Christian brotherhood in a nation often conceived as living "under God."

Affirmation of black ethnicity, then, is the cultural philosophy that is presupposed by black religion and the black church, and black identity is its critical element. Black religion may and often does travel with black nationalism, with inevitable confusion. However, their goals are not the same. Black nationalism is a political philosophy. Its goals are often amorphous and do not give primary consideration to the spiritual quest, even though religion may appear to be the focus of the movement. Hence, though the critical question is whether ultimate value is assigned to practical political goals or to the spiritual quest (with which political intent may be closely associated), for the black masses, black religion and black nationalism are not so clearly distinguished. Both are addressed to the sources of their distress, but they promise differing categories of relief. As a result, black nationalism often assumes the character of religion, because for those most distressed, ultimate value is whatever appears capable of a reversal of the circumstances they identify with their misery.

DOUBLE CONSCIOUSNESS AND A RELIGION APART

W. E. B. Du Bois made famous the theory of "double consciousness," a psychological phenomenon with which Blackamericans uniquely are affected through historical happenstance. They are part of two worlds, two cultures, living in and experiencing both, but frustrated in their constant struggle to reconcile the one with the other. It is one thing to be American; it is quite another to be black in America. In the black church the simple goal of every believer is to be Christian and regarded as such, but there is no precedent in the religious history of America that could provide real encouragement for that notion. The expression of the faith inevitably risks distortion by the racial prism through which black people are refracted. Thus, it may be less painful and more rewarding to the black Christian to think of himself as belonging to a religion apart—one that is peculiarly his own and therefore less vulnerable to the slings and arrows of racial prejudice.

The genius of ethnic feeling is that it can strengthen the ego of the group by accentuating its assets and assigning relatively minor value to whatever lies beyond its spectrum of possibilities. Indeed, the cardinal values of an ethnic group may be precisely those experiences of the group that have been belittled or devalued by outsiders. For example, most black churchgoers put great emphasis upon a rousing sermon with spirited singing and fervent praying as critical to the worship experience. They want to *feel* God's presence rather than reason about it. For this, the black church has been criticized as too emotional or too demonstrative. But black worshipers often find the worship services of conventional white churches cold and uninspiring. Hence, blacks are apt to devalue white styles of worship as generally unrewarding for black people and sanction instead the ritual patterns developed independent of white influence in the churches of the black diaspora.

There are vast disparities between the two sets of experiences and the derivative needs and interests that distinguish black and white

Christians in America. Religion is most satisfying when it is cognizant of, and responsive to, the realities that shape the concerns of those who look to it for relief and fulfillment. In that regard the black church, like dozens of other religious groupings that derive their identity from the internalization of group experience, functions as a critically important ethnic instrument. The ritual preferences of black religion require no justification, for the black church, like any other, can be authentic only when it is true to its own heritage. The expression of that heritage in appropriate ritual form is an expression of spiritual commitment and ingroup appreciation. This is a distinctive cultural achievement and a valued symbol of identity in the extensive spectrum of religious observance in America.

NOTES

1. Benjamin Mays, *The Negro's God* (Boston, 1938), 43–44.
2. "David Walker's Appeal," in Bradford Chambers (ed.), *Chronicles of Negro Protest* (New York, 1968), 69.
3. Gayraud Wilmore, *Black Religion and Black Radicalism* (New York, 1973), 106–107. See also Carter G. Woodson and Charles H. Wesley, *The Negro in Our History* (Washington, D.C., 1966), 131. Blacks could not belong to the Baptist Association of Savannah at that time.
4. Charles H. Wesley, *Richard Allen, Apostle of Freedom* (Washington, D.C., 1959), 52–53.
5. Wilmore, *Black Religion and Black Radicalism*, 113, 114.
6. Wesley, *Richard Allen*, 79–80.
7. Brown and his church were implicated in the plot charged to Denmark Vesey in 1822. Brown escaped to Philadelphia, but his church was closed.
8. William J. Walls, *The African Methodist Episcopal Zion Church* (Charlotte, 1974), 94. Compare Harry V. Richardson, *Dark Salvation* (New York, 1976), 135, which reports that "the annual meeting of the group of churches in 1828 is regarded by some as the first General Conference" of the AMEZ Convention.
9. B. F. Wheeler, *The Varick Family* (Mobile, Ala., 1906), 6–7.
10. Walls, *African Methodist Episcopal Zion Church*, 44.
11. The Christian (formerly Colored) Methodist Episcopal Church was the additional Methodist body. The Baptist conventions were the National Baptist Convention, Inc.; the National Baptist Convention in America; and the Progressive Baptist Convention.
12. Walls, *African Methodist Episcopal Zion Church*, 141.
13. Wesley, *Richard Allen*, 70, 72.
14. *Ibid.*, 72.

THE SOUTH ENCOUNTERS THE HOLOCAUST: WILLIAM STYRON'S *SOPHIE'S CHOICE*

Richard L. Rubenstein

There have been many literary explorations of the destruction of the Jews of Europe during World War II, but only William Styron's *Sophie's Choice* has been written from the singular perspective of an American southerner.[1] At first glance, given Styron's southern Protestant background and his previous writings, his choice of subject matter would appear to be surprising if not strange. Educated at Davidson College and Duke University, having served as a marine in World War II, Styron always has expressed in his writings his experience and sensibility as a southern writer. This is as true of *Lie Down in Darkness,* the story of beautiful, doomed Peyton Loftis and her Tidewater Virginia family, as it is of *The Confessions of Nat Turner,* the tale of a slave revolt that took place in 1831 in a Southampton County, near the part of Virginia in which Styron grew up and in which, as an adolescent, he became fascinated with Turner. Even Styron's least popular but by no means least significant book, *Set This House on Fire,* though set in Italy after World War II, expresses his perspective as a southern writer through its narrator, Peter Leverett—like Styron, a native of Tidewater Virginia.

As is well known, Styron's most famous and controversial work is *The Confessions of Nat Turner.* Undoubtedly, part of the controversy was due to the timing of its publication. The book was published at the height of the civil rights movement of the turbulent sixties. It won the Pulitzer Prize and was received with favor by many whites. It was, however, the object of vehement criticism from black intellectuals.[2] In the midst of their own mid-twentieth-century fight for civil rights, blacks saw Nat Turner as a nineteenth-century black freedom fighter. Styron portrayed Turner as sexually disturbed and sexually involved with the daughter of the owner of the plantation on which he had worked. During the revolt Turner captured and killed the girl. Although Styron was accused of racism, it would appear that his actual concern in the novel was the phenomenon of slavery and its continuing legacy. By describing Turner's impotent yearnings to possess the girl, Styron explored the distorting effects of slavery on a gifted but doomed leader. Styron thus added a sexual and psychoanalytic element to the story of one of the most important antebellum efforts by blacks at revolt and self-liberation.

Thirteen years separate the publication of *Sophie's Choice* in 1979 from the publication of *Nat Turner.* Styron is a careful writer who takes as long as he feels is necessary to write a book, unlike a number of authors who turn out a book every year or two. According to his own account, Styron worked on *Sophie's Choice* for the better part of a decade. When the book finally appeared, it received mixed reviews, though it was a popular success in both the hardcover and paperback editions. Because Styron had once again chosen an emotionally charged subject, it was not surprising that the reviews often told more about the reviewers than about the book. John Gardner saw the book as a southern gothic novel that took as its subject "the nature of evil in the individual and in all humanity." "In *Sophie's Choice,*" Gardner wrote, "it is no longer just the South that is grandly decayed, morally tortured . . . it is the world." Writing in *Midstream,* Alvin Rosenfeld saw *Sophie's Choice* as Styron's flawed attempt to compete with Jewish novelists by taking a subject that properly belonged to them. There is an edge of bitterness in Rosenfeld's comments: "Styron wants to beat the Jews at their own game, but in telling this story of the Polish girl who stole a ham and forever after suffered sexual, moral, and psychological abuse, he has written not so much a novel of the Holocaust but an unwitting spoof of the same. Reducing Hitler's war against the Jews to a literary war, he has turned the tables on his competitors and given us the Holocaust in whiteface, de-Judaizing Auschwitz and making it the erotic centerpiece of a New Southern Gothic Novel." With less bitterness but still faulting Styron for failing to emphasize the uniqueness of the Jewish catastrophe, Pearl Bell asserted in *Commentary* that Styron's emphasis on slavery at Auschwitz was a mistake: "By emphasizing not the end and the goal of the Nazi plan—mass murder—but rather the means of domination and enslavement which they settled on to effectuate that goal, Styron loses a sense of the enormity of the Holocaust."[3] While this is not the occasion to discuss the reviews in detail—a phenomenon worthy of independent treatment—one fact stands out glaringly in almost all of the reviews that appeared in the national media: few of the reviewers appear to have understood that in *Sophie's Choice,* a major southern writer continues and enlarges upon the literary exploration of the phenomenon that dominated *Nat Turner*—namely, slavery.

Sophie's Choice is a multidimensional novel embracing a host of themes. Nevertheless, both *Sophie's Choice* and *Nat Turner* are about slavery. Even Styron's choice of heroine, a Polish Catholic prisoner of Auschwitz, rather than a Jewish victim of Auschwitz, reflects his preoccupation with slavery. This does not mean that Styron ignored the phenomenon of mass murder at Auschwitz. He does explore the extermination of Europe's Jews, but his primary concern in *Sophie's Choice* is one that has been with him ever since, as a youth, he came to understand the legacy slavery had bequeathed to his own native region. Styron has on occasion been criticized for having written about a Polish Catholic rather than a Jewish victim of Auschwitz. There were, after all, far more Jewish than Polish victims at Auschwitz. Nevertheless, given his lifelong concern with slavery, his choice of Sophie—whose function at Auschwitz was that of a slave—rather than a Jew—who, no matter what task he or she might have been assigned at Auschwitz, was fated for extermination—gives the work a literary integrity and a continuity with *Nat Turner* that would have been far more difficult to achieve had Styron's protagonist been Jewish. It cannot be stressed strongly enough that *Sophie's Choice* is part of one of our most important southern writer's continuing attempt to explore the phenomenon of slavery.

The importance of the question of slavery is apparent almost from the beginning of *Sophie's Choice.* The time is 1947. Stingo, the narrator, has just graduated from Duke after having served in the marines during World War II. At Duke, Stingo had taken writing courses. Stingo tells us that William Faulkner and Thomas Wolfe were his literary models. With his college years behind him, Stingo has come to New York to pursue a writing career.

When Stingo first arrives, he supports himself by working as a very junior editor at McGraw-Hill, a publishing corporation that had prospered from its textbooks, industrial manuals, and business and technical journals. As a sideline, it did publish some novels and serious nonfiction, but the corporation's real interest lay in the more profitable enterprise of business and technical publication. Stingo's job consists of reading and rejecting manuscripts that such publishers of quality fiction and nonfiction as Knopf and Scribner's had already rejected. Stingo quickly realizes that the only way he could prosper at McGraw-Hill would be to work hard at fitting into the McGraw-Hill corporate mold. Put differently, Stingo realizes that corporate success at McGraw-Hill means the end of his prospects of becoming a serious writer. There is more than a hint of southern agrarianism in the image Styron draws of the honest, young, aspiring southern writer who finds it impossible to adapt to the gray, impersonal, money-making world of a New York corporation. The hint of agrarianism surfaces continually throughout the book. There is, for example, an unforgettable episode in which Rudolph Höss, the commandant at Auschwitz, bids Sophie, who is his slave secretary, to share his pride and delight as he gazes out of the window at his magnificent white Arabian stallion freely galloping about in the field reserved for him alone. This scene is in stark contrast to the view from another window, a view of the entrance to Auschwitz, at which freight trains ceaselessly disgorge their battered human cargo and, beneath the infamous entrance sign ARBEIT MACHT FREI, the selection is made of who is to be dispatched immediately to the gas chamber and who is to be condemned to the slower death of abusive slave labor.

After admiring the stallion, Höss returns to a letter he is dictating to Sophie concerning the disposition of some able-bodied Greek Jews. The letter reads in part: "The Greek Jews being such a pathetic lot and ready to die anyway, we hope that it is alright that they have been assigned to the death commando unit at the crematorium, where they will handle the corpses, and extract the gold from the teeth and feed bodies to the furnace until they too, exhausted beyond recall, are ready for the gas."[4] Clearly this is a new dimension in slavery undreamed of in the old Confederacy. The contrast between the dehumanized viciousness of the human world in which a slavery and mass death has been industrialized and rationalized and the vital beauty and dignity of the natural world could not be drawn more graphically.

Stingo quits McGraw-Hill with less than fifty dollars to his name and no immediate job prospects. But he need not have worried. Within a few days he receives a wholly unexpected gift that, he tells us, "like another instance of great fortune much later in my life . . . had its origins in the institution of American Negro slavery." The gift derived from an inheritance bequeathed to him by his grandmother, who was born in 1848 and, at the age of thirteen, possessed three Negro slaves—two sisters, Lucinda and Drusilla, and their brother, Artiste. Shortly after Artiste was given to Stingo's grandmother, he was falsely accused of having made an "improper advance" toward one of the town's white girls. As a result of the alleged impropriety, Stingo's great-grandfather sold Artiste for $800. Artiste was sent to labor "in the grinding hell of Georgia's turpentine forests." It later turned out that Artiste had been unjustly accused, but it was too late to reverse the sale. Stingo's great-grandfather had incurred the guilt of having broken up a family and having condemned the sixteen-year-old boy to the most miserable kind of servitude.

The $800 was converted into gold coins and hidden away. The Civil War came and went. For a while the coins appeared to have been lost, but as a result of research into family documents, Stingo's father was able to locate them. By the terms of Stingo's grandmother's will, the coins were to be divided among her grandchildren. Faithful to his mother's wishes, Stingo's father sold the coins (which had increased in value to $5,500) and delivered the proceeds to the proper heirs. Stingo's share came to $500. In 1947 that was a sum sufficient to permit Stingo to devote his entire time to writing. Thus, the proceeds from the sale of a slave in the antebellum South gave Stingo the financial independence with which to launch his career. One need not enter into speculation concerning whether this episode is auto-biographical; there can be no doubt that Styron has used it to dramatize the extent to which the slave system of the old Confederacy continued to affect the descendants of the masters as well as the slaves almost a hundred years after its official demise.

Stingo's inheritance offers him little more than a chance to get started. He proceeds to find a cheap room in Flatbush, a Jewish section of Brooklyn, in a rooming house run by Mrs. Yetta Zimmerman. As Stingo puts it, he becomes "another lean and lonesome Southerner in the kingdom of the Jews." He moves into the house to begin his writing. Settling into his room, he hears the sounds in the room above him of "the frenzy of two people fucking like crazy wild animals." Stingo quickly learns that the sounds above are to be a constant source of distraction. When the couple is not engaged in coupling, they are constantly involved in an unspeakably vicious and ultimately self-destructive, sadomasochistic quarrel. The woman is Sophie Zawistowska, a Polish Catholic woman who had been both a prisoner of the Germans at Auschwitz and a prisoner of the Russians after the war. Her tormentor-lover is Nathan Landau, a seemingly brilliant Jew with an infinite capacity for obscene verbal aggression, most of which he directs at Sophie. Nathan initially presents himself as a Harvard-trained scientist with an important position at the Pfizer Pharmaceutical Company, but appearances turn out to be very deceptive. Stingo learns from the number tatooed on Sophie's arm that she had been a concentration-camp inmate, but to his surprise, he discovers that she is Polish and Roman Catholic rather than Jewish. Like Nathan, Sophie is not as she first presents herself. She confides in Stingo and tells him about her life in Poland, but she is neither truthful nor candid. Nathan abuses her and constantly denounces her as a Polish whore and anti-Semite, but she cannot free herself from the degrading relationship. However, she does complain to Stingo of the injustice of Nathan's incessant accusations, claiming that her father was an antifascist who risked his life to save Jews before he was killed by the Nazis. She later admits that not only was her father pro-Nazi but that before the war he had written a pamphlet entitled *Die Polnische Judenfrage: Hat der Nationalsozialismus die Antwort? (The Polish Question: Does National Socialism Have the Answer?)*. In it he proposed outright extermination as the only way to "solve" the problem of Poland's 3,500,000 "superfluous Jews." Although prewar Poland was perhaps the most violently anti-Semitic country in Europe, not excluding Germany, there was a certain "old-fashioned" character to Polish anti-Semitism: it was long on emotion and short on method. In unmethodical, unsystematic, hate-ridden Poland, Professor Zbigniew Bieganski's proposal was more radical than even most of his anti-Semitic colleagues and students could stomach. Far from being the daughter of an antifascist, Sophie is the daughter of one of the most openly pro-Nazi Polish academics of the prewar period.

As Stingo comes to spend time with Nathan and Sophie, Nathan alternatively encourages his literary ambitions and subjects him to uncontrollable verbal abuse. A crucial incident occurs after Bobby

Weed, a young black, is lynched in the same part of Georgia to which Artiste had been sent almost a century before. While Bobby Weed was still alive, his genitals were cut off and stuffed into his mouth. He was then assaulted by the mob with a blowtorch and left to die. Nathan hurls at Stingo the accusation that "the fate of Bobby Weed at the hands of white southern Americans is as bottomlessly barbaric as any act performed by the Nazis during the rule of Adolf Hitler."[5] Over and over again, Nathan loses control of himself and gives vent to almost every conceivable distortion then current about the South. One of Nathan's worst moments comes when the newspapers reported that Senator Theodore Bilbo of Mississippi had resigned from the Senate because an incurable cancer of the throat had reached an advanced stage. Bilbo had been one of the most offensively racist demagogues in the Senate. His public utterances about blacks and Jews were almost as embittered in their way as some of the abusive things Nathan was saying to Sophie and Stingo. There was, of course, an important difference. As a United States senator, Bilbo possessed power and did real harm to large numbers of people. Nathan is a mentally unhinged Jew whose grotesque method of coping with life in the aftermath of the Holocaust includes extreme verbal abuse. Unfortunately, in the end, Nathan also does real harm, if only to himself and Sophie.

Stingo is shocked when Nathan proposes a toast to "the slow, protracted death of the Senator from Mississippi." When Stingo refuses to toast to any man's death, Nathan likens Bilbo to Hitler and begins another antisouthern diatribe, repeating once again his equation of the South with Nazi Germany. Knowing something about southern populism that Nathan cannot possibly know, Stingo, without defending Bilbo, sees another side to the man. Like James K. Vardaman, Cotton Ed Smith, and Tom Watson, Bilbo had started with populist idealism, a concern for the common man, and opposition to big money, big business, and monopoly capitalism. In Stingo's words, "These men, basically decent and even visionary to begin with, were brought down by their own fatal weakness in the face of the Southern racial tragedy; for each of them in the end, to one degree or another, was forced to play upon and exploit the poor redneck's ancient fear and hatred of the Negro in order to aggrandize what had degenerated into shabby ambition and lust for power."[6] Like the others, Bilbo fitted into this pattern.

Although it is easier for Stingo, as a white Protestant, to be objective about men like Bilbo, neither Stingo nor his literary creator can ignore the question implied in Nathan's accusations: in what ways was the system of slavery in the old Confederacy and its continuing legacy in modern times different from the racist system of domination and servitude in Nazi Germany? It must be remembered that Stingo has come into contact with Nathan and Sophie because he is a direct and immediate beneficiary of the slave system of the Old South. In Stingo's case there is no need to enter upon theories of class, status, and social causation to demonstrate that he has benefited directly from slavery. The gold coins that purchased Artiste in one century and provided sustenance for Stingo in another make theoretical speculation unnecessary. Nor is there anything abstract about Sophie's link in slavery. Sophie had been a twentieth-century slave in the most advanced and rationally developed institution of slavery ever created, Auschwitz, as Styron amply makes apparent in the novel. Nor is the demented Nathan free from the taint of slavery. The prototypical historical memory of the Jews is that of deliverance from Egyptian slavery. Nathan's verbal abuse and the resentments that motivate him are expressions of a religioethnic culture of the servile consciousness, in the technical sense in which that consciousness was understood by Hegel in his dialectic of the Master and the Slave and as the notion was developed and deepened by Nietzsche.[7]

In *Nat Turner* Styron explored the destructive distortions of personality that slavery caused in a gifted and resourceful young black. In *Sophie's Choice* most of the heroine's lies, deceptions, and guilt have their origins in the fact that Sophie has made the slave's fundamental choice—namely, the decision that survival *at any cost* is to be preferred to death. Moreover, there is an implicit judgment on this particular slave's choice in the tale Styron has to tell. The only justification for the slave's decision to become another person's animate tool is the hope that either one's self or one's progeny will outlive the condition and consequences of servitude. Of necessity, the slave lives for the future—that of progeny if not self—rather than the present. Unfortunately, there can be no future for Sophie. Her two children have been murdered by the Nazis, and she is unable to extricate herself from the sadomasochistic relationship with Nathan that ends when the couple take cyanide and find their final deathly peace in each other's arms. By contrast, at the beginning of the book, Stingo introduces himself in a way that is reminiscent of another narrator who alone survives to tell the tale. "Call me Stingo" reminds us of "Call me Ishmael," with which the survivor-narrator commences his tale in Melville's *Moby Dick.* In the last scene in *Sophie's Choice* Stingo, after the funeral, goes to the beach he had visited with Sophie and Nathan, weeps, falls asleep, dreams abominable dreams, but awakens the next morning to find that some children had protectively covered him with sand. Arising, he recalls the words:

> 'Neath cold sand I dreamed of death
> but woke at dawn to see
> in glory the morning star.[8]

At the end of the book the dream of death is a thing of the past, and there is a hint of resurrection for the heir of the masters but not for the heirs of the slaves. At least in *Sophie's Choice,* slavery appears to be a dead end. This idea would be in keeping with the aristocratic ethic that held that a short, victorious life is to be preferred to a long life of indignity and servitude.

One way to answer the question of how, if at all, modern slavery differs from that of the Confederacy is to examine the new slave masters. Two twentieth-century slave masters are portrayed in some detail in the novel. They are Rudolph Höss, for about two years the commandant at Auschwitz, and Dr. Walter Dürrfeld, the chief executive officer of I. G. Auschwitz, the vast industrial installation at Auschwitz-Monowitz where I. G. Farben, the German petrochemical cartel, attempted to manufacture synthetic rubber using a work force consisting primarily of slave labor from the death camps. Unlike the slaveholders of the Old South, neither Höss nor Dürrfeld owned the slaves in their charge. Both were functionaries of impersonal, bureaucratic institutions. This fact alone points to a fundamental difference between slavery in the South and modern slavery.

In the South the personal link between owner and slave, however, attenuated by the intermediate authority of overseers and by utilitarian considerations, was never completely severed. An identifiable human being was ultimately responsible for the slaves. In the Nazi world, the ownerless slaves were ruled by functionaries whose only imperative was to carry out their assigned tasks, no matter what the human consequences might be. This phenomenon was part of the larger modern phenomenon of the separation of the worker from ownership of his tools, or, put differently, the means of production. In an earlier age those who used tools owned them. In modern times impersonal institutions such as governments and corporations own the means of production. As animate tools of a modern corporation, the slaves at Auschwitz were no longer the possessions of private owners. They were the possessions of anonymous institutions. This simple legal fiction had as its social consequence the fact that no human being could be held responsible for their fate. In actuality, the new slaves were regarded as nothing more than finite, rationally calculated units of motive power or energy. The duration of each unit had been calculated to be about three months in the industrial plant and one month in the mines, after which it was expected that the average unit would expire and be replaced by a fresh unit. In the Nazi slave system, human existence was reduced to a system of wholly amoral, impersonal calculations of use and function. Even at its worst, the South was never like I. G. Auschwitz.

Because of her knowledge of languages, Sophie briefly serves as the slave secretary of the commandant rather than a common slave in the industrial installations of I. G. Farben. Sophie is thus the rationalized twentieth-century version of the antebellum house nigger. Höss is a thoroughgoing functionary. Styron describes him: "The Commandant was . . . dedicated blindly to duty and a cause; thus he became a mere servo-mechanism in which a moral vacuum had been so successfully sucked clean of every molecule of real qualm or scruple that his own description of the unutterable crimes he perpetuated daily seem often to float outside and apart from evil, phantasms of cretinous innocence."[9] Höss may have been a servo-mechanism, but he was not without a capacity for initiative as long as it lay within the scope of his duties. It was he who proposed Zyklon B gas as the means of dispatching the greatest number of victims with the least effort and expense to the system.

Höss had once been a Christian, but he is no longer. In conversation with Sophie he identifies himself as a *Gottgläubiger,* a term the SS used to affirm both their breach with Christianity and their own distinctive neopagan faith. Here we note another important difference between the slavery of the South and the new slavery. In the South the masters were Christian. As Eugene Genovese has pointed out, most of the masters could never entirely free themselves from Christian moral constraints in their dealings with the slaves.[10] No such constraints impeded the new masters.

Although Höss is one of the new masters, Sophie attempts to gain his favor under the misapprehension that she can thereby improve her situation. She first tells him about her pro-Nazi father and his pamphlet proposing the extermination of Poland's Jews. "My father was to the depths of his soul *Judenfeindlich* (anti-Semitic)," she says. Höss is annoyed. He responds: "*Judenfeindlich.* When will I cease hearing that word, 'anti-Semitic'? My God, I'm tired of that! Jews, Jews, will I ever be done with Jews?"

At a later point, Höss asks Sophie why she hates Jews with such intensity; she answers by telling him of her father's admiration for Julius Streicher. She also invents a story of how her younger sister was sexually assaulted by a Jewish butcher as she walked near the ghetto of Krakow.

But Sophie has completely misjudged the situation. Höss has nothing but contempt for Streicher's theories about the Jews as a sexual menace. In his autobiography, written in prison after the war, Höss claimed that he had never hated Jews. Although Styron has been criticized for accepting Höss's self-serving autobiography at face value on this point, most scholars who have studied the SS find little reason to doubt Höss. Styron's vignette is on target. Like so many of his SS colleagues, Höss was convinced that the Jews had to be eliminated from Germany. But extermination was not their preferred method. Of course, once the order was given, men like Höss regarded the extermination of the Jews as a technical problem to be solved as efficiently as possible, not as an occasion for the expenditure of needless emotion. Indeed, Styron quotes Höss as asserting that the emotion of hatred was foreign to him. Referring to Höss, Styron writes, "In the world of the crematoriums hatred is a reckless and incontinent passion, incompatible with the humdrum nature of the quotidian task."[11] Sophie gets nowhere by trying to gain Höss's favor on the basis of a shared hatred. Sophie also miscalculates in assuming that approval of Nazi ideology by a Polish slave would have made any difference to an SS commandant even if he had hated the Jews. Had the Nazis won the war, the Poles were destined for a slave existence at best and perhaps for extermination. The Nazis were not interested in what Poles thought, save as an aid in manipulating a captive population.

Sophie next attempts to seduce Höss. As is well known, in the slave system of the Old South, sexual liaisons of varying duration and intensity between masters and female slaves were fairly common. Although the power equation in these relations was always weighted in favor of the master, the liaisons testify to the fact that the system of dominance had not been completely rationalized and that an emotional element could from time to time complicate the relations of masters and slaves. Put differently, the system had yet to lose its last shred of humanity.

Through no fault of her own, Sophie is unable to comprehend how profoundly the world of slavery has changed. Höss is momentarily attracted to her. He admits to her that he has longed to have intercourse with her and is about to give in when he is interrupted by his adjutant's knock on the door. When he finishes talking to the adjutant, he tells Sophie that he is sending her back to the prisoner block for good. Höss overcomes his moment of weakness. He will not permit his work to be distracted by a Polish slave, no matter how attractive she may be.

The other slave master in the novel is Dr. Walter Dürrfeld, the chief executive officer of I. G. Auschwitz. Dürrfeld has been sent to Auschwitz to preside over a huge corporate enterprise, the I. G. Farben synthetic rubber plant. Before the war Dürrfeld had visited Krakow and for four hours had been the guest of Sophie and her father. During the brief interlude Sophie finds herself attracted to and moved by the powerful executive of one of the world's largest corporations. Dürrfeld is more than a business man. He is a man of broad culture, learning, and artistic sensibility. Nothing comes of the encounter. Sophie puts it out of her mind for six years. She next hears of Dürrfeld at Auschwitz through his constant telephone contact with Höss. Dürrfeld requires more Jewish slaves than Höss is able to supply. There is a conflict among the members of the SS elite between those who want to use able-bodied Jews for slave labor in Poland's wartime factories and those who want them exterminated with no

Richard L. Rubenstein

delay. I.G. Farben had invested over two billion dollars in the construction of the *Buna* (synthetic rubber) factory at Auschwitz. The corporate leadership of I.G. Farben had been persuaded that Auschwitz was the proper location for the construction of the industrial installation. Auschwitz was near the raw materials—coal and water—that were needed for the production of *Buna*. Auschwitz also offered the corporation a sure supply of skilled labor. By locating the factory at a death camp, it was possible for the corporation to achieve a maximum rationalization of its labor costs. The slaves were given minimum subsistence rations and nothing more. The average worker at I.G. Auschwitz was good for about three months before dropping dead or being so debilitated that he or she was dispatched to the gas chambers. Since the supply of death-camp inmates was being constantly replenished, there was no economic reason for the corporation to keep its workers alive any longer.

In one face-to-face interview with Höss, Dürrfeld demands more Jewish slaves. He says that he is responsible to his stockholders. Without a suitable labor force, there will be neither production nor profit. When Höss tells Dürrfeld that the SS is split between those who want to use Jews as slaves and those who want to exterminate them, Dürrfeld sees no conflict: "You and I know that, either way, they will be *dead.*" Even more than Höss, Dürrfeld is the completely rationalized slave master. In the late eighteenth and early nineteenth century, the classical economists had argued that labor is a commodity. The corporate executives at I.G. Farben had carried that doctrine to its logical conclusion. One buys a commodity at the best possible price; one disposes of it when it has no further value. At Auschwitz, perhaps for the first time, labor was nothing but a commodity.

When Dürrfeld then leaves Höss's office, he brushes past Sophie in the antechamber. He does not recognize her. She is shocked to see that he has become a bloated caricature of the handsome executive she had met six years before. At this point, I must add a personal note. *Sophie's Choice* includes a brief discussion of and quotation from my book *The Cunning of History.* In the middle of the narration of Sophie's encounter with Höss, Styron breaks off the story and offers some thoughts on Sophie's situation as a modern equivalent of the "house nigger": "In all slave worlds there soon develops a hierarchic design, a pecking order. . . . Because of her great fortune

88

Sophie found herself among a small elite." The slave elite was differentiated from the other slaves at Auschwitz by virtue of the fact that they fulfilled a function the SS regarded as relatively indispensable. This was in contrast to the vast majority of slave inmates, "who because of their very superfluity and replaceability had only one purpose: to labor to the point of exhaustion and then to die." Auschwitz thus served two functions. It was an extermination camp, and it was also "a vast enclave dedicated to the practice of slavery." Nevertheless, Styron asserts that this was "a new form of slavery—of human beings being continuously replenished and expendable." Styron then quotes from *The Cunning of History:* "Most of the literature on the camps has tended to stress the role of the camps as places of execution. Regrettably, few ethical theorists have paid attention to the highly significant political fact that the camps were in reality a new form of human society." [12]

I am honored and delighted that a writer of Styron's preeminent standing has taken my ideas seriously, but I find it significant that what he selects from *The Cunning of History* is the argument that slavery at Auschwitz was radically different from, and infinitely more rationalized than, the slave system of the Old South. He offers the following comment on the passage just quoted:

> That new form of human society of which Rubenstein writes (extending Arendt's thesis) is a "society of total domination," evolving directly from the institution of chattel slavery as it was practiced by the great nations of the West, yet urged on to its despotic apotheosis at Auschwitz through an innovative concept which by contrast casts a benign light on old-fashioned plantation slavery even at its most barbaric: this blood-fresh concept of the simple *expendability* of human life. . . . Bedevilled as they may have been at times by the dilemmas of surplus population, the traditional slaveholders of the Western world were under Christian constraint to avoid anything resembling a "final solution" to solve the problem of excess labor; one could not shoot an expensively unproductive slave; one suffered with Old Sam when he grew superannuated and feeble and let him die in peace. . . . The Nazis, as Rubenstein points out, were the first slaveholders to fully abrogate any lingering humane sentiments regarding the essence of life itself; they were the first who "were able to turn human beings into instruments wholly responsive to their own will even when told to lie down in their graves and be shot." [13]

As far as Stingo and Stingo's creator are concerned, Nathan is wrong about the South. Neither the antebellum nor the postbellum South can be compared with Nazi Germany. Stingo may have been a direct beneficiary of an exploitative system of domination, but the system to which Stingo is heir stands in the same relationship to the Nazi slave system as the old, precapitalist, privately owned bourgeois enterprise stands to the modern, fully developed, multinational corporation. As noted, the Nazi slave system represents the logical outcome of the thoroughgoing rationalization of the processes of production and distribution. Such rationalization demands the total depersonalization of all relationships within the system of production and distribution, the achievement of maximum economies of scale in the use of all commodities necessary for the process of production, and the reduction of labor to calculable units of energy that are freely available for use or elimination as needed. Only in a death camp with an abundance of freely disposable slaves who are absolutely dominated by the masters can such a perfect rationalization be achieved.

The abiding continuity of Styron's personal involvement with slavery is made explicit in what would seem to be one of the more important autobiographical passages in the book. While at Yetta Zimmerman's rooming house, Stingo's money is stolen. His initial reaction is rage, but later he is relieved that he no longer possesses the money that had come from the sale of Artiste. Stingo tells us, "I was glad to get shut of such blood money, to get rid of slavery." Stingo immediately corrects himself: "Yet how could I *ever* get rid of slavery? A lump arose in my gorge, I whispered the word aloud 'Slavery!' There was dwelling somewhere in the inward part of my mind a compulsion to write about slavery, to make slavery give up its most deeply buried secrets. . . . And were not all of us, white and Negro, still enslaved? I knew that in the fever of my mind and in the most unquiet regions of my heart I would be shackled by slavery as long as I remained a writer." [14] In the scene that follows, Stingo discusses Nat Turner with Sophie and Nathan. We do not have to speculate about the author's preoccupation with slavery or the link between *Nat Turner* and *Sophie's Choice.* Styron spells it out for us.

A number of Styron's critics have faulted him for his detailed and explicit descriptions of young Stingo's attempt to find sexual release. Stingo's efforts are frequently comic. Some critics have resented what they regard as the intrusion of this note of sexual levity in a book about a distinctively unfunny subject. It is my conviction that these critics have permitted their own distinctive preoccupation with and involvement in the Holocaust to interfere with their understanding of what Styron has achieved. Styron is not Elie Wiesel and could not have written an eyewitness memoir of what actually took place at Auschwitz, as did Wiesel. Styron is a southern Protestant who has written a *Bildungsroman*, a novel describing the hero's journey from innocence to experience. Styron did not experience the Holocaust at first hand, and he chose not to write about it as if he had. His hero, who in many respects is his younger self, came to know and become involved with a survivor of Auschwitz. In the journey from innocence to experience the hero's encounter with a woman is often a decisive element in the process, but few heroines in literature have ever been responsible for so complex and multifaceted an introduction of the hero to the world of experience as is Sophie. Stingo's encounter with Sophie is absolutely crucial to his journey. Moreover, Stingo's sexual struggles are inseparable from the other components of the journey. Styron neither vulgarizes nor trivializes his subject by weaving together Stingo's sexual story, Sophie's account of her experiences, and the older narrator's reflections on Auschwitz, his younger self, and the many other elements—experiential, historical, and ideological—of mature identity that he has been able to grasp as a result of his encounter with Sophie. Historical and philosophical ideas are more likely to be abstracted from sex, emotion, and personal self-exploration in college textbooks than they are in real life. Some of Sartre's best reflections on phenomenological ontology are embedded in his novel *Nausea*, but as in *Sophie's Choice*, the author has chosen to interweave them with the concrete experience of the protagonist. In historical, philosophical, or theoretical treatises, there is quite properly no place for information about the authors' sexual lives at the time they were formulating their ideas. Nevertheless, in real life ideas and feelings are inseparable, as is the case in Styron's descriptions of Stingo. Far from weakening the novel, Stingo's sexual struggles are integral to his unique voyage from innocence to experience.

Nor is there any reason why Styron would have emphasized the extermination of the Jews rather than slavery in his novel, as some of his critics have suggested. *Sophie's Choice* is his book, not theirs; there is no reason why their priorities should be his. On the contrary, the critics would have been better instructed had they attempted to understand the author's experience in its own terms—which is precisely what the author offers us in the book. As the heir of slaveholders, confronted with the bitter accusation that his native civilization was no better than that of the Nazis—an accusation young Styron must have heard from more than one northerner—slavery rather than the fate of the Jews was the immediate problem that Stingo had to deal with. From this perspective *Sophie's Choice* can be seen as less a novel about the Holocaust than a novel about how the Holocaust affected a highly gifted young southern writer. This fact does not mean that Styron's story is necessarily more or less significant than that of any other writer on the subject. Of necessity, Styron's story is different. Nor has Styron invaded anybody else's literary turf because his own literary tradition is played out and no longer offers a viable subject, as critic Alvin Rosenfeld has meanly and ungraciously argued. Styron came by his theme honestly and handles it with great artistry.

Some of Styron's vignettes are likely to offend some Jews or, at the very least, make them feel uncomfortable. One such scene depicts Sophie and Stingo freely giving vent to their own anti-Semitism. However, it must be remembered that Styron is not telling the story of how Jews experienced the Holocaust but of how Sophie experienced it and how she shared her experiences with Stingo. The author has by no means diminished the credibility of his tale by including vignettes such as these in his story. On the contrary, by telling the story of how a young southern innocent sought a place where he could find the peace to write his first novel and how this led him to the wholly unanticipated encounter with one of the most terrible historical catastrophes of all time through his involvement with one of its female victims, who had a rabidly anti-Semitic family background, Styron comes as close to universalizing the event for those who did not experience it directly as does any major novelist.

It is interesting to note that the public reception of this novel was more favorable than that of the critics. It is my conviction that, in this case, the public's instinct was better than that of the critics. In spite of critics like Rosenfeld, *Sophie's Choice* demonstrates that there is nothing played out about the southern literary tradition, at least as far as William Styron is concerned. In good measure, the importance of *Sophie's Choice* lies in the fact that it is a distinguished southerner's honest attempt to spell out what the Holocaust has meant to him. I know of no other such book. Only an artist of assured stature and courage could have written such a book. Only such a writer could have dared examine his own history and his own tradition in the light of the Holocaust.

As with any awesome event that defies simple conceptualization, there can be no single interpretation of the Holocaust. Every honest interpretation represents the weaving of this interpreter's own history and experience with what he or she knows of the event. I wonder how a survivor of Cambodia or one of the Vietnamese boat people might interpret the Holocaust were he or she to take it as a theme for a novel. Styron is not an ordinary writer. His works are part of the permanent legacy of American literature. We are all enriched because a son of the South and an heir of the slave tradition has found his own way of exploring this unique historical tragedy. What is amazing is how few of Styron's critics understood what he was doing.

NOTES

1. William Styron, *Sophie's Choice* (New York, 1979).

2. John Henrick Clarke (ed.), *William Styron's Nat Turner: Ten Black Writers Respond* (Boston, 1968).

3. John Gardner, *New York Times Book Review,* May 27, 1979, p. 1; Alvin Rosenfeld, "The Holocaust According to William Styron," *Midstream* (December, 1979), 43; Pearl Bell, "Evil and William Styron," *Commentary,* LXVIII (August, 1979), 59.

4. Styron, *Sophie's Choice,* 226.

5. *Ibid.,* 70.

6. *Ibid.,* 190.

7. See Frederick G. Weiss (ed.), *Hegel: The Essential Writings* (New York, 1974), 64–79.

8. Styron, *Sophie's Choice,* 515.

9. *Ibid.,* 149.

10. Eugene Genovese, *The World the Slaveholders Made* (New York, 1969), 98–99.

11. Styron, *Sophie's Choice,* 154.

12. Richard L. Rubenstein, *The Cunning of History: Mass Death and the American Future* (New York, 1975), 46; Styron, *Sophie's Choice,* 233.

13. Styron, *Sophie's Choice,* 235–36.

14. *Ibid.,* 420.

SLAVES IN BIRACIAL
PROTESTANT CHURCHES
John B. Boles

Religion was the heart and soul of the Afro-American's human triumph over chattel slavery. Religion provided a system of ideas and practices that gave directions for living; it marked with symbols and ceremonies significant events in an individual's life; it provided hope, fulfillment, and a special kind of freedom for people mired in chattel bondage. Although the importance and centrality of the slaves' religion recently has been recognized, the precise origin, nature, and function of their faith are still issues under active debate.

Black Christianity found many ways of expressing itself, but for most slaves throughout the antebellum period the normative worship experience was a joint worship service attended by both blacks and whites. African components persisted in the slave culture's naming practices, kinship systems, musical instruments, body language, folktales and other oral traditions, and carving, pottery, quilting, and basketmaking styles. The imprint of Africa lingered also in religion. In fact, certain aspects of African religious thought may have predisposed slaves to accept the evangelical Protestantism they were exposed to after the mid-eighteenth century. But the emerging Afro-American Christianity was greatly influenced by white practices and by black participation in southern churches—so much so that it is possible to speak of a biracial religious community in the Old South. Complete equality and true justice never existed, but black and white met more equally under the steeple than anywhere else in southern society. That relationship is the focus of this essay, which surveys a broad and complex topic that ranges across two continents and three centuries.

The West Africa from which most slaves came contained hundreds of different cultural systems and an awesome variety of religious practices. But there were several underlying common assumptions

Some of the material in this essay has previously appeared in the author's *Black Southerners, 1619–1869,* published by the University Press of Kentucky.

and, even more important, some striking similarities to the kinds of Protestant evangelicalism Africans encountered in the American South. Meaningful generalizations, even though they risk oversimplification, can be made. For the West African the world was infused with spiritual forces. Nature gods and ancestral gods gave a special value to one's kinship group and the physical environs of one's village. Every event—from cataclysmic natural disasters to minor personal misfortunes—had its roots, it was believed, in the realm of the spiritual. African societies in the seventeenth and eighteenth centuries appear to have been completely nonsecular; religion was all-encompassing, an aspect of every detail of life, an influence on every occurrence. Most Africans had a conception of time in which the present and the past were almost fused into one. Ancestors were almost literally still present. But the future was extremely foreshortened, hardly conceivable except in the most limited, day-after-tomorrow sense. In a triune conception of the supernatural, ancestral spirits and nature spirits were the most common supernatural beings; they were normally deemed responsible for the happenstances of life and supplicated. Yet, superior to these two types of gods reigned an omnipotent, omniscient god who could be appealed to when all else had failed.

Ordinarily, in African societies the gods spoke to persons by sending a spirit, and possession—often frenzied—was the human evidence of communication with the supernatural. Throughout West Africa, people considered themselves an organic part of the cosmos, but water had a special role, a mystical, symbolic one. Streams, rivers, lakes, and springs were often "aquatic temples" where various nature or ancestral spirits dwelled. Springs gushing from the center of the earth were often thought to be symbolic of rebirth, still waters represented creation, and water in general suggested life, fertility, and hope. Religious ceremonies often took place beside or even in water, were usually public, involved the community, and frequently were marked by participatory congregational singing. The religious ceremony bestowed and reinvigorated a sense of belonging by providing the individual with a sense of fellowship with contemporaries, ancestors, and the natural environment. Through spiritual possession, one encountered the supernatural essence of the universe.

Given the nature of American slavery, the specifics of African religions—the ritual specialists, the religious language, and the ritual paraphernalia—could not be transported intact to the American South. But the philosophical essence of the system was transplanted and slowly transformed. In the seventeenth century, slaves were too few and too intermixed with whites to be able to maintain much more than a haunting memory of Old World practices. On scattered occasions blacks were baptized as Christians, but the language barrier and the planters' lingering uncertainty about the continued slave status of a baptized bondsman minimized the Christianization of blacks. Also, there were few actively Christian whites in the South in the seventeenth century. By the third quarter of the eighteenth century, however, Baptist, Methodist, and Presbyterian evangelicals had established themselves and had begun the process of forming churches, recruiting ministers, and popular evangelizing that would eventually turn the Old South into a hothouse of religious orthodoxy and personal piety. The upsurge of African importations, the beginning of net population growth for American-born slaves, and the birth of Afro-American culture coincided with the commencement of the southern evangelical movement. These coincidental developments were to have a major impact on the evolution of Afro-American Christianity in the Old South.

In 1774 a young Princeton-educated tutor to the family of Councillor Robert Carter encountered an aged African-born slave, Daddy Gumby, on a Virginia plantation. The slave clearly had accepted Calvinistic teachings, as evidenced by his statement that "God yonder in Heaven Master will burn *Lyars* with *Fire & Brimstone*! . . . Men are wicked." When the tutor, Philip Vickers Fithian, said it was too hot to attend church, the old slave admonished him: "Too hot to serve the Lord! Why I that am so old & worn out go on foot."[1] Clearly, some Africans who had mastered the English language had also adopted the Christian world view, and for every African like Daddy Gumby who did so, there must have been also several American-born slaves who found comfort and purpose in Christianity. All three of the southern evangelical denominations that would soon be dominant in the region welcomed black worshipers and actively preached to bondspeople. Many planters were still skeptical of the utility and wisdom of converting the slaves. But the growing popular denominations, consisting primarily of non-slave-owning yeoman farmers, believed all were equal in the eyes of God. The early Baptists and Methodists, especially, often criticized slavery and felt driven to spread the gospel to all God's creatures. Most church services were joint services—and remained so throughout the antebellum period—but there were other factors besides the churches' welcoming black members that made evangelical Christianity attractive to increasing numbers of slaves.

If ever there was a situation in which Africans might feel that the lesser gods had proven unequal to the task and that as a consequence their omnipotent god was the one to be relied on, then capture, the middle passage, and enslavement in the New World was it. Increasingly, after the mid-eighteenth century both newly imported and already acculturated slaves came into contact with fervent evangelicals who preached of a benevolent, all-powerful God who reached out to the lost and forlorn and provided deliverance. It was easy to identify the supreme African god with the Christian's God. The idea was especially compatible with African views when the Christian God was proffered by ministers (and congregational members) whose zeal and spirit-infused exhortations bore a comforting resemblance to African possession. And the African concept of ancestral gods, nature gods, and an omnipotent creator god was transferable to the Christian Trinity of God the Father, God the Son, and God the Holy Spirit.

As the slave population increased and slave families became ever more common, blacks grew more concerned with cultural values and religious services. After all, not only were their lives now substantially more stable, but they were having children. Families became, if not quite the norm, an often realizable goal. With families came a desire to cement relationships ceremonially, to legitimate and maintain cultural values. Parents are always more concerned than young singles to preserve religious traditions. At the same general time that demographic forces were pushing slaves in the direction of family formation and creation of their own culture, Protestantism was penetrating the plantation South. The willingness of the evangelical churches to accept blacks as members and, by the use of such terms of address as brother and sister, to include them in fellowship gave slaves a sense of belonging and group identity that again resonated with African memories. The Baptist practice of immersion may well have recalled African water rites, whereas the emotional intensity, the vigorous congregational singing, and the joyful sense of spiritual release common to the Methodists as well as the Baptists appealed to the African sensitivity. New World realities and Old World recollections formed the matrix out of which Afro-American Christianity emerged.

In the 1770s and 1780s, as pioneer churches were organized, there were black members participating in the very acts of incorporation. The absolute number of black church members was small at first (and before the nineteenth century total church membership was only a tiny fraction of the population). But slaves were attending churches, taking communion, being baptized and confirmed, listening to sermons, singing hymns, and gradually accepting the Christian world view. The Great Revival at the beginning of the nineteenth century established the mode of revival piety that came to characterize the antebellum South. At the very peak of the revival, during the climactic Cane Ridge camp meeting of 1801, there was "a Black assembly, hearing the exhortations of the Blacks; some of which appeared to be convicted and others converted."[2] Thereafter, in steady, unspectacular fashion, the numbers of slaves worshiping in joint congregations grew, despite the fact that before the 1840s planters sporadically declared their unease about the potentially revolutionary implications of the gospel.

After the mid-1840s, when the three major denominations had splintered away from the national organizations and appeared safe on the issue of abolition, planters became even more supportive of efforts to Christianize the slaves, in part because they thought religion would make them better slaves. But there were reasons unrelated to plantation efficiency for sponsoring the preaching of the gospel to the blacks. Ministers advocated missionary activities both to rebut abolitionist charges that slaveholders left their bondspeople in heathenish conditions and out of genuine desires to enlarge God's Kingdom. Guilt and the urge to evangelize were both factors, their relative importance differing from person to person and at various times. During the final generation of the Old South, several hundred white missionaries preached regularly to slave congregations in the regions where the black population was high. In addition, by the eve of the Civil War perhaps as many as a quarter of all slaves were members of churches, principally in areas where average slaveholdings were small. But one should resist the temptation to interpret the resulting slave Christianity simply as an example of successful social control exerted by whites over blacks.

Slaves avidly accepted Christianity and made it their own because it served their purposes so well. Slaves understood that, as the white ministers often said and as the Bible proclaimed, in the eyes of God all are equal, slave and free alike. Likewise, salvation was available to everyone who had faith in Christ. In addition, slaves could identify with Jesus, particularly in his role as the suffering servant. With salvation came the promise of a better life after the earthly travail was finished, but just as important, the Christian faith provided a moral purpose for day-by-day living. As children of God, black men and women felt that their lives were not meaningless or of little worth. And because God was just, many slaves expected recompense in the end for the injustice of their present lives in bondage. The concept of the Chosen People was widely adopted by the slaves as descriptive of their own situation: for like the people of Israel they were enslaved, mistreated, and downtrodden, and if they kept faith with God, they could look forward to eventual triumph. The effect was to provide a healthy dose of self-respect for the slave community. Their identification with the people of Israel gave a certain sense of moral grandeur, even a feeling of moral superiority vis-à-vis haughty masters, to the slaves struggling to maintain their essential humanity amidst an institution that classified them as mere property. In the churches black men and women found persuasive reason to live as morally responsible adults, discovered arenas for the practice of black leadership, and enjoyed a status far closer to equality with whites than anywhere else in southern society. No wonder the church was the dominant institutional force in the lives of so many black southerners throughout the antebellum period and into our own time.

Historians have sufficiently recognized neither the role of the slaves in the southern churches nor the role of those churches in the lives of the slaves. From the inception of institutional church life, particularly among the soon-dominant Baptists and Methodists, slaves were active church members. Of course, the percentage of black members varied according to their percentage in the local population, but in every region blacks and whites worshiped together. Blacks commonly represented 20 to 40 percent of the congregation of Baptist churches; often they were the majority. Generally, blacks sat segregated at the rear of the church, in the balcony, or in a lean-to addition to the church. Blacks and whites heard the same sermons, took communion at the same service, were baptized or confirmed together, and were buried in the same cemeteries. Black delegates attended district association and quarterly meetings down to the Civil War. On occasion, when the white members built a new church building, the blacks were given the old building and allowed virtual autonomy over matters in the adjunct church. A white committee would be appointed to supervise the black congregation, which might be called, for example, the Stamping Ground African Baptist Church to distinguish it from the parent, white Stamping Ground Baptist Church. But such supervision appears to have been nominal. The slaves so separated were less the victims of segregation than the beneficiaries of whites' recognition that bondspeople had special needs and special interests best served by their own leaders. In the far more common biracial churches, black deacons and elders sometimes served alongside whites, and it was not unusual, when no white minister was available, for the whole congregation to listen with approval to a black preacher. In fact, sometimes biracial congregations requested certain black preachers. Across the South, especially talented black preachers gained great fame as pulpit orators, and whites agreed that black ministers such as John Jasper and Andrew Marshall had unrivaled power to move a congregation.

In its economic, political, and social realm the Old South was a deferential, hierarchical society. But distinctions of class and race counted for surprisingly less in the religious realm. Such relative democracy before God did not remove distinctions in what was called the "civil" world, but it helped reduce conflict there. There was more nearly a biracial community in the antebellum Protestant churches than in the society as a whole. Standards for admission to and dismissal from churches were essentially the same for both races. A measure of spiritual equality was accorded blacks even in the language of address: "Brother" and "Sister" were affixed to their given names, as with white comembers. Church clerks would write back to slaves' home churches to obtain letters of dismissal for slaves recently sold away, and when a letter arrived attesting to the slave's good standing, he or she would be admitted to the new church. The process of joining or removing from a church was the same for slave and free. A person made a profession of his faith and either was baptized or submitted evidence of his prior baptism at another church. The relationship of the church to slavery was filled with irony and contradiction. Even while churches had slave members and accorded them relative equality in the spiritual realm, the churches were always careful to recognize the realities of the slave society of which they were a part. Churches generally sought slaveowners' permission—and obtained it—before accepting slave members. Church minutes contain numerous letters like the following, entered in the Chestnut Grove (Virginia) Baptist Church books on the second Sunday of July, 1862.

> Rev Mr. Briggs
> My man servant Hubbard wishes to attach himself to your church; you can admit him if you think proper
> J. A. Michie

> Rev. Mr. Briggs:
> Harvard and Nelson have my permission to join the Baptist Church at Earlysville, and I pray that the Holy Spirit may guide and direct them through life—and that they may finally be saved in heaven.
> June 23rd 1862 Joshua Jackson[3]

The fact that the owners were called upon to grant permission indicates the pervasiveness of the master-slave relationship. But as these letters also suggest, slaves had significant autonomy, and some slave owners had genuine moral concern for the souls of their bondspeople. Like all human institutions, slavery was enormously complex and as varied as the persons involved.

An even more impressive example of how slaves entered into the life and spirit of the churches, and vice versa, is provided in the way the churches functioned as moral courts. The three dominant evangelical churches took seriously and tried to put into practice Jesus' directives as outlined in Matthew 18:15. Different denominations had differing procedures. A Baptist church, for example, would meet at least once a month on Saturday or Sunday afternoon in a "business" session in which the major business was the moral supervision of its members. Each member was expected "with love and charity" to watch over other members and counsel them to change if they had been seen to transgress some moral law. When there was a dispute or no quick confession was forthcoming, charges would be brought against the offending party at the business session. Most transgressions consisted of such human failings as drunkenness, profanity, breaking the Sabbath, fornication, adultery, stealing, and lying. Charges were made, witnesses heard, and testimony taken, and the defendant was judged either innocent or guilty. If judged guilty, the person either confessed and promised reformation or was excommunicated. Such activity was a significant part of religious life and responsibility in the Old South, and slaves participated in the whole process voluntarily and, to a surprising degree, as virtually the equals of whites. Bondspeople clearly took pride in their name and good character; it was one thing masters could not take away from them.

Blacks were held by whites—and apparently by other Christian slaves—to substantially the same moral standards as whites were. Testimony was taken from and about slaves in the same way it was for white communicants. When whites brought charges against a black member, the accused was not automatically assumed to be guilty. Rather, the case was decided on its merits. Baptist church minute books in Mississippi reveal several occasions on which charges by whites against slave members were dismissed and the slave deemed innocent. In like fashion, slaves bore testimony against whites, and the whites then underwent moral examination. All this happened in a society in which slaves could not testify against whites in civil courts. In 1819 one William West was denied a letter of dismissal from the Hephzibah Baptist Church in East Feliciana Parish, Louisiana, because the church had concluded he had unjustly whipped a "black brother of the church." Three years later another white member, D. Edds, was excommunicated after charges that he had abused one of his slaves were substantiated by examination.[4] The church records show that masters frequently brought charges against slaves for lying, stealing, and even running away, but in every case slaves were accorded at least a reasonable semblance of due-process trial and often were judged innocent. That masters would utilize the church in an attempt to maintain plantation discipline is not surprising, but that they accepted the authority of the church—where black testimony was given—suggests a social complexity not always appreciated by historians.

Moreover, slaves brought charges against one another, defended

103

themselves, and in general stood before their fellow members as free moral agents. Clearly, whites and blacks accepted the same moral code, identifying the same sins to be overcome. The churches' position on black adultery is highly significant. In a society in which slave marriages were not legally recognized and could be ended at the master's convenience, evangelical churches held slaves strictly accountable for adultery. Hence, in the eyes of many southern churchgoers, the slave marriage was sacred and its commitments firm (though slaves who had been sold and separated against their will could remarry). None of this indicates that the South was not racist, for in subtle ways whites were always in the ascendant position, and blacks were literally and figuratively at the back of the church. Nevertheless, what is more remarkable is the degree to which there existed a biracial religious community in the Old South.

Historians have been too prone to emphasize the differences between white and black religion in the Old South, contrasting joyful, emotionally demonstrative black services with stereotypical images of arid, lifeless white services. But most white southerners, including Baptists and Methodists, enjoyed fervent worship with spirited preaching and participatory singing. Predominantly white rural churches were more like the lively black services than the Episcopal ceremony or the more sophisticated urban churches. As the antebellum period drew to a close, all of the white denominations were moving toward trained ministers, more sedate worship, and shorter services, while black Christianity remained truer to the early revivalistic style. Even so, commonalities in belief, sermon structure, and worship style persisted. More than a century after the Civil War, remnants of these shared practices were visible in the clear affinity between Baptist presidential candidate Jimmy Carter and black church members in 1976.

Talented slaves rose to positions of leadership in the churches, serving often as elders and deacons and occasionally as preachers. In all regions from the 1770s through the Civil War there were black ministers who preached to black and mixed audiences. The absence of educational standards and the looseness of ecclesiastical organizations made it easier for blacks to become Baptist preachers and no doubt enhanced the popularity of that denomination for slaves. At some times in some states it was illegal for slaves to become preachers, but white church authorities bent the laws and permitted slave "exhorters" to preach and "testify." Although it was also illegal to teach slaves to read, literate bondspeople existed in all areas of the South. Often they had been taught by God-fearing masters or mistresses so they could read the Bible, though occasionally white children or other literate slaves were their tutors. When black preachers spoke to mixed congregations, they trod softly lest the gospel theme of liberation raise the hackles of the whites. But when unsupervised, most black ministers apparently preached of the freedom provided by redemption. No doubt the described "freedom from sin" and "spiritual liberty" often came near to being a double-entendre for freedom from slavery, at least to suspicious whites, especially after insurrection scares. But it would be a mistake to interpret slave religion simply as either an opiate for passive slaves or a training ground for rebel activists. This conclusion becomes increasingly evident when one considers the variety of institutional forms that slave religion took.

The overwhelming majority of slave worshipers practiced their faith with whites in the mainline Protestant churches, but in most good-sized southern towns and cities there were independent black churches under the control of free black leaders. Many of these churches benefited from white patrons. Saint James African Episcopal Church in Baltimore is a good example of such an autonomous church. Occasionally—as in Richmond and Louisville—the major black Baptist church was the largest congregation in town. Although only free blacks held the leadership positions in such churches, since the church charters discriminated against slaves, bondspeople found in the all-black churches a meaningful and uplifting kind of worship. White visitors often noted the decorum, the eloquent sermon, and the marvelous singing that characterized the black temples of worship. The theology preached was little different from that in biracial churches, though by the 1830s the old camp-meeting kind of fervor was practically absent from the urban white churches. Except for the fact that services were usually longer and more overtly emotional, the theology, ritual, and organization of the black churches closely resembled those of the white churches. Independent black churches added much to the cultural life of urban blacks, providing a sense of order and direction, an opportunity to practice leadership skills, a va-

riety of self-help organizations, and—most important—visible proof
to all blacks, slave and free, that they could govern important aspects
of their lives. Sometimes, as when the black church was a mission
church funded by a predominantly white denomination, a white minister officiated. But the usual pattern in these influential citadels of
black cultural life was for total black leadership, a secular as well as
religious leadership that continued well into the postbellum period.

An insufficiently understood and greatly exaggerated aspect of
slave religion is the so-called underground church, the invisible institution of covert worship services held deep in the woods or se-
cretly in slave cabins and urban cellars. Certainly the religious lives
of slaves extended beyond the church structures, beyond the formal
services where whites were present. Devout bondspeople in the pri-
vacy of their quarters surely had prayer meetings, sang hymns and
spirituals of their own composition, and pondered the dilemmas of
trying to do right in a world that did them so wrong. Weather permitting and master permitting, slaves on Sunday afternoons often
met together for songs and preaching to supplement what they had
heard in the morning worship hours. In these informal settings, black
preachers could preach with less constraint. This could mean that
they exhorted their listeners to rebel, but it probably more often
simply freed the slave ministers to preach the gospel with greater
ebullience, enlivening their messages with colorful imagery and
weaving into their texts stories of Old Testament heroes and New
Testament miracles that magnified the awesome power of God and
love of Christ. Black ministers proclaimed the terrors of hell and the
joys of heaven with a concreteness of detailed description that few
whites could match. In the manner of the rich African oral tradition,
the spoken word moved people and transmitted the heart of their
culture from one generation to the next, entertaining them in the
process. With consummate oratorical skills Afro-American preachers
utilized an African medium to spread and maintain a Euro-American
message. As might be expected, black Christians magnified the role
and importance of the preacher. Nowhere were their verbal skills
given more license than in the Sunday afternoon and nighttime meetings where they were not inhibited by the presence of whites. Here
black preachers developed their characteristic and distinctive homi-
letic style.

On other occasions—as perhaps when a master prohibited slaves from attending church or when the white minister at church showed scant respect for the blacks' true religious feelings by preaching little but self-serving doctrines, such as "Slaves, obey your master"— slaves sought in their own special brush-arbor service to explore and proclaim the full gospel message of repentance and joy. Extant testimony by slaves shows their dissatisfaction with ministers who foreshortened the Christian message. Maria, one of Mary Boykin Chesnut's slaves, had real affection for one white minister who "preaches to black and white just the same. There ain't but one Gospel for all," she said. But she despised another minister who "goes for low-life things—hurting people's feelings. Don't you tell lies—don't you steal. . . . Before God," she insisted, "we are as white as he is. And in the pulpit he has no need to make us feel we are servants."[5] In situations in which slaves were repeatedly subject to such truncated preaching, they slipped away, held secret services (sometimes turning a pot upside down in the belief that it would capture the sounds of their ceremonies and not betray their presence), relied on their own leaders, and created their own secret churches largely invisible to prying whites. The very attempt to do this, of course, indicates how false was the belief by some earlier scholars that slaves had no role models or cultural norms other than those provided by their masters.

In two small and isolated geographical regions, the sea islands of Georgia and South Carolina and the sugar-producing areas of New Orleans and rural Louisiana, where the ratio of blacks to whites was extremely high, African (or, in Louisiana, Caribbean) admixtures were strong enough to give slave religious services a decidedly un-European cast, as exemplified in the frenzied shouts of the sea islands and the voodoolike practices of south Louisiana. But with these two exceptions, perhaps in no other aspect of black cultural life had the values and practices of whites so deeply penetrated as in religious services. After all, black folklore, dance, art, basketry, and other practices flourished during those hours from sundown to sunup, when white supervision was least, and most readily identifiable Africanisms occurred in those areas of slave life whites found of marginal importance. Of what concern was it to a planter what kinds of stories slaves told in evenings on their cabin stoops or what kinds of motifs they wove into their baskets or sewed into their quilts? In this cultural twilight zone, which apparently had no effect on the plantation work routines or on the society's racial etiquette, blacks carved out a surprising and significant degree of autonomy. From this beachhead of cultural self-determination slaves resisted dehumanization and expanded control or at least influence over aspects of their life ranging from food supply to clothing styles.

With religion it was different. Whites did care what blacks believed, in part because the whites felt the truths of the gospel were too important to be left to "untutored" and "superstitious" slaves, in part because the masters correctly sensed the potentially liberating and even revolutionary implications of several scriptural doctrines. Whites worshiped with blacks and listened to the same sermons. Apparently slaves sat through the entire worship service, hearing the same theology the whites heard; only at the conclusion of the service, when the minister turned his special attention to the slaves in the gallery or back rows and addressed them in a short homily that was an addendum to the main sermon, did slaves have to endure the message of social control. Exhortations for slaves to obey their master and repeated admonitions not to lie or steal made religion seem safe to whites and also made many slaves doubt the intentions of the preacher. But the substance and the heart of the sermon was understood by the bondspeople, and that message of life-affirming joy, a message that obliterated one's this-worldly status and placed supreme value on steadfast faith, was more revolutionary than planters ever suspected.

Christianity taught that, in the eyes of God, slaves were the equals of their masters; it taught slaves that their souls were precious. It provided a context wherein slaves along with their masters struggled against the evil forces within themselves. Christianity was life-affirming for slaves as well as whites; it infused individuals of both races with joy and confidence. Strong emotions and fervent belief characterized the worship services of the free people as well as of the enslaved. In a social institution that defined them as no more than property, slaves found within the church powerful reassurance of their humanity. Within the church, one's earthly status was of less avail than one's spiritual status, and armed with faith, slaves discovered a profound guarantee of their worth as persons. Passivity and cynicism alike were overcome as bondspeople struggled to purify their lives through the discipline offered by the church. Slaves recognized the harmful effects of lying, stealing, violence against one another, drunkenness, and promiscuity, especially when fellow slaves were hurt. Consequently, they labeled such practices sinful, and when conversion promised to help them reform their lives, they, like all evangelicals, spoke of being freed from sin. Eloquent black preachers and devout laymen gave testimony to slaves' sense of responsibility, providing role models of enduring strength. The prototype of the Chosen People kept alive faith in a final retribution, and Jesus, as a personal friend and savior, offered daily encouragement to lives filled with suffering and toil. Religious slaves often felt themselves morally superior to their master, and the whites' disproportionate wealth and power had no effect on such self-confidence. Experiencing hope, joy, and purpose in their faith, Christian slaves found more than a will simply to survive physically. They survived as a people who amidst chattel slavery could find within themselves the power to love and care, the strength to forgive, and the patience to endure with their souls unshattered.

Psychologically, most slaves inwardly repudiated slavery and persevered remarkably intact. Certainly there were some whose sense of worth was gnawed away by the constant abuse, and these became virtual Sambos—spiritless, unresisting, and conforming to the white's desires. Other bondspeople displaced their anger at the institution of slavery onto those weaker than themselves and mistreated their spouses, their children, or the farm animals. Slaves occasionally fought among themselves, taking out their anger in blows against available enemies. Some committed suicide or lashed out blindly against offending whites and were killed as a consequence. Yet, the remarkable fact is not the expected social pathology, but the degree to which slaves succeeded in maintaining their families, their honor, and their sense of individual worth. As Thomas Wentworth Higginson recalled when he looked back on his wartime experience among black soldiers: "We abolitionists had underrated the suffering produced by slavery among the negroes, but had overrated the demoralization. Or rather, we did not know how the religious temperament of the negroes had checked the demoralization."[6] Perhaps more than any other factor, Christianity in several forms—the biracial church, the independent black church, and the so-called invisible church—provided slaves with a purpose and a perspective with which to overcome slavery psychologically and spiritually and survive as humans.

As some critics have charged, in one sense much slave religion was otherworldly and escapist. Partly because their life in this world was frequently broken by separation and hardship and partly because the African heritage of an extremely foreshortened view of the world made the expansive Christian view of the hereafter exhilarating, slaves in their songs and sermons often reveled in blissful descriptions of heaven. Such raptures were to some extent compensatory. But elements of the descriptions—the portrayal of heaven as a place where all God's children have shoes, for example, and where there is no more work and where families and loved ones are united never to be torn apart again—were telling comments on life in this world. Moreover, the clear implication that slaves were destined for, and deserved, "a home in glory land" reveals a profound rejection of images of degradation and worthlessness. Belief by slaves that in the end they would occupy seats in heaven spoke volumes about their sense of God's justice, and their sense of eternal reward again raised the uplifting theme of identification with the Chosen People. Such beliefs no doubt worked against suicidal assaults against bondage, but these beliefs also immeasurably armed slaves for a more profound, inner repudiation of the bonds of slavery.

There is also some truth in another view, that slave religion was primarily a staging ground for black revolt. Surely black Christians saw the contradiction between the gospel's view of equality and freedom and the preacher's injunction that slaves must obey their masters. Throughout the history of Christianity, oppressed peoples have been inspired by the teachings of Jesus to attack their oppressors and repudiate their earthly rulers. No one can deny that Christianity raises the possibility of rebellion for the sake of conscience, and slave owners certainly were aware of that. Church participation, moreover, gave slaves a chance to develop leadership skills, to communicate with one another, and to cultivate the sense of common purpose and of injustice that could stimulate insurrection. For some slaves in particular situations, religion did motivate and facilitate rebellion. Most slave revolts in the United States, both those that were only planned and those actually undertaken, had a religious dimension, from the Stono revolt in 1739 to Nat Turner's rebellion in 1831. There was a fateful ambiguity at the heart of the slave's response to Christianity; the fervent rebel and the passive, long-suffering servant were equally authentic expressions of black religion. But in the Old South the overwhelming majority of slaves internalized rebellion, for they recognized the imbalance of power that made armed insurrection sheer futility.

Submission was, in many instances, merely a conscious decision, a way of coping with the exigencies of life in a slave society. Submission was not total but partial and controlled; it reflected the limited possibilities for overt action and the kind of sublimated moral rebellion permissible. For the huge majority of slaves, their folk Christianity provided them both a spiritual release and a spiritual victory. They could inwardly repudiate the system and thus steel themselves to survive it. This more subtle, more profound type of spiritual freedom made their Christianity the most significant aspect of slave culture and effectively defused much of the potential for insurrection. Repeatedly the narratives tell of slaves' having their souls "freed." One aged ex-slave remarked that she had often heard her mother say: "'I am so glad I am free.' I did not know then what she was talking about. I thought she meant freedom from slavery."[7] It was precisely this belief that one was in the ultimate sense "free" that allowed countless slaves to persevere. In ways masters never suspected, the Christianity of blacks mitigated against slave uprisings and supported the essential humanity of a people defined as property.

The Civil War and emancipation brought many changes to southern blacks. Northern churchmen saw the South, with its four million freedpeople, as a fertile mission field. Northern churches—the Methodist Episcopal Church, the African Methodist Episcopal Church, the African Methodist Episcopal Church Zion, the Presbyterian Church, the Baptist Church, and the Reformed Episcopal Church—rushed to establish southern branches. Tens of thousands of ex-slaves withdrew from their former biracial churches and joined these new all-black churches. (Some white missionaries and scattered white northerners who had recently settled in the South were also members, but in the South churches affiliated with northern denominations became overwhelmingly dominated by blacks.) After the initial, formative stage, when northern missionaries were founding the churches, freedmen who had been slave preachers and exhorters led the new denominations. These men and their fervent congregations were part of the harvest of slave Christianity.

Across the South many thousands of freedpeople also withdrew from their former biracial churches and formed black versions of the southern denominations. The National Baptist Convention and the Colored Methodist Episcopal Church were the two largest of these new denominations. In all the black churches the theology, the ritual, and the organization were very similar to those of the white churches from which their membership was drawn. The numbers and devotion of the black worshipers and the adeptness of their ministers suggest the vitality of slave Christianity under the auspices of the parent southern churches. Even though slave members had not been accorded complete equality, they had practiced leadership roles, nurtured their sense of self-worth, and grown in faith. More a testimony to the humanity of the slaves than to their slaveowners' intentions, black participation in antebellum southern churches had been a critical proving ground for slave survival skills and cultural growth. The burgeoning of black churches after the Civil War points back to the centrality of Christianity in the slave community.

It should be pointed out that the blacks withdrew from the churches; they were not initially excluded. Many whites tried to persuade the freedpeople not to separate, both because they feared losing control over them and because they doubted the ability of blacks to preach the gospel "pure and undefiled." Still others genuinely hated to see a racial division in the church. But freedpeople had chafed under white control—even under well-intentioned white paternalism—for too long. Black faith was strong, black leaders were capable, and the black need for self-direction and autonomy was manifest. Consequently, southern churches became significantly more segregated after the Civil War, and the move away from joint worship was black-instigated. Despite the similarities in theology and organization, the two races have continued down separate denominational paths ever since. The differences between white and black Christianity—especially the expressed emotion, sermon style, and music—were greater in 1960 than they had been in 1860. Contemporary differences have obscured historical similarities. But that is only another one of the ironies of southern history.

NOTES

1. Hunter Dickinson Farish (ed.), *Journal and Letters of Philip Vickers Fithian, 1773–1774: A Plantation Tutor of the Old Dominion* (Williamsburg, 1965), 151–52. See also 1–35.

2. *An Account of an Extraordinary Revival of Religion in Kentucky* (New York, 1801), 2.

3. Minutes of Chestnut Grove Baptist Church, July, 1862, on microfilm in Alderman Library, University of Virginia, Charlottesville.

4. Minutes of Hephzibah Baptist Church, November 20, 1819, December 22, 1822, March 15, 1823, in Department of Archives and Manuscripts, Louisiana State University, Baton Rouge. Larry James, a former graduate student at Tulane University, brought these cases to my attention.

5. C. Vann Woodward (ed.), *Mary Chesnut's Civil War* (New Haven, 1981), 260.

6. Thomas Wentworth Higginson, *Army Life in a Black Regiment* (Boston, 1870), 253.

7. George P. Rawick (ed.), *God Struck Me Dead* (Westport, Conn., 1972), 60. Vol. XIX of *The American Slave: A Composite Autobiography,* 19 vols.

CATHOLICS IN A PROTESTANT WORLD:
THE OLD SOUTH EXAMPLE
Randall M. Miller

American Catholicism has been a religion of immigrants. More than anything else, that fact has shaped the social and cultural contours of American Catholicism and fixed its place in American consciousness. For much of its history in the United States, Catholicism also has been at odds with the dominant religious culture. During the high tide of Catholic immigration in the nineteenth century, Catholics entered a culture cast in an Anglo-Saxon evangelical mold. In the northern states this mold never held firm, partly because the flood tide of Catholic immigrants in the mid-nineteenth century made Catholicism the majority religion in the North by 1860. By dint of numbers Catholics became a major political and social force in northern society, and indeed their strong presence contributed significantly to the fragmentation of northern religious culture and society. In the Old South, for a variety of reasons, the evangelical mold already had set by the time Catholic immigrants found their way to southern cities in the 1840s and 1850s. Perhaps that fact partly explains why so few Catholic immigrants ventured South. It surely explains why Catholicism never moved from the perimeter of southern culture and why it is impossible to understand southern Catholicism except in terms of its response to the pervasive evangelical culture of the South and that culture's response to it.

Throughout their history southern Catholics have struggled with the peculiar tension of being both native and alien, southern and Catholic, at the same time. They have never quite resolved that tension. On one hand, they have lived in a society in which place conquered time, in which evangelicalism and racism have been the almost unbroken themes of the region's religious history, at least from the nineteenth century through the 1950s. On the other hand, they have held to a religion founded on universalism, on church authority that transcends both time and place.

Caught between traditional Catholicism and southern traditions, southern Catholics responded in two ways. One response followed the advice of Archbishop John Carroll of Baltimore and other early American Catholic church leaders, who encouraged Catholics to adopt the ways of American society and who, like Bishop John England of Charleston, even tried to incorporate American republicanism into the church's ecclesiastical structure. The other response resulted from a hard fact of southern life: the evangelical southern society resisted any accommodation with outsiders except on its own terms. Conscious of their status as a social and numerical minority, the Catholics developed a ghetto mentality of sorts. In areas of Catholic concentration around Louisville, Kentucky, and in southern Louisiana, the church tried to insulate its members in a Catholic subculture of church, schools, and piety. In fact, both adaptation and exclusion proceeded simultaneously. But in the end, southern Catholics, to a greater degree than their northern counterparts, sacrificed elements of their private traditions to win acceptance in the secular world.[1]

It had to be so. The dispersed nature of the Catholic population in the rural South, the subregional variations of southern Catholicism from French Louisiana to Anglo-American Maryland, the poverty of priests and parishes, the existence of an indigenous French Catholic establishment unresponsive to Catholic immigrants, and other factors weakened an already fragile Catholic church in the South. In addition, of course, southern Catholics confronted a rigid society inextricably bound up with slavery and evangelical Protestantism. That made all the difference.

Evangelical religion formed the marrow of southern culture. As early as the 1830s an evangelical unity and a conservative doctrinal orthodoxy gripped the South. Spiritual awakenings periodically tightened and extended the evangelical hold. Even the unchurched shared evangelical beliefs concerning sin, conversion, and scriptural authority. By 1860 the evangelical religious ethos permeated southern society, thanks to the numerous religious associations, schools, and revivals. A glance at a religious atlas reveals the extent of the evangelical dominion. Except in southern Louisiana, no Catholic county existed in the South, and only a few southern counties showed even one Catholic church in 1850. Lutherans and Jews were also too few for notice. When immigrants did come to the South, they settled in cities—on the territorial and social fringes of regional identity. The lack of religious and ethnic diversity strengthened the evangelical consensus, of course, but it also led to a narrow world view and to an exaggerated sense of southern distinctiveness.[2]

As the evangelical consensus strengthened in the South, religious leaders emerged as prominent intellectual and moral authorities in society. They assured their place within the inner circle of social power by declaring for slavery. That was to be expected. However, ministers derived social authority also from the public's conviction that society needed moral guardians. Ministers did not determine southern political policies, but they did imbue them with a sense of destiny or divine favor. Ministers set the standards of public morality and private belief. They established the agenda for social concern in the evangelicals' world.[3]

From their pulpits and through their religious associations and publications the evangelical ministers elaborated on the southern definition of a proper social order. Ministers extolled the uniqueness of the South as a stable, God-fearing society in a rapidly disintegrating, godless world. From the 1830s on, they described southern social harmony or public virtue as the product of an evangelical consensus rather than of a republican political economy, thereby parting company with the "liberal" thought of Jefferson's day. The ministers envisioned a glorious future of southern prosperity and piety. Indeed, they viewed southerners as God's new Chosen People. With this promise of destiny, however, came obligation. To fulfill their social covenant of order, southerners needed to retain their simplicity of religious doctrine and practice, their cultural uniformity, and their deferential society. God demanded this of them—or so the ministers said.

With its evangelical consensus based on biblical authority, the South possessed the essential ingredients of public virtue. The North had none of them. Beginning in the 1830s, southern ministers regularly commented on the moral decay of northern society. The liberal theologies insinuating themselves into northern pulpits, the high rates of crime and social dislocation in northern cities, and the corruption of northern religious bodies by politically motivated reformers, especially abolitionists, all convinced southern ministers that a deep moral and social malaise afflicted northern society. With its ethnic and religious diversity the North was clearly on the road to social disorder. The South must go the other way, the ministers warned. It was within this context that southern responses to Catholicism took form.

Few in numbers, teetering on the territorial edges of the region, and outside the evangelical Protestant ethos of southern culture, for a time Catholics rarely entered into southern consciousness or history. The slavery debate changed all that. To combat northern criticism of slavery and southern life, and perhaps to assuage their own guilt concerning slavery, southerners constructed the idyllic image of the paternalistic plantation society. Ministers had a large hand in this, for their evangelical assumptions suffused southern assertions about the virtues of the South's "golden age." The gathering political storms of antislavery agitation quickened the South's closing ranks to defend its peculiar institution. Regional self-consciousness degenerated into paranoia. The presence of so many slaves in the South almost guaranteed such a result. Slaves chafed at their shackles, and the southern proslavery arguments notwithstanding, most southerners knew it. Concern over rebellions—real and fancied—tormented white southerners. In such a circumstance, southerners hardly tolerated any breaches in local customs, looked upon all outsiders with suspicion, and crushed dissent. The Catholic church, with its loyalties and structure transcending the South, needed watching.[4]

A general anti-Catholic prejudice further hobbled Catholic prospects for complete acceptance in southern society. Everywhere in the English-speaking Protestant world, Catholicism loomed as a hydra, as the Beast of the Apocalypse bent on devouring progress and enlightenment and menacing the social order. For centuries such anti-Catholic images had been the mother's milk of Anglo-American Protestantism. They nourished southerners along with the rest. This development is hardly a surprise, since few southerners met any Catholics except in the lurid literature of nativists and professional Catholic baiters. In an examination of the letters and diaries of approximately two hundred Protestant Southerners, James W. Patton did not find "a single statement complimentary to the church." Catholics had an image problem.[5]

In many parts of the South where few or no Catholics lived, Protestant southerners considered Catholics akin to freaks in a raree-show. When a Catholic clergyman ventured out to speak in a public place, he often caused a sensation. For example, Charles Manly recalled that the appearance of a Catholic bishop at the baccalaureate service at the University of North Carolina set off a "great rush to see the animal as if he was the big bull of Bashan or the Pope of Rome." Catholic priests, draped in "womanly" cassocks and pledged to an unnatural celibacy, were out of step with the masculine southern culture.[6]

To southern evangelical sensibilities, Catholic worship reeked of superstition and magic. A typical reaction was recorded by a Georgia woman touring Catholic Europe. She dismissed Catholic mass as "most amusing and funny," yet trembled to enter a Catholic church again, lest Lucifer seize her soul. Even in Louisiana, where they should have been more sensitive to Catholic ways, Protestants ridiculed Catholic services. The "rank idolatry" and "nonsensical mummery" of Catholic worship simply disgusted members of more austere churches.[7]

The vortex of southern anti-Catholicism, however, centered on the fear that Catholics threatened disorder and moral corruption wherever they settled. The genteel Catholicism of the Carrolls and Taneys and Brents of Maryland did not conjure up dark images of Catholic evil so much as did a new breed of Catholics whom southerners met in Creole Louisiana and in immigrant ghettos in southern cities. The Creole Catholic culture did not measure up to southern standards of racial and social propriety. The racial mixing of Catholic Creole New Orleans stirred southern anti-Catholicism and particularly outraged evangelicals concerned with social purity and unity. Methodist minister William Winans, for example, could hardly overcome his shock upon meeting Catholic Creoles. He drew back from this "mongrel race, compounded of French, Spanish, and Negro, with a slight sprinkling of Anglo-Saxon ruffians and outlaws" who were all "illiterate and profligate." This was not the stuff of a chosen people and virtuous society.[8]

Even more worrisome to evangelical builders of southern harmony was the heavy influx of poor Irish and German Catholics into southern cities. Southerners feared that the immigrants carried the demon of social disruption with them. For example, the editor of the Tallahassee *Florida Sentinel* blamed the urban ills plaguing the North almost entirely on Irish Catholic rowdyism and warned his readers to stay alert to Catholic demons in their midst. Major election riots involving Irish Catholics in Louisville, Memphis, and New Orleans in the 1850s gave credibility to such fears. The presence of foreign-born priests, who controlled the Catholic church completely in the South, heightened southern suspicions of evil Catholic intentions.[9]

Some southerners marched as a vocal, if poorly organized, company in the nativist phalanx, but the region's heart was not really in Know-Nothingism. Catholics were too few and too scattered outside of Louisiana to pose much danger to southern life, and as Avery Craven observes, they were "too well integrated into Southern life to produce serious hostile reaction." It has always been the thought of Catholic danger rather than the facts of Catholic existence in the South that fueled southern anti-Catholicism. As long as Catholics remained few in number, stayed isolated in Catholic enclaves, and supported southern political and social arrangements, they were safe from anything more pointed than verbal barbs directed at them. Still, anti-Catholicism lingered in the public mind—which is to say the evangelical mind—to remind southern Catholics that they would always remain aliens in the Protestant South.[10]

Interestingly, a few southern intellectuals and ministers tried to draft Catholic doctrine into the cause of anchoring the region's conservative social order. George Fitzhugh, the eccentric but seminal proslavery apologist, admired Catholicism for its social discipline and respect for hierarchy. Fitzhugh's stridently antidemocratic musings found few takers in the South, but other southern intellectuals discovered and applied Catholic thinking. George Frederick Holmes, for example, recanted his youthful anti-Catholic writings and read Catholic writers almost exclusively in the late 1850s, partly because his social conservatism and "flights of mysticism" drew him to Thomist philosophy. For the southern Protestant gentlemen theologians, Catholic philosophers offered guides to the kind of classical rationalism they were urging on their urban congregations. Thomist scholasticism fit nicely into the literary parsons' prescriptions for reasonable proofs of God's work and goodness. The Catholic insistence on obedience and authority particularly won favor among men of a conservative social stripe. L. Silliman Ives, the Episcopal bishop of North Carolina, converted to Catholicism for that reason.[11]

Lines of communication existed between some Catholic and Protestant churchmen and intellectuals of the Old South. Bishop John

England, a classical scholar, found congenial company in Charleston's literary and philosophical society and mixed easily with the great men of estate and mind in the city. Protestants often enrolled their children in Catholic schools because the priests and sisters enjoyed reputations as good teachers and because they were considered sound in their social views. Numerous prominent southerners of the 1850s and 1860s, including Jefferson Davis, were among the alumni of Catholic schools and colleges. Such connections probably helped to dissipate anti-Catholic hostility to a point.

But too much should not be made of such connections or of the rationalistic enterprises of the gentlemen theologians. These men only moved on the periphery of southern religious and social culture. Their intellectual elitism, their small numbers, and their urban ministries placed them outside the mainstream of southern Protestantism. Even they accommodated their theology to the social order. As was the case with all things southern, the shadow of slavery hung over them. It is likely that the principal reason that they and Catholic leaders received a hearing in the South was because, paradoxically, both groups of men also helped to prop up slavery, even as their very presence seemingly undermined the social order built on an evangelical consensus.

Slavery was the shibboleth of southern civilization. Acceptance in the Old South meant getting right with slavery. As H. Shelton Smith has shown, southerners tolerated some straying from theological orthodoxy on the part of their ministers, but they lashed out at the slightest defection from the doctrine of white supremacy. The ministers did not disappoint them. In the two decades before the Civil War, evangelical ministers—a strategic elite functioning as teachers, preachers, and guardians of morality and order—forged a social consensus on slavery. The ministers sanctified the South's peculiar institution in ways intended to make southern acceptance of slavery and the social order ingrained and natural. Southern ministers shouldered much of the burden of defending the racial arrangements in the South, before and after the Civil War, thereby acquiring their social authority in a world consumed by racial concerns.[12]

Catholics were no different. Without blushing, Catholic churchmen proclaimed the rightness of slavery, passing into the political orbit around the world the slaveholders made. Catholic leaders opposed antislavery reform as a New England Protestant movement closely aligned with nativism and anti-Catholic activity. In addition, many Catholic clergymen who came from Europe linked abolitionism in America with the rationalism and anticlericalism that threatened Catholic teaching in Europe. Like the dominant churches of the Old South, the Catholic church mirrored the racial values of its followers and reinforced planter hegemony by supplying biblical justifications for slavery and a conservative social order.[13]

In this, Catholics merged with the most salient feature of southern Protestant ethics. Samuel Hill has recently argued convincingly that southern churches refused to claim responsibility "for the health and direction of the society at large." Of course, the clergy responded to social conditions by defining and disciplining moral behavior, but they always did so within the social context. To preserve public order, they promulgated a theology of individual sin and conversion that subordinated ethical responsibility to personal salvation. Religious leaders did not abdicate their ethical responsibility for society altogether, for they inveighed against demon rum, dueling, and Sabbath breaking. But evangelicals conceived their social role narrowly, and by the 1850s, according to Anne Loveland, they had backed off from public efforts to arrest moral decline. Ministers chose not to entrust the reform of humanity to such human instruments as revivals and reform associations, the latter of which were fast becoming secular and formal. Southern evangelicals made peace with their social world by disclaiming any special obligation to transform it. They turned to God's grace and power to eradicate social evils and invoked the doctrine of the spirituality of the church, which bound over the profane to the state. This limited conception of public responsibility encouraged evangelicals generally to support existing social and political relations and, when combined with the southerners' sense of destiny, obviated self-criticism. The evangelicals' formula for social change ended up stressing personal holiness and the individual's accommodation with the temporal order.[14]

So did American Catholics generally. Most American Catholic writers viewed society as static and beyond human ability to alter it. Indeed, Catholics were expected to accept their condition in life as an expression of God's will. Such thinking directed individual interest toward piety and away from the affairs of this world, and it bred social complacency and an uncritical acceptance of society. Catholic theology stressed personal salvation through the sacramental system. It required no critique of the social world and even discouraged it. The church might ameliorate a social ill, such as slavery, but it lacked the theological and ethical thrust to destroy it. Catholics extracted from their theology a conception of social reform directed solely toward improving the lot of the individual as a means to his salvation. Catholic social vision focused on charity, not reform, and hardly threatened the southern social order.

Religious voluntarism in America shattered the congenital connection between the whole people (embodied in the state) and the church that had existed in Catholic Europe. As a result, the Catholic church in America neither felt nor claimed an ethical responsibility for the whole society. The church did not try to create a Catholic conscience for a Protestant nation. The church shifted its emphasis to cultivating its inward spiritual plantation and relegated civil welfare to the state. Southern Catholic churchmen labeled slavery a political issue and accordingly placed it outside the church's province. Whatever their personal attitudes regarding slavery, southern Catholic clergy invariably followed the church's conservative policy.[15]

Bishop John England of Charleston, the most articulate and formidable Catholic spokesman in the South, stated the church's position as early as 1840. When several southern critics intimated Catholic complicity with abolitionism because Rome opposed the African slave trade, Bishop England, acutely sensitive to local political arrangements, wanted no misunderstandings about the church's willingness to conform to local cultural and social arrangements. In a long series of public letters he assured his fellow southerners that Catholics were determined to resist the "mischief" of the antislavery movement. England confessed a personal distaste for slavery, but he recognized the institution as compatible with man's law and divine will. Slavery's fate rested with the legislature, not the church.[16]

The most ambitious explanation of the church's relation to slavery came in 1861. In a sermon that was subsequently printed and widely circulated in the South, French-born Augustin Verot, who several months later became bishop of Savannah, described the reciprocal nature of southern bondage and the place of Catholics in it. Although Verot assailed the evils of the African slave trade, he fastened on a paternalistic, idyllic image of southern slavery and society rooted in familial trust and loyalty. Slavery was both a duty and a burden. Masters were obligated to feed, clothe, and shelter their slaves decently and, most important, to raise them in the true faith. Verot especially enjoined masters to keep slave families together—an implicit criticism of southern practice. The slaves, in turn, owed obedience and industry to their masters, or so Verot insisted.[17]

Verot's argument fitted the general southern presentment of slavery. Like the Protestant ministers, Verot and other Catholic clergymen had abandoned any interest in emancipating the slaves and concerned themselves with converting them to Christ and to obedience. These men believed that bringing the gospel to the slaves promised the rescue of heathen Africans from savagery and sin. Christian slavery, argued Protestant and Catholic alike, would improve the tone of society by providing moral discipline for both masters and slaves. Catholics and Protestants joined hands to win grudging acceptance from planters for their mission to the slaves. They did so by assuring planters that pious and well-treated slaves would be orderly and well-behaved ones. The convergence of Catholic and Protestant arguments on the benevolence of slavery speaks volumes on the social constraints slavery imposed on religion generally.

The Catholic and Protestant defense of slavery as a duty and a burden was intended primarily for home consumption. Catholics, like Protestants, discovered that Christian masters too often neglected their duties to the slaves. In 1785 John Carroll reported that the three thousand or so black slaves held by Catholic masters were "dull in faith and depraved in morals" because Catholic masters kept them "constantly at work" and gave them no time for religion. The situation did not improve in the next seventy-five years. In 1866, at the Second Plenary Council, the American bishops echoed Carroll's lament on the sad history of Catholic instruction and charity among the slaves.[18]

Bishop William Henry Elder of Natchez summed up the problem in 1858 in a letter to the Society for the Propagation of the Faith. He observed that in rural areas few slaves of Catholic masters—indeed few white farmers—received regular spiritual instruction. Several planters hired preachers to attend to their plantations by delivering sermons on Sunday, but the preachers were generally Protestants. Many masters refused to let their Catholic slaves attend services off their plantations, because they feared that the slaves might run away. Planters occasionally encouraged slaves to preach, but slave religious leadership naturally excluded the Catholic priest from control or direction of the religious concerns of slaves. Such leadership by slaves was not widespread among Catholics anyway. The southern bishops discouraged black lay preaching because they feared unlearned preachers would debase Catholic doctrine. As teachers of catechism, the masters performed poorly if at all. The masters failed to do their part in bringing up their slaves as Catholics. With widely scattered churches, few priests, and no money, Elder and the other bishops could not meet the needs of either the slave or the free Catholics. The priests who were available devoted their attention to winning and holding white Catholics, and some priests evoked fear or, worse, ridicule among the slaves who did not understand them or perceived them to be arms of the masters' authority.[19]

By neither teaching nor example did the church create a moral climate conducive to manumissions or humane treatment of slaves. Individual clergymen interceded on the slaves' behalf and called for Christian charity, but their numbers were few and their power illusory. Catholic masters remained the sole arbiters of discipline and treatment on their plantations and in their communities. The church did not figure much in the strategies of enslaved blacks for survival. It was a white institution geared to white supremacy. After all, even religious orders owned slaves, and the church defended slavery.[20]

Slavery corrupted clergy as well as lay people. Consider the case of Brother Joseph Mobberly of the Society of Jesus. Mobberly, along with another Jesuit and an overseer, ran a plantation owned by Jesuits in rural Maryland. He made much of the master's obligations to prepare the slaves for the sacraments and to encourage them in their devotions, but he did not do very well with his black wards. The slaves' repeated thefts, lackadaisical work habits, and running away exasperated Mobberly, who bemoaned the lax discipline of the South and thought that slaves were becoming "more corrupt and more worthless" by being spared the rod. Mobberly was relieved of his plantation duties after repeated complaints about his harsh treatment of the slaves. He was not a bad man. But the vagaries and frustrations of managing a troublesome property eroded his good intentions and high ideals and converted him to the slaveholders' side of the issue.[21]

Foreign-born Catholics did not escape slavery's corrosive effects. Strong aversions to blacks lurked in the Western European mind, to be summoned up in New World slaveholding societies. William Cohen has recently demonstrated that, for all their sniping at slavery and racism in America, French intellectuals of the eighteenth and nineteenth centuries expressed grave misgivings about the intelligence and malleability of black Africans. The numerous French missionary priests and the religious orders of French women who served the South inherited such doubts, priming them to accept southern racial values.[22]

The rapid, but unthinking, conversion to southern racial norms by the French nuns of the Daughters of the Cross mission in Avoyelles Parish, Louisiana, makes the point. At first, southern slavery shocked the French women, but several years in rural Louisiana worked wonders in the sisters' attitudes. When the mission purchased a slave named Simon and his eight children in 1856, the mother superior almost wept as she signed the bill of sale, but she warmed to the challenge of bringing up Simon and his children as good Catholics. As it turned out, Simon also needed guidance in his work. Minor tensions between the slave and his masters cropped up, but they did not seem threatening to the good sisters. After all, they provided well for Simon's spiritual and physical growth and expected only his gratitude in return. For their part, the sisters adapted to local customs on race and supported the Confederacy. During the war Simon fled the mission, thereby exposing the contradictions in the paternalistic ethos of this slave society. Suddenly, Simon became "ugly" and "tired of being happy." The sisters' outrage at their slave's betrayal underscored the self-delusion of southern slaveholders generally, the ministers being the worst among them: they were trying to impose static conceptions of order on a dynamic social situation.[23]

The Catholic support for slavery extended to support for southern nationalism. During the sectional crisis, southern Catholics stood with their region. A few Catholics whispered misgivings about unbridled southern nationalism, and several others flinched when they had to choose secession over union. But most southern Catholics lined up with the Confederacy for reasons of expediency if not of conviction. The Catholic bishops blessed the flags of Confederate regiments and prayed for Confederate victories. They joined their Protestant counterparts at the altars of the cause. After the war Catholic clergy added their mite to the Lost Cause apotheosis, even contributing a priest-poet in Abram Ryan, who outdid many evangelicals in celebrating the virtues of the old slave regime.[24]

The church's entanglement with slavery illustrates a central point about southern Catholicism and about southern religion in general. The church developed its social ethics as a response to the social world in which it lived. Its theology, which was almost entirely a product of the church in Europe, permitted a wide latitude of response and did not determine or harness its stand on social issues. Without a religious establishment, all American churches of necessity attuned themselves to the social and cultural environment in order to remain relevant and viable as churches. Southern Catholics made their bows to the age. They adopted a social posture befitting their position as members of an immigrant church on Protestant soil. In so doing, Catholics gained the social space to plant and nurture a Catholic religious culture free from political intrusions.

The church's response to slavery was more than a surrender to an unfriendly host society demanding public acts of deference, and it was more than a manifestation of a conservative social mentality formed by catechism and reinforced by church leaders—though it surely was those things, too. Rather, the Catholic response to southern slavery grew out of its peculiar experience of settling in the South. The church was an immigrant institution with only Old World models to guide its growth in a New World setting. In the Protestant world of the Old South the immigrant church was compelled to invest its energy in preserving its Catholic identity. So many internal problems sapped the church's strength that it was forced to make a rapid adjustment to its social environment.

The striking fact about the Catholic church in the Old South is its lack of visibility, even in southern cities where Catholics congregated. Not one Catholic challenged the social world the Protestant divines and slaveholders had built. To be sure, John England tilted lustily against nativism, but save for that, he always preached Catholic accommodation with the local social and political environment. Individual Catholics rose to prominence in agriculture, business, and politics expressly because they did so adapt. Their Catholicism counted for nothing as they entered the secular world. Even in New Orleans, where the church possessed the numbers, wealth, and prestige to withstand social and political ostracism by Protestants, the Catholic establishment tendered no critique of southern culture. In the South there was no one like Bishop John Hughes of New York to battle state legislatures for public money to support Catholic education. That southern Catholics did not clash with southern leaders over public policy or Catholics' rights was not due to cowardice; rather, the issues were not available in the South. Southern Catholics sought acceptance and anonymity rather than full participation in public affairs. Besides, as long as the contact points between Protestant and Catholic were political, not doctrinal, the church readily conceded politics to society in order to preserve doctrine to itself.

As Peter Berger once suggested, a church faced with challenges to its identity or to its true beliefs traditionally responds in one of two ways. It tries to maintain its credibility in the world by adjusting belief to current trends, or it resists the social and intellectual world by stubbornly defending traditional doctrines. In the South the Catholic church did both. It yielded up its social conscience to the status quo and devoted itself to the City of God. At the same time, the church tried to build a set of institutions paralleling those of Protestant society. It tried to wrap Catholics in a religious and cultural tissue of church, school, and social associations that would seal them off from Protestant intrusions. Creating a Catholic subculture became the principal preoccupation of the church for the next one hundred years.[25]

More than anything else, the internal dynamics of Catholic church-building determined the church's external social and political relationships. The Catholic church in the South lacked cohesion. It had to build an ecclesiastical structure almost from scratch, and it had to do so while contending with the different cultural expressions of Catholicism that immigrants and Creoles brought to the church. This developmental pattern contrasted markedly with the regular progression of internal expansion among evangelical groups. By the 1850s the southern evangelical churches rested on a solid institutional foundation. Schools, seminaries, and religious associations supported a regionwide evangelical establishment so that the evangelical churches, though built largely as democratic and congregational polities, spoke almost with one voice on matters of doctrine and discipline. The Catholic church, though constructed on a hierarchical and universal model, had to struggle to assert its authority over its members, indeed even to serve them at all. Its institutional voice met challenges from within in the form of lay trusteeism and cultural tribalism among various immigrant groups, all of which confused and compromised the church's authority throughout the region. By 1860 the church had gained the upper hand over many dissident elements, but it never entirely subdued them. As a result, church leaders remained inordinately preoccupied with internal and disciplinary issues.[26]

Building the institutional church was especially important to Catholics. Without an ecclesiastical structure in which to disseminate and enforce doctrine, without formally trained and officially consecrated priests to administer the sacraments, and without schools to teach catechism, Catholicism could not exist. The church was an institution. Such needs fostered a bricks-and-mortar mentality among southern bishops, who became little more than organization men seeking consensus and cooperation everywhere. The hostile social environment provided a justification for excessive attention to shoring up the ecclesiastical structure and reinforced a habit of Catholic parochialism that kept the church outside the influential spheres of southern life and culture.

In the end, the Catholic position in the Old South was ironic. The Catholic response to the Protestant world legitimated further the evangelical consensus by adhering to the evangelical ministers' definitions of proper social behavior. Southern culture, flowing from the matrix of evangelicalism and racism, always needed—no, craved—such confirmation. Each public ritual of approval from outsiders (be they Yankees, foreign travelers, or minorities) proved that what the ministers, keepers of the South's cultural and moral keys, did and said was indeed true. The Catholic response of political and social accommodation with the southern Protestant world order, like the response of the Yankees who settled and stayed in the Old South, thus strengthened a culture of which neither Catholics nor Yankees could ever be fully a part. Such has always been the force of the southern, and the American, environment. And such is the reason why southern Catholics, perhaps deservedly, passed into historical obscurity.

NOTES

1. The literature on American Catholicism is vast. See especially Andrew Greeley, *The Catholic Experience: An Interpretation of the History of American Catholicism* (Garden City, N.Y., 1967); Edward Wakin and Joseph F. Scheur, *The De-Romanization of the American Catholic Church* (New York, 1966); David J. O'Brien, *The Renewal of American Catholicism* (New York, 1972); Thomas T. McAvoy, "The Formation of the Catholic Minority in the United States, 1820–1860," *Review of Politics* X (1948), 13–14; Martin E. Marty, "The Catholic Ghetto and All the Other Ghettoes," *Catholic Historical Review,* LXVIII (1982), 185–205; Jay P. Dolan, *The Immigrant Church: New York's Irish and German Catholics, 1815–1865* (Baltimore, 1975); and Dolan, *Catholic Revivalism: The American Experience, 1830–1900* (Notre Dame, 1978). The best surveys of American Catholicism are John Tracy Ellis, *American Catholicism* (2nd ed. rev.; Chicago, 1969); and James J. Hennesey, *American Catholics: A History of the Roman Catholic Community in the United States* (New York, 1982). For southern Catholicism the literature is surprisingly thin. But see Randall M. Miller, "Roman Catholic Church," in Samuel S. Hill (ed.), *Encyclopedia of Religion in the South* (Macon, Ga., 1984), 647–57; and Randall M. Miller and Jon L. Wakelyn (eds.), *Catholics in the Old South: Essays on Church and Culture* (Macon, Ga., 1983), especially Miller, "A Church in Cultural Captivity: Some Speculations on Catholic Identity in the Old South," 11–52, for an interpretive overview of the Catholic responses to southern culture and society. On the continuity of southern history see especially Carl Degler, *Place over Time: The Continuity of Southern Distinctiveness* (Baton Rouge, 1977).

2. The central place of evangelical Protestantism in southern culture is well known. See Donald G. Mathews, *Religion in the Old South* (Chicago, 1977); Anne C. Loveland, *Southern Evangelicals and the Social Order, 1800–1860* (Baton Rouge, 1980); Samuel S. Hill, Jr., *The South and the North in American Religion* (Athens, 1980), 49–89; Charles R. Wilson, *Baptized in Blood: The Religion of the Lost Cause, 1865–1920* (Athens, 1980), 1–17; and Edwin S. Gaustad, *Historical Atlas of Religion in America* (Rev. ed.; New York, 1976), 105. On the significance of southern ethnic and religious homogeneity see George B. Tindall, *The Ethnic Southerners* (Baton Rouge, 1976), 1–21.

3. See Mathews, *Religion in the Old South;* Loveland, *Southern Evangelicals and the Social Order;* Hill, *The South and the North in American Religion;* and Wilson, *Baptized in Blood.* This and the following paragraphs rely on those works.

4. The South's descent into paranoia about slavery is best described in Clement Eaton, *The Freedom-of-Thought Struggle in the Old South* (Rev. ed.; New York, 1964); William Freehling, *Prelude to Civil War: The Nullification Controversy in South Carolina* (New York, 1965); and Steven Channing, *Crisis of Fear: Secession in South Carolina* (New York, 1972). On

the crippling effect the slavery issue had on religion, see Mathews, *Religion in the Old South;* Loveland, *Southern Evangelicals and the Social Order;* and Hill, *The South and the North in American Religion.* See also Drew Gilpin Faust, *A Sacred Circle: The Dilemma of the Intellectual in the Old South* (Baltimore, 1978), for discussion of that effect on ministers and lay thinkers. For an explication of the literature on southern guilt over slavery see Barbara S. Byrne, "Charles C. Jones and the Intellectual Crisis of the Antebellum South," *Southern Studies,* XIX (1980), 274–85.

5. James W. Patton, "Facets of the South," *Journal of Southern History,* XXIII (1957), 12–19. My own examination of another hundred or so diaries and collections of letters from southerners traveling abroad confirms Patton's conclusions.

6. Eaton, *The Freedom-of-Thought Struggle in the Old South,* 323.

7. Kate Jones Diary, July 22 and 29, 1851, in Southern Historical Collection, University of North Carolina, Chapel Hill; Priscilla "Mittie" Munnikhuysen Bond Diary, January 4, 1864, in Department of Archives and Manuscripts, Louisiana State University Library, Baton Rouge; Patton, "Facets of the South," 12.

8. William Winans Autobiography (Typescript in Millsaps College Library, Jackson, Mississippi), 56–57. Winans was an itinerant preacher in the Natchez country.

9. Tallahassee *Florida Sentinel,* May 21, 1844, June 23, 1864; New Orleans *Daily Crescent,* March 21, 1854.

10. W. Darrell Overdyke, *The Know-Nothing Party in the South* (Baton Rouge, 1950); Eaton, *Freedom-of-Thought Struggle,* 323–26; Avery Craven, *The Growth of Southern Nationalism* (Baton Rouge, 1953), 238–39. On the connections between anti-Catholicism and slavery see David Brion Davis, *The Slave Power Conspiracy and the Paranoid Style* (Baton Rouge, 1969), 32–51. See also William G. Bean, "An Aspect of Know-Nothingism: The Immigrant and Slavery," *South Atlantic Quarterly,* XXXIII (1924), 319–43.

11. Eugene Genovese, *The World the Slaveholders Made: Two Essays in Interpretation* (New York, 1969), 191–93; Neil C. Gillespie, *The Collapse of Orthodoxy: The Intellectual Ordeal of George Frederick Holmes* (Charlottesville, 1972), 45–47, 102–104; E. Brooks Holifield, *The Gentlemen Theologians: American Theology in Southern Culture, 1795–1860* (Durham, N.C., 1978), 101–109.

12. H. Shelton Smith, *In His Image, But . . . : Racism in Southern Religion, 1780–1910* (Durham, N.C., 1972). See also William S. Jenkins, *Pro-Slavery Thought in the Old South* (Chapel Hill, 1935), 200–41.

13. Madeleine H. Rice, *American Catholic Opinion in the Slavery Controversy* (New York, 1944); Timothy J. Holland, "The Catholic Church and the Negro in the United States Prior to the Civil War" (Ph.D. dissertation, Fordham University, 1950). See also Edward J. Misch, "The American Bishops and the Negro from the Civil War to the Plenary Council of Baltimore (1865–1884)" (Ph.D. dissertation, Gregorian University, Rome, 1968), Chs. 1–3.

14. Hill, *The South and the North in American Religion;* Loveland, *Southern Evangelicals and the Social Order,* esp. 84–90, 155–58, 173–74.

15. A good discussion of Catholic social thought is James E. Roohan, "American Catholics and the Social Question" (Ph.D. dissertation, Yale University, 1952).

16. *United States Catholic Miscellany* (Charleston, S.C.), October 10, 1840, February 17, 1841; Sebastian G. Messmer (ed.), *The Works of the Right Reverend John England, First Bishop of Charleston* (7 vols.; Cleveland, 1908), III, 191. See also England's posthumously published *Letters to the Hon. John Forsythe on the Subject of Domestic Slavery* (Batimore, 1844).

17. [Augustin Verot], *A Tract for the Times: Slavery and Abolitionism, Being the Substance of a Sermon Preached in the Church of St. Augustine. . .* (Baltimore, 1861). For an excellent analysis of Verot's thought see Michael V. Gannon, *Rebel Bishop: The Life and Era of Augustin Verot* (Milwaukee, 1964), 31–55. Nobody outdid Bishop Auguste Martin of Natchitoches, Louisiana, however. He insisted that slavery was "an arrangement eminently Christian by which millions pass from intellectual darkness to the sweet brilliance of the Gospel." Benjamin Blied, *Catholics and the Civil War* (Milwaukee, 1945), 25.

18. John T. Gillard, *Colored Catholics in the United States* (Baltimore, 1941), 63; Misch, "American Bishops and the Negro," Ch. 3.

19. William Henry Elder to the Society for the Propagation of the Faith, 1858, in William Henry Elder Papers, Archives of the Diocese of Natchez-Jackson, Jackson, Mississippi; *United States Catholic Miscellany* (Charleston, S.C.), September 10, 1831; William H. Elder to John M. Odin, May 13, 1866, in New Orleans Papers, University of Notre Dame Library, Notre Dame, Indiana.

20. On southern Catholicism and slaves see Randall M. Miller, "The Failed Mission: The Catholic Church and Black Catholics in the Old South," in Edward Magdol and Jon Wakelyn (eds.), *The Southern Common People: Studies in Nineteenth-Century Social History* (Westport, Conn., 1980), 37–54; and Albert Raboteau, *Slave Religion: The "Invisible Institution" in the Antebellum South* (New York, 1978), 271–75.

21. Diary of Brother Joseph Mobberly, vol. 1, pp. 140–42, in Georgetown University Library, Washington, D.C. The Jesuit plantation experience is analyzed in Joseph Agonito, "St. Inigoes Manor: A Nineteenth-Century Jesuit Plantation," *Maryland Historical Magazine*, LXXII (1977), 83–98; and especially in R. Emmett Curran, "'Splendid Poverty': Jesuit Slaveholding in Maryland, 1805–1838," in Miller and Wakelyn (eds.), *Catholics in the Old South*, 125–46.

22. William Cohen, *The French Encounter with Africans: White Response to Blacks, 1530–1880* (Bloomington, 1980).

23. Sister Dorothea Olga McCants (ed. and trans.), *They Came to Louisiana: Letters of a Catholic Mission, 1854–1882* (Baton Rouge, 1970), 39–40, 168. For another good example of a European-born Catholic clergyman's acceptance of southern attitudes regarding race and slavery, see Giovanni Antonio Grassi, *Notizie varie sullo stato presente della repubblica degli Stati Uniti dell' America. . .* (Rome, 1818), 13–14, 111, 115–16.

24. Willard E. Wight, "The Churches and the Confederate Cause," *Civil War History*, VI (1960), 367–68, 371–73; Blied, *Catholics and the Civil*

War, 53–69; Oscar Lipscomb, "Catholics in Alabama, 1861–1865," *Alabama Review,* XX (1967), 278–88; Willard E. Wight (ed.), "Some Wartime Letters of Bishop Lynch," *Catholic Historical Review,* XLIII (1957), 20–37; Wight (ed.), "Bishop Elder and the Civil War," *Catholic Historical Review,* XLIV (1958), 290–306; Wight (ed.,), "Some War Letters of the Bishop of Mobile, 1861–1865," *Mid-America,* XLIII (1961), 61–68; Cornelius M. Buckley (ed. and trans.), *A Frenchman, A Chaplain, A Rebel: The War Letters of Père Louis-Hippolyte Gache, S.J.* (Chicago, 1981). On Ryan see Wilson, *Baptized in Blood,* 58–61.

25. Peter L. Berger, *The Sacred Canopy: Elements of a Sociological Theory of Religion* (Garden City, N.Y., 1967), 153–69. On Catholic subcultures in the South see Miller, "A Church in Cultural Captivity," 28–42.

26. Miller, "A Church in Cultural Captivity," 20–37; McAvoy, "The Formation of the Catholic Minority in the U.S.," 13–34; Greeley, *The Catholic Experience,* 63–86.

SOUTHERN PROTESTANTISM AND REFORM, 1890–1920
J. Wayne Flynt

W. R. Meroney spent 1919 writing his doctoral dissertation at Southern Baptist Theological Seminary in Louisville, Kentucky. Facts gathered, analysis complete, he took up his pen and began to write. His work was entitled "The Old Church in the New Era," and as he warmed to his subject, the paragraphs flowed. The church that he loved must come to terms with the new age: She "must wage common war with socialism against the festering evils of human society. She must preach the gospel to the poor in a far richer way than she has ever yet done. She must proclaim liberty to those who are bound and make as her supreme social task the elevation of human society." [1]

Of course, every religious group produces its nonconformists, and the Reverend Dr. Meroney was by no means typical of Southern Baptist ministers. But those who judge the character of the past by the conservative uniformity of the present ignore the many W. R. Meroneys who flourished in the South between 1890 and 1920. Although they were atypical, they challenged southern Christianity at numerous points, sometimes with frenzied prophecies like those of Jeremiah, sometimes with quiet reasonableness like that of Luke.

To look at the South without discussing religion is like examining modern American culture without reference to sex: it is possible, but one certainly misses the drift of things. All scholars of the South interested in the dynamic interaction of religion and society owe a debt to Samuel S. Hill, Jr. Although others had made the point earlier, no other work so changed the direction of scholarship on southern religion as did his *Southern Churches in Crisis.* Hill insisted that historians, in their efforts to understand the shaping of the South, had taken religion too lightly. Along with white supremacy, the biblical

The author is grateful to Lynn E. May, Jr., editor of *Baptist History and Heritage,* for permission to use material published in that journal in an article entitled "Southern Baptists: Rural to Urban Transition," XVI (January, 1981), 24–34. Printed by permission of the Historical Commission of the Southern Baptist Convention, Nashville, Tennessee.

heritage was central to southern continuity. Hill postulated that the frontier, a rural mode of life, and cultural insulation have been as influential on southern religion as the Puritan covenant, immigrant subcultures, and other factors have been on religion elsewhere in the nation.

Hill's chief premise—that there has been a symbiotic relationship between biblical Christianity and secular southern culture—is now conventional wisdom. When George Tindall described the reformist Southern Sociological Congress, he noted, "One finds in the annals of this and later social reform movements a fundamental conditioning influence of the churches which gave to middle-class liberalism in the South a unique moral-religious tone." Charles R. Wilson has examined the rise of a civil religion in the South between 1865 and 1920 that developed quite separately from the mainstream American version. The variety based in Dixie was less optimistic, less liberal, less democratic, less tolerant, and more homogeneously Protestant. Applying southern liberalism exclusively to the complex question of race, Morton Sosna observed that most twentieth-century southern racial reformers were either newspaper editors, academics, "or people with a religious motivation who took ideas about Christian brotherhood seriously." Furthermore, as race increasingly became the quintessential issue of southern liberalism, those who viewed it in terms of the ethics of Christian brotherhood were more likely than journalists or academics to transcend the old separate-but-equal stance to embrace one of true racial brotherhood. Finally, the late John Lee Eighmy insisted that southern campaigns for social justice in the first decades of this century, though conducted generally under the "secular banner of Progressivism," sprang from the "South's religious resources." [2]

In years past, when historians generally agreed on the nature of progressivism, the task of relating religion to southern progressivism would have been simple enough. I could construct my syllogism as follows: the Progressive Era was a period of political, economic, and social reform; southern Protestants endorsed and even pioneered some of these reforms; therefore, many southern Protestants were social reformers. But there is wide disagreement among historians today over the nature of progressivism. The most widely accepted recent interpretation has it that the Progressive Era, which lasted from approximately 1900 to about 1916, was essentially conservative, concerned with preserving traditional values, restoring status to middle-class professionals and business groups, and asserting social control. By applying expertise, scientific data, and professional skills, middle-class reformers hoped to create a rational new social order out of a chaotic urban, industrial, immigrant society. Yet, such a view displays an enormous amount of presentism. Progressivism may now appear to have been bland and conservative and bureaucratic, but in its day it challenged many established ideas and institutions. Nowhere is this more evident than in what happened within the southern churches.

For my purposes, progressivism needs to be defined in more specific, regional ways. Southern progressivism, like all things southern, is a bird of a different feather, no matter how much it may resemble the rest of the flock.

In 1972 Jack T. Kirby published the first general survey of southern progressivism. His conclusions provide a useful structure for analyzing social Christianity. First, he contends, the scope of southern reform was unusually broad, in several ways running deeper and wider than in other regions. Second, in the South the problem of race was central to progressivism. Third, a superficial order appears within progressivism based upon the historic dichotomy between the populistic, rural, antitrust reformer and the urban professional reformer who sought to rationalize the new order by bureaucracy and centralization. But at a deeper level, Kirby insists, this dichotomy between traditional, rural progressives and urban, business progressives is misleading, because there were so many styles of reform within each category, so many overlapping goals, that efforts at labeling are meaningless. The "movements" encompassed far too many complexities, contradictions, and compromises. Kirby's galaxy of "reformers" includes the following: reactionary members of the elite who wished to reassert their values and regain lost control; paternalistic uplifters, including Protestant ministers and social workers who were terrified by the violence of poor whites and sought to defuse their revolt with humane reforms while at the same time keeping blacks from their bloody grasp; professional experts who sought to heal society's hurt with scientific cures; and patricians whose clean-government campaigns promised a simple political solution.[3]

When ministers appear in Kirby's study, as they often do, they are not very attractive. Their drive for social control and order, for stability and social hierarchy, is portrayed as essentially conservative, even when pursued on behalf of ostensibly liberal causes such as racial justice. Most Protestant pastors "remained evangelical in emphasis, orthodox in doctrine." Ministers with commitments to social reform were "quite extraordinary *even* among Episcopalians and Presbyterians" (emphasis added).[4] Perhaps Kirby looked for his reformers in the wrong places. Amid what Samuel Hill has called the lower-class hegemony of Methodists and Baptists, and even more frequently among Pentecostals, angry, sensitive consciences struggled with strange new visions.

The people's visions were not entirely of burgeoning cities and a new industrial order. Down endless dirt roads, among countless sharecroppers, on small farms where depressed agricultural prices and rural blight threatened to drive children to cities and parents to tenancy, alienated Baptists, Methodists, and Pentecostals were angry.

Because the evangelical gamut stretched from sharecroppers to millionaires, rural religion was not homogeneous. Among better-educated ministers who were pastors of affluent "First Churches," edited denominational newspapers, or held state convention posts, one was more likely to find traces of liberal theology mixed with conservative economic and social ideas. But at the forks of the creeks, where the poorly educated jackleg preachers held forth, other views were common.[5]

One reason historians ignored this story so long is that though they assumed that religion is heavily conditioned by culture, they did not follow the assumption to its logical conclusion, which is that different subcultures produce different religious expressions. Beyond the prevalent conservatism of the Redeemer South were different views, in coal-mining camps, in textile mills, and on tenant farms. These environments spawned labor unionism, Populism, socialism, racial demagoguery, and other nontraditional by-products that sometimes also provoked new tasks for the church.

In Bibb County, Alabama, Baptist pastor Samuel M. Adams served as president of the state Farmers' Alliance, as head of the Populist party in the 1890s, and as a state legislator. A reporter for a conservative Democratic newspaper listened to Adams address a farmers' institute in 1891 and wrote: "Mr. Adams is an easy and fluent speaker, but if he had stuck to his text we think it would have been more in accord of our idea of a Farmer's Institute. He is so full of politics that it was a hard matter for him to keep in the road."[6]

Adams was not an isolated case. Robert H. Jackson, a Baptist minister from Heard County, was elected to head the Georgia Farmers' Alliance in 1887. He also was elected county judge and a member of both houses of the state legislature. Another Baptist preacher, Richard Manning Humphrey, was chosen general superintendent of the Texas Alliance. Mrs. Bettie Gay, of Columbus, Texas, managed a large farm after her husband's death, represented her church at the state Baptist convention in 1886, and became a champion of woman suffrage, prohibition, the Farmers' Alliance, and the Populist party. One enthusiastic southern churchwoman spoke for many Baptists when she announced, "I am going to work for prohibition, the Alliance, and for Jesus as long as I live."[7]

Baptists and Methodists whose interests lay with more conservative causes chastised their reformist brothers and sisters. The editor of the *Alabama Baptist* worried about reports of unrest in the rural churches. He warned that many Baptist pastors had "gone wild over politics." Laymen were so engrossed with secular affairs that "they talked politics during Sunday School and outside church, not coming into worship until after the prayer and Scripture reading." A county preacher wrote that his members had become so divided over politics that bad feelings and a general coldness prevailed. In 1893 the pastor of Shiloh Church in Pike County wrote, "The dreadul political excitement of last year had almost torn the church to pieces." A state denominational leader returned from a mission tour and summarized conditions in almost exactly the same words: "Many of our churches are torn to pieces on account of last year's politics."[8]

Conservative Protestant leaders branded Populism a radical heritage and insisted that pastors had no business forsaking hallowed sanctuaries for tarnished legislative chambers. State denominational papers were full of such admonitions, and "First Churches" rang with denunciations of political parsons.

The Reverend Cary C. Lloyd, a physician and graduate of Philadelphia's Jefferson Medical College who deserted medicine for the ministry, pegged his argument to a traditional Baptist principle. In a sermon titled "Separation of Church and State: Soul, Liberty and Equality," he said that the Populist revolt had shaken Alabama "from center to circumference." He asked parenthetically, "Are ministers of the gospel, set apart to be messengers of peace on earth and good will to men, to abandon the sacred desk and entering the political arena, transform themselves into messengers of confusion, strife and discord, to advance a cause that bids fair to forever sunder the life-long ties of Christian love and Christian fellowship?"

Yet, Lloyd sometimes committed the same sin that he saw in others, though certainly not on behalf of Populism.

How true the prediction of a prominent Senator some two years ago: "the tendency is to the disruption of the Democratic Party." Today we find that faithful custodian of our liberties, disrupted, divided, torn with dissensions, the freedom of our citizens, both civil and ecclesiastical, threatened with destruction and a reign of civil and religious intolerance set up in the Commonwealth of Alabama, and this too accomplished largely in the churches whose duty it is to exalt Christ, not themselves, and point dying men to the cross. Let preachers return to their pulpits long prostituted to political ends, hold up the Banner of Christ now trailing in the mire and filth of political shame and disgrace.[9]

Obviously, evangelicals were not of one mind in the 1890s; nor did they reach a consensus with their urban brethren in the years to come. The crisis in rural America attracted attention on two levels between 1900 and the 1920s. The initial response came from religious leaders who perceived the complex crisis threatening southern rural life and believed that the churches must adopt new strategies to cope with this danger.

Although agricultural conditions improved after the 1890s, they remained bad. Rural people, especially the young, left farms for alluring cities; many of those who remained behind believed cities to be centers of crime and vice, where people were depersonalized, couples were divorced, and families were broken. One religious leader, J. C. Hiden, expressed the opinion of many Baptist rural folk when he proclaimed, "Men, like hogs, are bred in the country to be consumed in the towns."[10]

The malaise in rural America caused general concern about all areas of country life. In 1908 President Theodore Roosevelt appointed a Country Life Commission to study rural America, diagnose its problems, and propose solutions. One of the commission's recommendations was that the institutionalized church should exert social as well as spiritual influence on rural life.

Rural-life reformers, most of whom were urban, educated, middle-class Protestants with roots in rural America, blamed country churches for much of the crisis. Country churches clung to a narrow doctrinal emphasis and outworn orthodoxy, which admitted no link between religious and social problems. Poorly paid ministers presided over declining congregations worshiping in dilapidated buildings. Their vision was no broader than criticism of Saturday-night dancing or Sunday-afternoon baseball. Such attitudes among rural clergymen were understandable; seminaries offered no courses in rural sociology or the rural church.[11]

Religious leaders documented the problems of the rural church with statistical surveys. They condemned farm tenancy, which was robbing the church of thousands of members, and urged churches to consolidate and become concerned for the welfare of their communities.[12]

The earliest Southern Baptist treatment of the crisis of the rural church was Victor I. Masters' insightful book *Country Church in the South.* Masters was superintendent of publicity for the Home Mission Board, and his book, published in 1916, belonged to the literature of the national country life movement. He compiled statistics to document the decline of rural Baptist churches, stressing their inadequate programs, absentee pastors, and dilapidated buildings. He traced many of the problems to the Baptist pioneer legacy of excessive individualism, exclusive concern for personal salvation, and the notion that ministers should not be paid.

Masters illustrated the troubles resulting from this legacy with poignant case studies. One untrained, dedicated pastor in the mountains of southwest Virginia preached at two churches for a year, conducted three weeks of revival annually, and received a total salary of $13.20. He lived with his family in a two-room cabin on thirty acres of rented land. He worked for a neighbor part-time in exchange for a horse to plow his cornfield. On Sundays he walked to his churches, one of which was six miles away, the other five. Another pastor in the same region worked at a gristmill during the week and earned a salary from his part-time churches that totaled less than $30. A 1913 survey of 5,400 Southern Baptist churches with quarter-time pastors indicated that the average pastor's salary was $378, but that some made less than $30 a year.[13]

Even when rural pastors were promised an adequate salary, they did not always receive it. Baptist farmers were subject to capricious weather and fluctuating agricultural prices. Pledges made in the winter were contingent upon good crops and high prices the following fall. Even in good times pledges were not paid until harvest, and in bad times they were not paid at all. Masters recalled a case where a rural pastor with seven children and a salary of $700 received only $555 because of poor crops. He preached three times each Sunday at different part-time churches, a feat he accomplished by walking thirty miles each Lord's day. Another rural pastor with two children was promised $600 but received only $340. He raised $500 to buy lumber to repair the church, and the deacons offered to pay him $2.50 per day as carpenter. Ironically, the church agreed to pay him more per day as a carpenter than he earned as a pastor. But the irony was only theoretical: after he worked eighty-three days as a carpenter and was due $207, the deacons paid him only $5.

Masters acknowledged that part of the problem could be traced to rural poverty. He called the growth of farm tenancy the most alarming fact in southern rural life. Tenancy meant "the serious crippling, or the actual destruction of the treasured social, religious, and personal resources of the country." Tenancy was developing a class of white peasants that would in time destroy southern civilization. The country church must find ways to halt the growth of tenancy if rural religious life was to be stabilized, Masters believed.

Besides cataloging problems, he also advanced a number of proposals to rescue the country church. Rural churches should discuss frankly the "fictitious and harmful" elements of city life, he said. They should enlarge their social ministry to include women's societies and activities for the young. They should encourage organizations of farm people, which would improve community morale and reduce isolation. They should encourage better schoolhouses and salaries for teachers, give moral sanction to efforts to improve farming practices, use lay preachers on Sundays when pastors were unavailable, create circulating libraries to educate members, and standardize hymnbooks. Country pastors should take courses in rural sociology and economics at agricultural colleges and should have "an intelligent comprehension of . . . the problems of soil fertility, animal husbandry, and the growth of crops." Although the social function of the church must be recognized, Masters maintained, he cautioned against a social gospel that promised "a millennium without the cross of Christ."

Masters used his own position with the Home Mission Board to strengthen rural church work. Begun through his efforts in 1913, the board's Enlistment Department (actually a country church department) immediately began to spend $20,000 annually to aid rural churches. The department also inaugurated annual financial canvasses of all members of rural churches. The board employed twelve enlistment workers, who were paid jointly by the board and the state conventions. One each served in North Carolina, Georgia, and Kentucky, two each were employed in South Carolina, Mississippi and Louisiana, and three served in Alabama. Masters recommended that state boards refuse to provide aid to missionary pastors unless the local churches were willing to pay an amount that would provide a salary of at least $900 annually when combined with state funds. For years he used the monthly magazine of the Home Mission Board to emphasize country church problems and propose solutions.

Not everyone was so interested in country life. Masters criticized the Southern Baptist Convention for devoting little time to rural church problems. Denominational colleges and seminaries drew from the country but turned little back to it. They tended to produce graduates who were ashamed of their rural heritage and sought urban pastorates.

Masters was responsible for another step forward in July, 1922. At a joint meeting of the Home Mission and Sunday School boards in Atlanta, members agreed to sponsor a survey of rural church life to be undertaken by the Sunday School Board's Department of Survey, Statistics, and Information. This massive statistical survey of 2,043 white Southern Baptist rural churches was published in the *Southern Baptist Handbook* for 1923. The publication provided graphic, incontrovertible proof of the problems facing the rural church.

John W. Jent was the first person to mine the new information. Born on a farm in southern Kentucky and reared in rural southwest Missouri, Jent was a third-generation rural Baptist preacher. Although his father and grandfather had little education, Jent obtained degrees from Baylor University and Southwestern Baptist Theological Seminary. He continued his training in rural sociology at Columbia University and then joined the faculty of Oklahoma Baptist University, where he taught applied Christianity and conducted church conferences.

In 1924 Jent was invited to deliver the Holland Lectures at Southwestern Seminary. The lectures were published as *The Challenge of the Country Church*. Although he spent more time on the theological rationale of his proposals and elaborated them in more detail, his analysis of the crisis in the rural church and his recommendations closely paralleled Masters' earlier work.

Using statistics from the 1922 survey, Jent developed a point system for evaluating a "standard" rural Baptist church. The church received points for having a full-time, resident, college- and seminary-trained pastor; an adequate church building with kitchen, sanitary water, toilets, and a parsonage; a complete organizational structure and a regular program of community service; organized activities for young people to help keep them in the country; a regular budget system; and a minimum pastor's salary of $1,200 a year. A score of less than fifty points indicated that the rural church was "inefficient." As a result of his role at conferences on the country church and his call for more attention to rural sociology, Jent became a major authority on the subject within the Southern Baptist Convention.[14] Unfortunately, the proposals of Masters and Jent came as the South was entering a prolonged agricultural depression that drove millions of rural white southerners off the land and left the rest too impoverished to upgrade churches.

Doubtless many Protestant leaders were surprised and disappointed by the reaction of rural people to their attempts to save farm life. Reformers did not convince the rural churches that they should consolidate or become more socially conscious. Traditional evangelical religion, with its appeal for salvation of the soul, still dominated the rural churches' vision.

This fact did not mean that the rural church of the Progressive Era was of one mind any more than it had been in the 1890s. The same social and economic cleavage remained, as was demonstrated in a bitter political conflict brewing in the Southwest.

Too often the Fundamentalist mind has been depicted as theologically warped, and little attempt has been made to comprehend its mainsprings or its complexity. The life of one of Fundamentalism's greatest champions, J. Frank Norris of Fort Worth, Texas, suggests how rural poverty affects religious perceptions. Norris was born in 1877 at Dadeville in east-central Alabama. Eleven years later his family moved to Hubbard, Texas, where his father drowned the sorrows of sharecropping, not in the balm of Gilead but in the tonic of John Barleycorn. He lived with his wife and children in a dilapidated, unpainted shack. The boy grew up in a setting of deep family tension. On one occasion his father beat young Norris so severely that he broke the boy's nose and lacerated his body. Yet, when horse thieves threatened his father's life, the boy went to his aid, receiving three bullet wounds in the process. Gangrene set in, followed by inflammatory rheumatism that left Norris speechless and paralyzed. He spent two years in a wheelchair and a third year completing his recovery. In his thirteenth year he had been converted in a brush-arbor revival, and his mother sustained his faith by assuring him that someday he was destined to be a leader of men.[15] The J. Frank Norris of the Fundamentalist 1920s is well known, but the tortured young boy, growing up in the grinding poverty, demented violence, and wracking pain of the southern tenancy system is barely remembered. Norris' response to rural poverty—flamboyant Fundamentalism and repudiation of social reform—is familiar; in fact, it has become a stereotype. Other responses are less well known.

In the latter years of the Progressive Era agrarian socialism swept across the parched prairies and rolling hills of Oklahoma and Texas, blossoming like young cotton in the first warmth of summer. From 1912 to 1916 the Socialist party captured nearly 20 percent of statewide votes in Oklahoma. The party's primary strength was in rural counties with high rates of tenancy. Although fiercely partisan, socialism in the Southwest differed in many ways from the predominantly urban, eastern variety, which was often oriented toward immigrants. For one thing, Socialist ministers in the Southwest used camp-meeting fervor and a Fundamentalist idiom to create a "Socialist Gospel" that transformed secular socialism into a millenarian and transcendent faith in the possibility of reform. They generally ignored the genteel and intellectual brand of communitarianism advocated by men like George D. Herron. While clinging tenaciously to their

individualistic cultural traditions, they also resisted the encroachments of capitalistic commercial agriculture and mainstream urban
values on the rural community.[16]

Baptists, Methodists, and the Churches of Christ produced more
than their fair share of Socialists from rural congregations, despite
the conservatism of most of their leaders. But the Holiness wing of
revivalism produced the most converts to socialism. "The radical
asceticism and hopeful postmillennialism" of the Pentecostals provided fertile ground for the radical Red seed. Eugene V. Debs held
one of his 1905 rallies in southern Oklahoma in a Holiness taber-
nacle. A few years later a Socialist organizer reported that he had
founded a local among tenants near Romney, Texas, and had left "a
holiness preacher in charge to keep them right." He added that "holiness people make good Socialists." One Oklahoma newspaper concluded that Socialists were like simple-minded children who "took
up one enthusiasm after another." After leaving the Socialist party,
they would probably "join up with Holy Rollers," the writer specu-
lated.[17] He was probably right about the close association of these
two enthusiasms, though he almost certainly had their chronology
reversed.

When historians speak of progressivism, they usually do not mean
the radical agrarianism spreading across the South's impoverished
farm belt. They usually mean the political and bureaucratic reforms
sponsored by urban businessmen and professionals. But even the urban South, home of the more traditional progressive reforms, did not
escape the attention of concerned clerics.

Across the entire nation the social gospel emphasized the achievement of the Kingdom of God in this world, the relevance of Christian
ethics to everyday life, and the power of Christianity to reconcile
classes at war. It sought to replace the stress on church membership
with the idea that all citizens could be part of the Kingdom of God,
which would establish justice and love as the basis of all of American
society. It arose primarily in response to the plight of industrial labor
in cities and largely ignored the question of race. Most blacks still
lived on farms, and the social gospel, even in the South, was tilted
toward the emerging crises of the cities.[18]

If Samuel Hill is right—if the South's frontier, its rural life-style, and its cultural insulation produced a unique southern religion—it follows logically (albeit incorrectly) that there was "virtually no recognition of any responsibility to redeem the secular dimensions of community and national life, inasmuch as life and the Christian life are construed to be essentially individualistic."[19] Such a conclusion assumes a static quality in southern religious thought; yet, during the intellectual ferment of the early twentieth century, southern religious thought was not static. Even southern ministers were attending the University of Chicago, studying rural sociology, attending conferences on social reform, and reading books.

The Reverend G. C. Hamilton, a Methodist minister from Crowell, Texas, conducted several heated debates with a Socialist lawyer in 1911. After one particularly spirited exchange, Hamilton accepted his antagonist's challenge to read Walter Rauschenbusch's *Christianity and the Social Crisis.* Shortly after finishing the book, Hamilton announced his conversion to socialism. The parson's new conversion experience did not sit well with the stewards of his Crowell church, who expelled him; afterward, he was welcomed as a lecturer by the local Church of Christ.[20] Such conversions occurred with increasing frequency between 1900 and 1920.

The fact that the social gospel did indeed flourish in the urban South (though with some opposition from rural people) demonstrates that southern religion was far more resilient and flexible than its confined roots in the rural frontier might suggest. Although they seldom accepted liberal theology—with its "higher criticism" of scripture, its attempt to rationalize science with religion, and its humanism—well-educated Protestant divines were receptive to the new and more relevant gospel message.

The issues that most often attracted the attention of reformist ministers were the obvious ones: prostitution, alcohol abuse, child labor, and the convict lease system. Campaigns against prostitution and Demon Rum often have been dismissed as pietist attempts to enforce private moral standards in the entire community. But it was precisely these movements, requiring political involvement and shrewd use of ecclesiastical power, that first caused many ministers and lay people to apply Christian ethics to social problems. Having entered the fray, they found it difficult to disengage.

During the two decades in which Frank W. Barnett served as editor of the *Alabama Baptist,* he conducted a successful campaign to restrict child labor in Alabama. Barnett was an early ally of Montgomery's Episcopal priest Edgar Gardner Murphy, who launched the national campaign to end child labor. In 1907 Barnett waxed eloquent during a debate in the Alabama legislature on a bill to control such work: "The South is harboring a system of slavery more horrible than that which existed before the civil war, or which now exists in the Siberian mines—the slavery of child labor. Children from five to twelve years of age, working twelve and fourteen hours a day; babies . . tramping wearily all day, before flying and buzzing machinery, pitiful little wrecks of humanity that wring the hearts of all who behold their thraldom, save their brutish masters, the mill owners. [21]

As in the 1890s, conservative ministers and laymen chided pastors like Barnett for moving beyond the proper ministerial sphere, the salvation of souls. But the times had changed, and Barnett responded that any sincere minister must sometimes enter aggressively into the struggle over grave social issues. He had no use for "ultra-conservative and timid church members who elevate their eyebrows and rub their pious hands in deprecation" every time their pastor entered politics to improve the moral quality of life. Nor did he accept a definition of Christianity that assumed that religion had nothing to do with business and politics, "as if it were simply a question of private life, with no social obligations." [22]

Barnett was not exceptional. In 1882 Baptists from North and South had organized the Baptist Congress. By 1893 the congress had attracted enough southern delegates to move the meeting south, gathering at the First Baptist Church of Augusta, Georgia. Walter Rauschenbusch opened the session with an address entitled "The Church and the Money Power," which included a scathing attack on the church's acquiescence to wealth. Dr. James B. Gambrell, president of Baptist affiliate Mercer University in Macon, Georgia, praised the speech in his response. [23]

Over the years the social activism and intellectual ferment of the congress influenced a new generation of Southern Baptist leaders, including Edgar Y. Mullins, William O. Carver, William J. McGlothin, John R. Sampey, all of Southern Baptist Theological Seminary, and

Dr. William L. Poteat, who was later to head Wake Forest College. Professors and ministers from throughout the Southern Baptist Convention imbibed an activist theology that contributed directly to the creation of the church's Social Service Commission in 1908.

Although the Social Service Commission focused more narrowly on temperance in later years, it did include a broader social agenda in the teens. In 1913 Poteat became chairman of the commission and attempted to address the South's social distress, but he met increasing resistance from fellow Baptists.

In search of a more daring organization, many ministers, including Poteat, joined the Southern Sociological Congress, whose motivation was religious. Poteat addressed the congress in 1913, maintaining that "in the thought of Jesus, the Kingdom of God is not formal or institutional. . . . It is rather a social spirit which will transfigure" all institutions, he said. Furthermore, the local church was responsible for making its community "a little province of the Kingdom of God." Dr. Arthur J. Barton, at that time superintendent of Southern Baptist educational work in Texas, helped write a report that called attention to the need for health services, equitable justice, an end to lynching, and welfare and economic reforms.

Charles S. Gardner, professor of sociology at Southern Baptist Seminary, also attended the Southern Sociological Congress. He praised the social gospel as "the insistent Christian ideal . . . not only for the individual, but for the social life." Gardner's *The Ethics of Jesus and Social Progress,* published in 1914, argued the primacy of the Kingdom of God. The Kingdom, as he defined it, was a "social order, a system of human relations, progressively realized, in which the will of God is the formative principle and all the functions of which are organized and operated for the purpose of helping all men to realize the spiritual possibilities of humanity."

John N. Prestridge, editor of Kentucky's *Baptist World,* served with Poteat on the Social Services Commission. At the 1908 Southern Baptist Convention, Prestridge agreed with Gardner's definition of the Kingdom. As the chairman of the Committee on Civic Righteousness, he reported to the convention that "Civic righteousness and the Kingdom of God are bound up in each other. We are learning anew that Christ's commission to his followers is not primarily to increase the census of heaven, but to make down here a righteous society in which Christ's will shall be done, his kingdom come."

Southern Baptist Theological Seminary's biblical scholar, Archibald T. Robertson, was not renowned for his liberalism. Yet, even he caught a new vision of the Kingdom. In his book *The New Citizenship,* published in 1919, Robertson argued that Christians need not wait for the millennium to achieve social justice. They should go to work immediately to deal with "the white-slave traffic, the bondage of childhood in the factory, the oppression of labour by capital," he said. "The rights of labour are unquestioned and the labouring man must have the opportunity of educating his children," he added. Robertson advocated woman suffrage and praised Woodrow Wilson's New Freedom: "At least we can all do our part as citizens of the colony of heaven to make our commonwealth and our world as nearly like heaven as possible. This [the New Freedom] is the new crusade of the new citizenship and it is worth the best that is in the statesman and social reformer. And more, it has the promise of the blessing of the King of the Kingdom of God."

Since they were under the tutelage of professors with such views, it is no wonder that a new generation of Baptist ministers arose with a social definition of the Kingdom of God. Doctoral dissertations written at Southern Seminary during these years confirmed the new influences. In 1919, along with Meroney's essay advocating a Christian-Socialist alliance, there was a dissertation by James C. Stivender titled "The New Interpretation of Democracy." It called for applying the Christian perception of the brotherhood of man to the complex social problems of the day. "The Christian religion is working for the realization of the brotherhood of men which will take form in an ideal social order—the Kingdom of God." Also in 1919, James E. Welsh's dissertation, "Our Future Toward the Criminal," applied Christian ethics to another arena. The problem of criminality, he reasoned, "is a social one, and must be solved, to no small degree, by principles social."

In 1916 James R. Quisenberry submitted a dissertation grounded in the sociology of religion. In "The Primitive Church Congregation as a Social Organism," he probed the relation of the New Testament church to society and social conditions. He concluded that the task of Jesus had been "to establish the reign of heaven on earth; he taught his followers that loyalty to *him* was that alone which constituted them citizens of the Kingdom of God, and he taught them that the purpose of their lives was to be the promotion and reign of God."

The same winds of change that stirred Southern Baptist life swept with greater velocity through the Methodist denomination. Kirby noted in his study of southern progressivism that women professionals played a key role in reform. Specifically, Methodist laywomen launched a widely based social-settlement ministry in the South.[24]

The earliest concrete effort by Methodist women to initiate a ministry to the South's cities occurred in 1893. Meeting in Saint Louis, the women entrusted the new urban evangelical emphasis to the Woman's Parsonage and Home Mission Society. Economic depression delayed the work until 1900, when three pioneer settlements were begun in Nashville, Dallas, and Atlanta. Four others were opened in 1904. Predicated on the notion that ministers must live near settlement houses, Methodist social workers tackled the problems of the inner city.

One of their first controversies concerned the term *settlement house,* which had a nonevangelical and even secular connotation to Methodists, and as a result many pastors criticized the work. The women employed a shrewd stratagem in 1906; noting that Presbyterians did their downtown settlement house work in what was called Church House and Episcopalians in the Parish House, they changed the name of their facilities to Wesley House. In later years they distinguished mission efforts in black communities by the name Bethlehem House.[25]

The New South industrial city of Birmingham was a perfect setting for expanded social ministries. As early as 1877, women of the Home Mission Society of First Methodist Church had begun an industrial school for deprived children. The women gradually broadened their work to include home visitation and poor relief. They organized the Board of City Missions in 1903 and rented a cottage in a working-class neighborhood. This cottage became the city's first settlement house. A deaconess and a city missionary were employed as residents. They operated a day school for children whose parents worked, a night literacy school for working boys, and a free kindergarten. By 1905 three thousand children from lower-class families had attended the church-sponsored kindergartens. Funding proved a major problem, and the work was closed from 1905 to 1908, when the Board of City Missions opened a Wesley House in a different neighborhood. The ministry grew rapidly, requiring a larger house, which was purchased in 1909. A deaconess and assistant were employed, and Wesley House broadened its scope to include the textile operatives at Avondale Mills.[26]

In 1912 the Board of City Missions established a Wesley House to minister to five thousand Italian immigrants employed at the Ensley mills of the Tennessee Coal and Iron Company. The company donated a house, a playground, heat, lights, and two thousand dollars. The Board of City Missions employed a trained social worker— Dorothy Crim—and two assistants. The house staff conducted a night school three evenings a week, formed a community band, sponsored games, and set up two free medical clinics, the first in the Birmingham district. Behind the house, a 50-by-150-foot block of land was divided into plots so the children could learn gardening. Classes in cooking, sewing, first aid, and home nursing were conducted for women. In 1916 Wesley House established a housekeeping center consisting of a bedroom, kitchen, and dining room. There young women learned housekeeping skills, which were important in their social and cultural assimilation. On Sunday afternoons, Bible stories and songs attracted the children of Ensley for more traditional religious services.[27]

Such ministries quickly spread throughout the urban South. By 1920 there were at least twenty-six Methodist settlement houses for whites and blacks in southern cities. Methodists also constructed other types of facilities, all essentially rescue missions, during these years.[28]

Training workers for ripe urban mission fields was a major task. Scarritt Bible and Training School, which opened in Kansas City in the fall of 1892, provided a steady supply of Methodist social workers for inner-city work. In 1902 Belle H. Bennett, who headed the Woman's Board of Home Missions, petitioned the general conference for creation of the office of deaconess. The conference granted the request and consecrated the first five young women in 1903. The deaconesses provided the staff for most urban social work. They received no salary at first, only room and board and ten dollars a month. Belle Bennett could not understand how the church could insist on adequate compensation for laborers while refusing deaconesses a living wage, and in time the monthly stipend became a regular salary.[29]

By no means were these pioneer ventures of Southern Baptists and Methodists the only regional expressions of the social gospel. Many Episcopal and Presbyterian congregations sponsored "institutional churches," which were open each day of the week to provide social services. In fact the growth of these institutional churches is one of the notable achievements of the Progressive Era in the South.[30]

As with the rural church, this urban progressivism can be viewed as a genteel movement of social uplift growing from middle-class paternalism. But as with agrarian Socialist church folk, the urban social gospel produced its radical underside.

The Reverend S. R. Emerson, Alabama's state chaplain to prisoners, penned an essay in 1910 on the state's twenty thousand miners. Few of them attended church, he maintained, because they had no respect for pastors. If Methodism wanted to reach the miners, he wrote, pastors of churches in mining camps should each purchase a miner's lamp, suit, and cap, and enter the mines where their people worked. The denomination should build its own churches and reject offers to use buildings owned by the company. Such arrangements had caused miners to view ministers as company men, "and it is a known fact that in many places there is not the best of feeling between the men and the company." Furthermore, the pastor should be an advisory member of the United Mine Workers. Emerson believed that "the pastor makes a great mistake to oppose" the union.[31]

In 1907 another Methodist minister, the Reverend W. P. Blevins, addressed a district conference of his church meeting in the mining center of Dora, Alabama. There were fewer converts in mining camps than in foreign mission fields, he said. Even the membership figures for mining-camp churches were misleading, because Methodists in such churches were mostly farmers from adjacent areas or company officials. Miners preferred not to worship in the same congregation with company men. Mining communities needed institutional churches devoted exclusively to miners, with reading rooms, games and tables, a small gynmasium and baths, a night literacy school, a glee club, and religious services two evenings a week conducted "as often as possible by a miner in the interest of miners."[32]

Such sophisticated institutional churches usually developed in urban textile mill communities rather than mining towns. But in both types of communities bivocational ministers did supply a pastorate more sympathetic to workers. Because Baptists maintained a strong anti-intellectual tradition, one commonly found pastors in the denomination who made their living the same way as their parishioners: as tenant farmers, cotton mill operatives, or coal miners. Because depression, injustice, low wages, poor housing, and company oppression affected their lives the same way it did their members, they often expressed their anger in identical fashion. When Florida phosphate miners struck for higher salaries in 1919, the pastor of the church attended by most of the strikers offered his building in case of rain. He attended their rallies and led them in prayer.[33]

A West Virginia strike by coal miners in 1922 degenerated into bloody civil strife. The leader of the miners was John Wilburn, pastor of the Baptist church in Blair, West Virginia. A bivocational minister who earned his living as a miner, he employed his organizational skills in a sphere beyond the Sunday school. He established armed patrols, which gained control of Blair Mountain and the passes leading to it. Weeks of effort by the National Guard and a bombing strike by the army air force were necessary to restore order. Wilburn was tried for treason and other crimes, convicted of murder, and later pardoned.[34]

But Wilburn was no more typical of Baptist reactions to new economic realities than was the pie-in-the-sky evangelical who for so long has furnished the stereotype of southern religionists favored by American intellectuals. During the Progressive Era, new thoughts were circulating among the evangelical denominations of the South, which had been spawned by the great revivals of 1801 and nurtured by frontier individualism and isolation. Although these groups were more conservative, more emotional, and more oriented toward salvation than their counterparts in other regions, important new ideas charged the atmosphere. Many of the better-educated ministers who had been exposed to European and northern thought came to believe that the concept of the Kingdom of God applied to the social conditions of this world. And among uneducated rural church people—who were staunchly Fundamentalist and barely literate—millennialistic and Pentecostal religion fueled a raging fire of Populist and Socialist radicalism.

In later decades prohibition would become a central focus for religious reformers rather than only one element of a broad reform movement. Baptists and Methodists would move into the middle class, leaving the voice of social prophecy, as well as religious ecstasy, to the Pentecostals. But for a brief historical moment between 1890 and 1920, many southern evangelicals sounded more like Jeremiah than Jerry Falwell.

NOTES

1. Billy Storms, "Southern Baptists and a Social Gospel: An Uneasy Alliance" (Seminar paper, Southern Baptist Theological Seminary, 1975), copy in author's possession. This splendid study explores many aspects of Southern Baptist social thought between 1900 and 1920 and provides a valuable overview of the subject. Although this essay touches on several denominations, it emphasizes the Methodists and the Baptists, who have dominated the South both numerically and in terms of religious social thought.

2. George B. Tindall, *The Emergence of the New South, 1913–1945* (Baton Rouge, 1967), 8. Tindall emphasizes the religious element in southern progressivism more than other recent historians. Charles R. Wilson, "The Religion of the Lost Cause: Ritual and Organization of the Southern Civil Religion, 1865–1920," *Journal of Southern History,* XLVI (May, 1980), 219–22; Morton Sosna, *In Search of the Silent South: White Southern Racial Liberalism, 1920–1950* (New York, 1977), 198; John Lee Eighmy, "Religious Liberalism in the South During the Progressive Era," *Church History,* XXXVIII (September, 1969), 361. For a recent study of progressivism that also emphasizes the importance of religion to social and political reform, see Dewey W. Grantham, *Southern Progressivism: The Reconciliation of Progress and Tradition* (Knoxville, 1983).

3. Jack T. Kirby, *Darkness at the Dawning: Race and Reform in the Progressive South* (Philadelphia, 1972), 1–3, 47, 54, 60–68.

4. *Ibid.,* 87.

5. Frederick A. Bode examined Baptist and Methodist opposition to radical agrarian protest in *Protestantism and the New South: North Carolina Baptists and Methodists in Political Crisis, 1894–1903* (Charlottesville, 1975). Unfortunately, the book is flawed by its exclusive emphasis on Protestant elites. For a different view of how lower-class Protestant rhetoric and religious vision served the Populist cause, see Robert C. McMath, Jr., *Populist Vanguard: A History of the Southern Farmers' Alliance* (Chapel Hill, 1975); Robert M. Saunders, "The Ideology of Southern Populists, 1892–1895" (Ph.D. dissertation, University of Virginia, 1967); and Bruce E. Palmer, "The Rhetoric of Southern Populists: Metaphor and Imagery in the Language of Reform" (Ph.D. dissertation, Yale University, 1972).

6. Carrollton (Alabama) *West Alabamian,* July 1, 1891.

7. McMath, *Populist Vanguard,* 68.

8. *Alabama Baptist,* July 21 and 28, 1892, December 10, 1891, August 10 and 24, 1893.

9. Cary C. Lloyd, "Separation of Church and State: Soul, Liberty and Equality" (MS of a sermon preached in Alabama, probably in the 1890s, in possession of author).

10. Victor I. Masters, *Country Church in the South* (Atlanta, 1916), 40.

11. See William L. Bowers, *The Country Life Movement in America, 1900–1920* (Port Washington, N.Y., 1974).

12. L. G. Wilson *et al.,* "The Church and Landless Men," *University of North Carolina Extension Bulletin,* I (March 1, 1922), 1–27; Edmund Brunner, *Church Life in the Rural South* (New York, 1923), 177.

13. This and the following paragraphs are based on Masters, *Country Church in the South,* 54–59, 76, 98, 143, 149–50, 171, 180–84, 197.

14. John W. Jent, *The Challenge of the Country Church* (Nashville, 1924).

15. C. Allyn Russell, "J. Frank Norris: Violent Fundamentalist," *Southwestern Historical Quarterly,* LXXV (January, 1972), 272–73.

16. Garin Burbank, *When Farmers Voted Red: The Gospel of Socialism in the Countryside, 1910–1924* (Westport, Conn., 1976).

17. James R. Green, *Grass-Roots Socialism: Radical Movements in the Southwest, 1895–1943* (Baton Rouge, 1978), 172–73. Green's analysis places less emphasis on the role of religion than Burbank's, but both agree that evangelicals played a significant role.

18. Robert T. Handy, "The Social Gospel in Historical Perspective," *Andover Newton Quarterly* IX (January, 1969), 170–80.

19. Samuel S. Hill, Jr., *Southern Churches in Crisis* (New York, 1966), 82.

20. Green, *Grass-Roots Socialism,* 169–70.

21. *Alabama Baptist,* July 24, 1907.

22. *Ibid.,* October 6, 1909.

23. This and the following paragraphs are based on Storms, "Southern Baptists and a Social Gospel."

24. Kirby, *Darkness at the Dawning,* 54.

25. Noreen Dunn Tatum, *A Crown of Service: A Story of Women's Work in The Methodist Episcopal Church, South, from 1878–1940* (Nashville, 1960), 241–42.

26. *Ibid,* 242–43. See also *Alabama Christian Advocate,* March 6, 1902, November 26, 1903, January 21, July 22, 1909, June 9, 1910, February 8, 1912.

27. *Alabama Christian Advocate,* November 17, December 12, 1912, March 6, September 25, 1913; Tatum, *A Crown of Service,* 243–44.

28. Tatum, *A Crown of Service,* 244–81.

29. *Ibid.,* 325–27. And see John Patrick McDowell, *The Social Gospel in the South: The Woman's Home Mission Movement in the Methodist Episcopal Church, South, 1886–1939* (Baton Rouge, 1982).

30. For more detailed discussion of the social gospel in the urban South, see my series of articles in the *Alabama Review:* "Organized Labor, Reform, and Alabama Politics, 1920," XXIII (July, 1970), 163–80; "Alabama White Protestantism and Labor, 1900–1914," XXV (July, 1972), 192–217; and "Religion in the Urban South: The Divided Religious Mind of Birmingham, 1900–1919," XXX (April, 1977), 108–34. See also my "Dissent in Zion: Alabama Baptists and Social Issues, 1900–1914," *Journal of Southern History,* XXV (November, 1969), 523–42.

31. *Alabama Christian Advocate,* April 28, 1910.

32. *Ibid.,* June 6, 1917.

33. Tampa *Morning Tribune,* July 2, September 3, 1919.

34. For an example of church-labor radicalism see Richard D. Lunt, *Law and Order vs. The Miners: West Virginia, 1907–1933* (Hamden, Conn., 1979), which contains a complete account of Wilburn's role in the strike.

WILLIAM PORCHER DUBOSE AND A SOUTHERN THEOLOGICAL TRADITION, 1840–1920
Ralph E. Luker

In 1908, Oxford University's Lady Margaret Professor of Divinity, William Sanday, told Americans that there dwelled among them a prophet whom they ought to take more seriously. They should do so, said Sanday, precisely because "there are features about him that are not in the narrower sense American." Europeans knew Americans as a restless type and found this restlessness understandable: "They have a big continent to subdue; and they feel its promise; and it is not strange that they should also feel that no time is to be lost in subduing it," commented Sanday. But if America was to realize her true self, he insisted, she must look beyond the restlessness of her empire builders to something embodied in another type of American. "That something is wisdom; and wisdom is not to be had without calm," he believed; "all the more where, as in the case of Dr. DuBose, it is calm of the right kind—active and not passive, a quiet self-contained and self-controlled creativeness, that hastes not and rests not, like the great Creator Himself." [1]

Whether William Porcher DuBose embodied virtues of an American type meriting even analogous comparison with divine majesty is, one supposes, a matter of personal taste. The fact remains that he was the central figure in what Samuel Hill has called "a thin gray line" of southern theologians whose work won considerable recognition abroad but was widely ignored here in the United States and even in the South. Like the frustrated spirits in Drew Gilpin Faust's "sacred circle," and despite the indifference of their fellow southerners to their intellectual enterprise, they struggled to articulate an apology for the southern social order in terms of the most enlightened thought of their era. The result was a body of theological literature that was distinctly comparable with any other body of theological work in the world of its day. [2]

The roots of this southern theological tradition lie in, of all places, the undirected study of the oldest son of a South Carolina plantation

158

owner. Schoolmaster James P. Waddel reported to the father in 1835 on a conference with sixteen-year-old James Warley Miles: "I told him that I feared he was too much absorbed in the study of German . . . not that I would discourage the study of the noble language—but . . . nothing should interfere with the prescribed duties of our school."[3] From James Waddel's academy, young Miles went to the College of South Carolina in Columbia. There, before being expelled over a dueling challenge, he came under the influence of Francis Lieber, the professor of history and political economy. His own thinking largely influenced by the brilliant faculty of the university in his native Berlin, Lieber planted the seeds of his political thought in young Miles.[4]

From the College of South Carolina, Miles went to New York's General Theological Seminary, where he encountered comparative linguistics and contemporary biblical criticism, the high church Oxford theology, and the evangelical missionary movement. It must have been a heady atmosphere for the twenty-year-old South Carolinian. Ordered home by his bishop, the young seminarian shed the Oxford influence while serving South Carolina parishes, but in 1843 the missionary spirit beckoned him to join Horatio Southgate's Protestant Episcopal mission to Constantinople. His farewell to Charleston condemned the Oxford theology and affirmed the Reformation doctrines of *sola scriptura* and justification by faith.[5]

During his three years in Constantinople, Miles's considerable linguistic skills were put to good use in the production of Armenian translations of the Book of Common Prayer, the American communion service, a treatise on the Anglican church, and Bishop Samuel Seabury's sermon on Christian unity. However, the Eastern metropolis confronted the young South Carolinian with a remarkable pluralism: half a million Turks, 200,000 Armenians, 100,000 Jews—the latter said to have come "from every nation under heaven"—28,000 Greeks, and 18,000 Franks, including Germans, Italians, Maltese, Austrians, French, Russians, Scotch, English, Irish, and Americans.[6] In this cosmopolitan society, Miles's assumptions must have been challenged by its nonracial and relatively nonrestrictive slave system. "Nubians are frequently found in the very highest posts of the army and commanding and leading white men," said an English observer. "Some of our American friends . . . who came from slave-holding states, were at first much perplexed at finding that 'niggers' could be majors, colonels, generals, great pashas; and I believe they never got quite reconciled to a very common sight—a jet-black, hideously faced Nubian officer, with an embroidered coat and a diamond nishan, riding in great pride and stateliness through the streets, followed by two or more white servants running on foot. This seemed to them a turning of the world upside down."[7] But if Miles's racial attitudes were affronted in Constantinople, his mature theological position was established during those three years abroad.

Upon his return to the United States, Miles joined the faculty at the College of Charleston and began to publish his work—a book and ultimately over three dozen articles and pamphlets that articulated his way of thinking. His *Philosophic Theology* received a cold reception in the domestic press.[8] But it won the praise of Sweden's Fredrika Bremer; it combined, she thought, a "pure German spirit" with "English clearness and precision." More important to Miles was its reception by German church historian Johann August Wilhelm Neander. "We esteem it as an important publication in the field of Christian philosophy, Theological and Apologetic," said Neander. "It is evident that the influence of a Kant, a Jacobi, a Schelling, a Schleiermacher has . . . already diffused itself far beyond Europe." It was evident, too, wrote the German theologian, that Miles united a deep Christian earnestness with a clear and independent mind. "His whole theological way of thinking is of one piece," Neander concluded. "We tender to him our hand, as to one of those dispositions and spiritual relations who, in the great, hot battle of the present time, will ever draw more and more together, as one band. This work, as a remarkable sign of the times, deserves to be also known in our own land." And so it was. Neander reviewed *Philosophic Theology* in his *Deutsche Zeitschrift fur Christlich Wissenschaft und Christliches Leben* and encouraged his student, W. A. Lampadius, to publish a German translation of Miles's work, to which Neander's review was attached as a preface.[9]

Neander's enthusiasm came naturally, for while Miles was abroad, he had been deeply influenced by the mediating theology of Schleiermacher's followers in Germany, including Neander, as well as by Coleridge's disciples among the English broad churchmen. Following Schleiermacher, he began with human self-consciousness as the basis of knowledge, and from Coleridge he borrowed the distinction between reason as the subjective experience of supersensual truth and understanding as the objective sense of scientific knowledge. Miles argued that as Perfect Being, God cannot become the object of sense perception and must remain the subjective truth of intuition. Nevertheless, the idea of Perfect Being must manifest itself incarnate in the world of experience and does so in all the phenomena of human experience. This approach gave birth to four theses that framed Miles's thought. First, phenomenal existence is an expression of divine thought. The phenomenal world is like a field planted with the seed of divine thought. Second, history is the course of the fulfillment of the divine ideas. The organic growth of the seed led to a fruition guaranteed by its divine source. Third, the process of development is not subject to arbitrary redefinition but is directed by an informing law of development leading toward the fulfillment of all phenomena. Finally, human reason can perceive by intuition the divine intention evident in the course of history. Miles's wide interests—in theology, moral philosophy, social theory, linguistics, biblical criticism, and race relations—were all expressed in terms of this pattern of thought.[10]

Frustrated and angered by the impoverished quality of southern intellectual life, Miles resigned his position at the College of Charleston in 1854 and fled to Europe for two years of study at Berlin. Unable to find fulfillment in the South and yet unable to live apart from it, he returned to the college in 1856 as librarian. In that capacity he would develop an apology for the southern social order and interpret the world-historic meaning of the Confederacy during the Civil War.

Drawing upon a tradition from Aristotle through Aquinas and Richard Hooker through Burke, Coleridge, Thomas Arnold, and Francis Lieber, Miles's political theory located the origins of the state in the family in nature. Interpreting society in organic and hierarchical terms, he rejected the individualism of social contract theory. Particular states, language groups, races, and religions were divine ideas, each moving toward their perfection—to their freedom—in history.[11] Miles had learned to read scripture, not so much as the authoritative word of God, but as a record of a people in the process of moving toward perfection. Together with his experience in Constantinople, where Miles had seen white slaves and black masters, this attitude toward the authority of scripture convinced him of the inadequacy of biblical sanctions for slavery and led to his acceptance of the latest scientific evidence for the plurality of racial origins. Insisting that a natural inferiority was written into the origin of black people, Miles argued that the perfection of the master-servant relationship was the fulfillment of racial potential.[12] The Confederacy, then, was God's new idea in history that would enable the people of the South to reach toward the fulfillment of their potential—Anglo-Saxons to perfect their mastery, Africans to perfect their servility. Miles's Confederate vision was a nightmare of perfectionist racism.[13]

While James Warley Miles fought the Civil War in his mind, William Porcher DuBose fought it on the battlefields of Virginia. Between the Seven Days campaign of June 25 to July 1, 1862, and the defeat at Vicksburg a year later, he was captured once and thrice wounded. Then, accepting Episcopal ordination as a deacon, DuBose became a chaplain with Kershaw's Brigade. Only after the defeat at Cedar Creek, Virginia, on October 19, 1864, could he contemplate the failure of the Confederacy and, with it, the shattering of his whole world. "In class one day he told us that after the war, he had lost his fortune and his civilization," said a Sewanee student. "The Church was all that he had left."[14]

For the young Miles the evangelical and churchly influences among South Carolina Episcopalians were dichotomous alternatives between which one was forced to choose. But for his kinsman and heir, DuBose, they were dialectical influences to be drawn upon and synthesized. Late in life, he told his former students that he had gone through three theological phases. The first, or evangelical, phase extended from his childhood through a conversion experience that took place while he was a student at the Citadel in 1854, through his years as a student at the University of Virginia and the diocesan seminary at Camden, and through his rich engagement with the thought of Saint Paul during the Civil War. Confederate defeat appears to have led to the second, or churchly, phase. DuBose and Miles had vested belief in the Confederacy as the bearer of the Spirit in history. For DuBose, this faith was transformed by defeat into devotion to the church as the extension of the Incarnation in history.[15] Writing under the influence of the churchly continental theologians

Neander, Herman Ohlshausen, and Isaac August Dorner, and the Mercersburg theology of John Williamson Nevin and Philip Schaff, DuBose offered the New South an ecclesiology in the place of its lost polity. In the rich liturgical and hierarchical traditions of the churchly life, he found a saving remnant of the best that he had known of "his home, his own, his native land." "The Church was to me simply the divine institution that claimed and attracted all the fealty and devotion of my heart, mind, soul, and life," said DuBose. "The more divine it could be made to appear, the more willing and satisfied was my loyalty." [16]

Called from the parishes of South Carolina to the University of the South at Sewanee, Tennessee, in 1872, DuBose proclaimed his theology for the New South from his mountain outpost. Although his thought was not so wide-ranging as that of Miles, DuBose's whole theological approach sanctioned the overthrow of Reconstruction. In his first two books, *The Soteriology of the New Testament* and *The Ecumenical Councils,* for example, he spoke of freedom, of salvation, in terms of the fulfillment or perfection of potential. Christ is generic man in whom that fulfillent is accomplished for and in us. Miles would have approved all of the assumptions in DuBose's metaphorical apology for the return of white rule to the South. "Put oil under water," wrote DuBose, "and (right or wrong) it will come to the top." [17] In the thought of Miles and DuBose, what is given in the order of nature must be saved in its own terms and in appropriate relation to the other. Oil will be redeemed as oil, water will be saved as water, and the latter in appropriate subordination to the former.

In the maturity of his old age, DuBose believed, the evangelical and churchly phases of his thought were synthesized in a broad church or catholic phase whose theme was unity. Between the ages of seventy and eighty, the old theologian who had spent forty years teaching in the mountains of east Tennessee, reached out in five new books, in an important series of articles, and through the growing influence of his students, to make his southern theology available to the nation and the world.[18] In response to Adolph von Harnack's *What is Christianity?* DuBose argued that the gospel must be understood not simply as the message of Jesus, but in terms of the Incarnation, life, and Resurrection of Christ.[19] In his doctrine of the Atonement, DuBose joined English theologians of the Lux Mundi group, particularly Robert Campbell Moberly, in developing the generic understanding of Christ to suggest that his atoning work is not so much that of substitutionary sacrifice or moral example as that of vicarious representative.[20]

By 1910 DuBose had begun to make his mark, not only in his books, but also through the influence of his students. Theodore DuBose Bratton, Thomas F. Gailor, William A. Guerry, and Henry Judah Mikell became the Episcopal bishops of Mississippi, Tennessee, South Carolina, and Georgia respectively. But his influence was not limited to the South or to southerners. In 1921 the redoubtable William T. Manning, a native of England and one of DuBose's ablest students at Sewanee, would step down after thirteen years as rector of Manhattan's Trinity Church to begin his twenty-five-year reign as the Episcopal bishop of New York.[21]

Through Edgar Gardner Murphy, who gave up the priestly office for a career in child labor, educational, and racial reform efforts, DuBose's influence extended into America's progressive social reform movements at the turn of the century. A conservative critic of capitalistic individualism, Murphy attacked child labor's disruptive effect upon the organic ties of community.[22] His keen sense of the mutual obligations of culture and democracy led Murphy to devote the most productive decade of his short career in the South to education as a conserving influence in a dynamic society.[23]

A moderating influence in the South's racial climate at the turn of the century, Murphy nevertheless accepted the assumptions in James Warley Miles's justification of slavery. Tracing racial distinctions back to history's horizon and projecting them into the distant future, Murphy argued that the Negro's salvation lay not in assimilation but in separation. Thus, he became one of segregation's most sophisticated apologists. The coincidence of modern democracy and imperialism in his own time, Murphy believed, offered the South a new world historic opportunity—to tutor the world in the development of a biracial society.[24] As the white South more and more approximated its destiny as political mentor to the modern world, so the black South would more and more approximate whatever destiny it had been given. Thus, Murphy reconciled the assumptions of James Warley Miles with the values of the Progressive Era. Murphy's work won widespread praise not only in America but from English intellectuals as well. Lord James Bryce praised his application of Christianity and "sound political philosophy" to contemporary social problems. Joseph Houldsworth Oldham, editor of the *International Review of Missions,* sought to persuade Murphy to publish a work on race relations in an international perspective.[25]

If Manning took DuBose's theological attitude to his New York diocese and Murphy extended its influence in social reform, Silas McBee, as editor of the *Churchman* and the *Constructive Quarterly,* gave it a national and an international platform. In 1896 McBee left Sewanee to become editor of the *Churchman,* the semiofficial voice of the Protestant Episcopal Church. In that capacity he opened its columns to DuBose, handled the publication of his mentor's books, promoted their sale, and saw to it that they were favorably reviewed. Through McBee's growing international contacts, the books were reviewed in journals published in London, Edinburgh, Dublin, Liverpool, Brisbane, Sydney, Paris, Berlin, and Copenhagen.[26] "What is to be desired," DuBose wrote McBee in 1908, "is a *Movement* towards the Theology and Philosophy of which I am recognized as an Exponent."[27]

McBee introduced William Sanday to DuBose, and shortly thereafter, Sanday was singing the Sewanee theologian's praises as "the wisest writer (in his field) on the other side of the Atlantic" and "the wisest Anglican writer on both sides of the Atlantic." Others—Lord Bryce, the bishop of Manchester, Scotland's Marcus Dods, and France's Abbé Henri Bremond—joined in a chorus of praise for DuBose.[28] By 1911 Sanday's enthusiasm had made DuBose perhaps the most influential American theologian in England, and in that year McBee undertook a tour of Christendom that would extend his influence well beyond the English-speaking world. From London to Berlin, Saint Petersburg to Alexandria, and Jerusalem to Constantinople, McBee touched base with the historic centers of Christianity, reflecting upon the problem of Christian unity in the terms he learned from DuBose and returning to the United States with an imaginative plan to foster that unity.[29]

In March, 1913, McBee published the first issue of the *Constructive Quarterly,* an international ecumenical journal. Its editorial board reflected his intention to publish representative treatments of Christianity from all branches of the church. Rather than seeking "neutral territory," the effort was to find "common ground, where loyalty to Christ . . . will be secure from the tendency to mere compromise." The initial editorial board included thirteen Americans of various denominations, eleven British churchmen, five Germans, and five Russians. Eventually, it included representatives from Scandinavia, North Africa, India, and China. Among the leading members of the board and contributors to the journal were DuBose, William Adams Brown, Francis J. McConnell, Shailer Matthews, Arthur James Balfour, James Denney, William Ralph Inge, William Sanday, William Temple, Adolph Deissmann, Freidrich Loffs, Nicholas Gubakovsky, and Nathan Soderblom. A committee of Roman Catholic cooperators with the journal included Pierre Batiffol and Wilfred Ward. Yet, a closer look at the journal throughout its ten years reveals a parochial bias. Ninety of the 445 articles were published by its thirteen most prolific writers, and among them DuBose published eleven—by far the largest number. McBee's *Constructive Quarterly* was essentially a vehicle for putting DuBose's southern theology before catholic Christendom.[30]

As William Hutchison's theological modernists had done, Miles, DuBose, Manning, Murphy, McBee, and the others sought to adapt religious ideas to contemporary culture. They believed that God was immanent in and revealed through human cultural development, and they thought that human society was moving toward realization of the Kingdom of God.[31] But the adaptation of religious ideas to contemporary culture is a perilous enterprise—particularly when that culture is deeply rooted in racist and class-conscious assumptions. As the beneficiaries of such assumptions, convinced that they epitomized the latest—and therefore highest—human cultural development, these southern theologians and churchmen saw themselves, no doubt, as harbingers of the Kingdom. Even the indifference of their fellow southerners to their intellectual enterprise failed to produce a sense of divine judgment upon all human cultural achievement. Only their own social conservatism led them to have reservations—about industrial capitalism's use of child labor, about the feared possibility of unbridled competition manifesting itself in racial violence, even about the essential rightness of the southern social order.

They found recognition, not from their fellow southerners, but from Europe's liberal intellectuals. William Sanday's appreciation for William Porcher DuBose as a different type of American and the praise of other liberal European intellectuals for James Warley Miles and Edgar Gardner Murphy revealed the intellectuals' recognition that they had found kindred spirits in these southern spokesmen for an embattled social elite. Murphy died in 1913, DuBose in 1918, the *Constructive Quarterly* in 1922, and Silas McBee in 1924. World War I marked the demise both of Europe's liberal intellectual aristocracy and of the southern tradition in theology and social thought represented in their American kinsmen.

NOTES

1. William Sanday, *The Life of Christ in Recent Research* (New York, 1908), 281–82.

2. Drew Gilpin Faust, *A Sacred Circle: The Dilemma of the Intellectual in the Old South 1840–1860* (Baltimore, 1977). I have surveyed this southern theological tradition in "Theological Liberalism and Social Conservatism: A Southern Tradition, 1840–1920," *Church History* (June, 1981), 193–204, and *A Southern Tradition in Theology and Social Criticism, 1830–1930: The Religious Liberalism and Social Conservatism of James Warley Miles, William Porcher DuBose, and Edgar Gardner Murphy* (New York, 1984).

3. James P. Waddel to James S. Miles, March 18, 1835, in William Porcher DuBose Papers, Southern Historical Collection, University of North Carolina, Chapel Hill. On Miles's life and thought, see my "God, Man, and the World of James Warley Miles, Charleston's Transcendentalist," *Historical Magazine of the Protestant Episcopal Church,* XXXIX (June, 1970), 101–36. See also E. Brooks Holifield, *The Gentlemen Theologians: American Theology in Southern Culture, 1795–1860* (Durham, N.C., 1978), 66–71.

4. While Miles was his student, Lieber was at work on volume one of his *Manual of Political Ethics Designed Chiefly for the Use of Colleges and Students at Law* (2 vols.; Boston, 1838–39). As late as 1857, Miles signed a letter to Lieber "Most respectfully and affectionately your pupil." J. W. Miles to Francis Lieber, June 26, 1857, in Francis Lieber Papers, Huntington Library, San Marino, California. See also Frank Freidel, *Francis Lieber: Nineteenth-Century Liberal* (Baton Rouge, 1947); and Charles B. Robson, "Francis Lieber's Theories of Society, Government, and Liberty," *Journal of Politics,* IV (1942), 227–49.

5. Powel Miles Dawley, *The Story of General Theological Seminary* (New York, 1969), 11–179; Samuel H. Turner, *Autobiography* (New York, 1863); Charles Breck (ed.), *The Life of the Reverend James Lloyd Breck . . .* (New York, 1883), 8–39; E. Clowes Chorley, "The Oxford Movement in the Seminary," *Historical Magazine of the Protestant Episcopal Church,* XXV (September, 1961), 177–201; Charles T. Bridgemen, "Mediterranean Missions of the Episcopal Church from 1828–1898," *Historical Magazine of the Protestant Episcopal Church,* XXXI (June, 1962), 95–126; James Warley Miles, *Farewell Sermon* (Charleston, 1843), 3, 11; Luker, "James Warley Miles," 101–106.

6. For contemporary American comments on the city's pluralism, see John P. Durbin, *Observations on the East, Chiefly in Egypt, Palestine, Syria, and Asia Minor* (2 vols.; New York, 1845), II, 189–92, 239–43; Greene Wheeler Benjamin, *The Turk and the Greek; or, Creeds, Races, Society, and Scenery, in Turkey, Greece, and the Isles of Greece* (New York, 1867), 24–26; and Horatio Southgate, *Narrative of a Tour Through Armenia, Kurdistan, Persia, and Mesopotamia . . .* (2 vols.; New York, 1840), I, 80.

7. Charles MacFarlane, *Turkey and Its Destiny: The Result of Journeys*

Made in 1847 and 1848 to Examine into the State of That Country (2 vols.; Philadelphia, 1850), II, 198. See also MacFarlane's interesting account of an attempt by a South Carolina doctor to establish a model plantation near San Stephano with four slaves from an American plantation. *Ibid.,* I, 46–52, 224, II, 18–19, 104–105, 131–42, 248–53, 368–75.

8. James Warley Miles, *Philosophic Theology; or, Ultimate Grounds of all Religious Belief Based in Reason* (Charleston, 1849). For a sample of reviews, see *True Catholic: Reformed, Protestant and Free,* VII (April, 1850), 558–60; James Smith Rhett, *Southern Quarterly Review,* XVII (April, 1850), 145; and *Charleston Gospel Messenger and Protestant Episcopal Register,* XXVII (May, 1850), 45–47, 171.

9. Fredrika Bremer, *The Homes of the New World: Impressions of America,* trans. Mary Howett (2 vols.; New York, 1854), I, 378–79; Johann August Wilhelm Neander, "Philosophic Theology," *Southern Quarterly Review,* XVII (September, 1850), 259–60; James Warley Miles, *Philosophische Theologie, oder die letzen Grunde alles religiosen Glaubens in der Vernunft beruhend,* trans. W. A. Lampadius (Leipzig, 1850), iii–viii.

10. Miles, *Philosophic Theology,* 13, 75, 102–103; Miles, "The Danger and Safety of the Republic," *Southern Quarterly Review,* XIV (July, 1848), 168–69; Miles, *Annual Oration: Delivered Before the Chrestomatic Society of the College of Charleston, February 22, 1850* (Charleston, 1850), 16–23; Miles, *Discourse, Delivered Before the Graduating Class of the College of Charleston, at Their Request in the College Chapel, February 23rd, 1852* (Charleston, 1851), 5–8; Miles, *The Ground Morals: A Discourse Delivered Before the Graduating Class of the College of Charleston, at Their Request in the College Chapel, March 28th, 1852* (Charleston, 1852), 9–11, 13, 16–36; Miles, *The Student of Philosophy: Annual Oration Delivered Before the Literary Societies of the South Carolina College, in the College Chapel, Columbia, December 7th, 1852* (Charleston, 1853), 8–10.

11. Miles, "Union of Church and State," *Southern Quarterly Review,* XV (July, 1849), 319–45; Miles, *The Discourse on the Occasion of the Funeral of the Honorable John C. Calhoun, Delivered Under the Appointment of the Joint Committee of the City Council and the Citizens of Charleston, in St. Phillip's Church, April 26, 1850* (Charleston, 1850), 14–19.

12. On Miles's racial thought and apology for slavery, see Miles, *Philosophic Theology,* 230–31; Miles, Review of Leiber, Nordheimer, and Donaldson, *On the Philosophy of Language,* in *Southern Quarterly Review,* XX (October, 1851), 392–93, 403–404, 527; Miles, *Student of Philology,* 18–30, 48–49; Miles, *The Relation Between the Races of the South* (Charleston, 1861). In his correspondence, Miles returned periodically to this theme, each time attempting to find just the right words to express it. See, for instance, Miles to Mrs. Thomas John Young, July 23, 1864, July 24, 1864, August 12, 1864, [ca. 1864], February 6, 1865, all in James Warley Miles papers, Manuscript Division, Duke University Library, Durham, N.C. On the antebellum debate on racial origins, see William Stanton, *The Leopard's Spots: Scientific Attitudes Toward Race in America, 1815–1859* (Chicago, 1960)

13. James Warley Miles, *God in History: A Discourse Delivered Before the Graduating Class of the College of Charleston on Sunday Evening, March 29th, 1863* (Charleston, 1863).

14. William Porcher DuBose, "Reminiscences, 1863–1878" (Typescript in Southern Historical Colection, University of North Carolina, Chapel Hill), 134; DuBose, *Turning Points in My Life* (New York, 1912), 49–50; George Boggan Myers, "The Sage and Seer of Sewanee," in DuBose, *Unity in the Faith* (Greenwich, Conn., 1957), 19.

15. DuBose, *Turning Points,* 16. George Boggan Myers incorrectly interpreted the three phases as "Evangelical, Broad Church, and High Church," Myers, "Sage and Seer of Sewanee," 16. Had he reversed the last two terms, Myers would have been more faithful to DuBose's own interpretation of the direction his thinking took.

16. DuBose, *Turning Points,* 54–55; Theodore DuBose Bratton, *An Apostle of Reality: The Life and Thought of the Reverend William Porcher DuBose* (New York, 1936), 106. See also DuBose, *Turning Points,* 52, 61–62; and Bratton, *An Apostle of Reality,* 104–107. A key early document, important in this regard and often overlooked in DuBose studies, is DuBose, *The Christian Ministry: Sermon Preached at the Ordination of Rev. O. T. Porcher, Abbeville, S.C., May 15, 1870* (Charleston, 1870).

17. DuBose, *The Soteriology of the New Testament* (New York, 1892); DuBose, *The Ecumenical Councils* (New York, 1896); DuBose, "Wade Hampton," *Sewanee Review,* X (July, 1892), 8. See also DuBose to Mrs. Joseph A. Huger, March 5, 1898, in the Habersham Elliott Papers, Southern Historical Collection, University of North Carolina, Chapel Hill; and DuBose, *The Reason of Life* (New York, 1911), 36–37.

18. The books were *The Gospel in the Gospels* (New York, 1906); *The Gospel According to St. Paul* (New York, 1907); *High Preisthood and Sacrifice* (New York, 1908); *The Reason of Life;* and *Turning Points.* The series of articles, originally appearing in Silas McBee's *Constructive Quarterly,* were published posthumously as *Unity in the Faith.*

19. DuBose, *Gospel in the Gospels,* 3–7. See also DuBose to Silas McBee, July 26, 1901, August 5, 1901, August 21, 1901, August 27, 1901, McBee to DuBose, August 26, 1903, all in Silas McBee Papers, Jessie Ball duPont Library, University of the South, Sewanee, Tennessee.

20. Useful treatments of this problem include Robert Campbell Moberly, *Atonement and Personality* (London, 1901); John Kenneth Mozley, *The Doctrine of the Atonement* (London, 1901); Robert Mackintosh, *Historic Theories of Atonement* (London, 1920); John Stewart Lawton, *Conflict in Christology: A Study of British and American Christology, from 1889–1914* (London, 1947); and George S. Hendry, *The Gospel of the Incarnation* (Philadelphia, 1952).

21. John H. Seabrook, "William Thomas Manning: A Study of Christian Unity," *Historical Magazine of the Protestant Episcopal Church,* XXXIV (June, 1965), 147–70; Seabrook, "Bishop Manning and World War I," *Historical Magazine of the Protestant Episcopal Church,* XXXVI (December, 1967), 301–21. See also Manning's appreciation of DuBose in Manning, "An Apostle of Reality," *Living Church,* XCV (October 24, 1936), 457–58, 361.

22. Edgar Gardner Murphy, *Problems of the Present South: A Discussion of Certain of the Educational, Industrial and Political Issues in the Southern States* (New York, 1904), 105–24, 129, 131–36, 139, 141–44, 148–49;

Murphy, *Child Labor in Alabama: The Nichols-Sears-Murphy Correspondence* (Montgomery, 1902), 4–5, 13–15, 17, 19, 28–37.

23. Murphy, *Problems of the Present South,* 48–50, 264–88. See also Hugh C. Bailey, *Edgar Gardner Murphy: Gentle Progressive* (Coral Gables, 1968).

24. Edgar Gardner Murphy, *The White Man and the Negro at the South* (N.p., n.d.), 19, 45–46; Murphy, *The Task of the South: An Address Before the Faculty and Students of Washington and Lee University, Lexington, Virginia, December 10th A.D., 1902* (N.p, n.d.); Murphy, *Problems of the Present South,* 34–37, 63–64; Murphy, *The Basis of Ascendancy: A Discussion of Certain Principles of Public Policy Involved in the Development of the Southern States* (New York, 1909), 222–23.

25. James Bryce to Edgar Gardner Murphy, November 30, 1909, in Edgar Gardner Murphy Papers, Southern Historical Collection, University of North Carolina, Chapel Hill; Joseph Houldsworth Oldham to Silas McBee, February 1, 1912, in Silas McBee Papers, Southern Historical Collection, University of North Carolina, Chapel Hill. Eventually Oldham would publish the work he had in mind for Murphy, and in it the influence of the southern reformer's thinking is evident. See Joseph Houldsworth Oldham, *Christianity and the Race Problem* (Chautauqua, N.Y., 1926).

26. A substantial portion of the McBee Papers in the Southern Historical Collection reflects these activities.

27. DuBose to McBee, March 7, 1908, in McBee Papers, Sewanee.

28. Sanday, *Life of Christ in Recent Research,* 281. See also Bryce to McBee, June 19, 1911, in McBee Papers, Chapel Hill. Dods and Bremond are quoted in Silas McBee, "William Porcher DuBose," *Constructive Quarterly,* VIII (1920), 522; Bishop Moorhouse of Manchester is quoted in Manning, "Apostle of Reality," 458.

29. Silas McBee, *An Eirenic Itinerary: Impressions of Our Tour with Addresses and Papers on the Unity of Christian Churches* (New York, 1911), esp. ix–x, xiv, 19.

30. Silas McBee, "Introduction," *Constructive Quarterly,* I (March, 1913), 1. DuBose's essays were collected and published posthumously as *Unity in the Faith.*

31. William R. Hutchison, *The Modernist Impulse in American Protestantism* (Cambridge, 1976), 2.

PERSPECTIVES ON THE
ELECTRONIC CHURCH
William Martin

The top religious news story in 1980 was the electronic church. Americans were told that almost everybody watched Jerry Falwell, Pat Robertson, or Oral Roberts, or one of their brethren on television and, depending on who was doing the telling, that this was either going to save or ruin the country. The discovery that millions of people were not only listening and watching the media ministers but apparently were believing what they said and sending money to help them keep saying it stirred a vigorous response, mostly critical, in what has come to be called the mainline churches. Some of the criticisms were well-founded, some were based more on fear than fact, and some had the ring of a tinkling cymbal hit by a sour grape.

There has been a wide range of statements concerning how many and who are members of the Great Church of the Airwaves. Ben Armstrong, the executive director of the National Religious Broadcasters, began his book *The Electric Church* with the assertion that "starting in the predawn hours of each Sunday morning, the largest religious gathering in America takes place, drawing almost 130 million people to their radio and television sets."[1] Most people who have written or commented publicly on the phenomenon of electronic religion seem to have taken Armstrong at some version of his word. This enormous estimate of the size of the weekly audience for broadcast religion has been repeated uncritically by people who should have known better, and similarly outsized figures on specific television evangelists—Jerry Falwell is a prime example—have been accepted as gospel truth and allowed to stir unrealistic alarm or false hope, depending on one's point of view.

The New York *Times* has quoted Armstrong's figure of 130 million without challenging it, though it has noted that some estimates for individual ministers, including Falwell, appear to be inflated. The *Wall Street Journal* has credited television ministries with 128 million viewers. *U.S. News and World Report* has spoken of "TV gospel shows beamed to 50 million viewers each week by evangelicals such as Falwell, Robertson, and [James] Robison." A United Press International (UPI) story estimated that "about 115 million persons listen to at least one religious radio show and about 40 million watch at least one religious TV show each week." *New York* magazine not only set the American membership of the electronic church at 130 million, but credited Rex Humbard with "an audience of 100 million worldwide." A *Saturday Evening Post* article assigned 50 million viewers to Oral Roberts.[2]

Since early 1980, most media attention to the electronic church has focused on Jerry Falwell and the Moral Majority. Although few reporters professed to know any Falwell supporters personally, they were sure the woods and towns and cities were full of them. In a strident article about the New Right, *Penthouse* said the audience for evangelical television was between 40 and 60 million, and *Playboy* reported that "each week as many as 30,000,000 Americans tuned into Jerry Falwell's *Old-Time Gospel Hour.*" Jimmy Breslin whittled Falwell's audience down to 25 million; the "Today" show and Bill Moyers gave him only 20 million; and Joseph Sullivan and Anthony Lewis of the New York *Times* and various reporters at *Newsweek* and the Knight-Ridder newspapers seemed finally to settle on 18 million as the appropriate estimate. On occasion, however, the *Times* noted that Falwell's actual audience might be as small as 6 million.[3]

These high estimates appalled mainline church leaders, who were already anxious over the trend among television stations to air paid evangelical broadcasts instead of furnishing free time for programs produced by more liberal religious bodies. One of the trend's most vocal critics has been Dr. William Fore, head of communications for the National Council of Churches. Despite his extensive acquaintance with religious broadcasting, Fore wrote in *TV Guide* that "some 47 percent of Americans see at least one religious program a week on TV." Another influential mainliner, James M. Wall, editor of the *Christian Century*, wrote that "these fundamentalist television preachers now reach over 100 million persons each week." Wall's editorial, ironically, was based on Richard Hofstadter's essay "The Paranoid Style in American Politics."[4]

Some TV ministers avoid such claims, but others do not, a fact that has contributed to the confusion. For example, Jim Bakker has boasted that his PTL Club has an audience of 20 million, even though associates have admitted the figure was "a total fabrication." Rex Humbard's press materials once claimed his program was seen by "up to 100 million"; his current promotional literature makes the more modest and supportable claim of 1.4 million. Jerry Falwell's aides have estimated his audience at 15 million, though Falwell admits he really does not know how many people watch and hear him. James Robison's publicity claims his television show has a potential audience of 50 to 60 million people, without noting that considerably less than a million actually tune in. In fact, in a recent fund-raising letter, he stated that "over ten million homes are reached and helped each week by our TV program." Other evangelists make even more extravagant claims. For example, Frances Swaggart asked supporters of her husband Jimmy's ministry to send money to purchase TV equipment that would "reach approximately 300 million people with God's love in 1981." But no media preacher outstrips Bert Clendennen, who has often reminded radio listeners that his program reaches "one out of every two people on the face of this earth."[5]

Claims such as these would be more understandable if we had recourse to nothing more substantial than faith, hope, and guesswork. Fortunately, that is not the case. In the course of a decade of research on the electronic church, I have examined a substantial number of audience surveys—some conducted by academics, some by the Harris and Gallup organizations, and some by private market-research companies. I have also looked closely at data published by Arbitron and Nielsen, the two major rating services for broadcast media, on the television preachers' audience over the course of several years. The results are remarkably uniform, and the conclusion to which they point is that the audience estimates cited in the major media, however much they may differ from one another, share one feature in common: they are all absurd.

Several polls have indicated that between 45 and 50 percent of adult Americans listen to some type of religious radio program at least once a year, but the regular audience is much smaller. A 1978 survey conducted for *Christianity Today* by the Gallup Organization revealed that 79 percent of a sample designed to represent the adult general public of America indicated they did not listen to religious radio at all, an additional 5 percent claimed to listen less than one hour per week, and only 5 percent reported they listen three hours or more per week.[6] When projected to an adult population of 155 million people, this survey indicates that approximately 32.5 million people say they listen to religious radio at least occasionally, but that only 7.75 million claim to listen as much as three hours per week.

The best recent data on religious radio and television are those gathered for the American Research Corporation by the Gallup Organization and published in *Profile of the Christian Marketplace, 1980.* Within the audience of listeners to religious radio, most of whom describe themselves as regulars, the sexes were about evenly divided, with women outnumbering men only slightly (53 percent to 47 percent), a variation that could easily be accounted for by more convenient access to radio among nonworking women. Other demographic patterns are more distinctive. Blacks were almost twice as likely as whites to listen to radio preachers, and people over 50 were more than twice as likely to listen as those in the 18-to-34 age bracket. One-third of listeners' households had a total income of less than $10,000, only 15 percent reported income greater than $25,000, and less than 1 percent had incomes above $50,000. Education levels were also modest, with only 23 percent of listeners having attended college; 19 percent had not completed high school. People involved in professional occupations were less than half as likely as other occupational groups to listen to radio preachers. Thus, the audience for religious radio is seen to be drawn overwhelmingly from the lower-middle class, the working class, and the lower classes. It is also disproportionately populated with southerners, who constitute 36 percent of all listeners and are almost twice as likely to listen as residents of the East. Finally, the likelihood that a given individual will listen varies significantly with the size of the population in his or her locale: 48 percent of moderate-to-regular listeners live in towns or cities with less than 25,000 inhabitants; only 11.8 percent live in cities of a million or more. Whatever their sex, age, or social class, 86 percent identify themselves as Protestants and 82 percent say they have made a commitment to Jesus Christ and have attended church within the six months prior to the survey.[7]

The audience for religious television, though not identical with that for religious radio, bears a strong resemblance to it. The Gallup *Christianity Today* poll found that as many as 29 percent of the general public (45 million people) watch some religious television, that one in four watch at least one hour per week, and that 12 percent (18.6 million) watch two or more hours per week. The demographic patterns that emerge from the Arbitron and Nielsen data and the *Christian Marketplace* poll reveal that, on the average, the audience for religious television is over 60 percent female. As with radio, black women are more likely to watch religious television than are white women (16.3 percent to 10 percent), but black males are less than half as likely as white men to watch religious television as to listen to religious radio (8.9 percent to 21.5 percent), a finding probably attributable to the fact that none of the major television ministries caters particularly to blacks.[8]

People over 50 comprise 64 percent of the adult audience, compared with only 15 percent from the under-35 category. Less than 10 percent reported a total household income in excess of $25,000, and 41 percent reported less than $10,000. Predictably, this lower income level corresponds to modest educational and occupational attainment. Only 15 percent of those who express a strong preference for televised religion have attended college; 26 percent did not complete high school. Laborers are more than four times more likely to view religious programs than are professional people, and two categories, "labor" and "non-labor/retired," provide 83 percent of the viewers of religious television. Thus, as was the case with radio, the audience for religious television is drawn predominantly from the lower-middle class, the working class, and the lower classes. It also manifests distinct regional patterns, with southerners four times more likely to watch than easterners and three times more likely than westerners. In fact, over 80 percent of those who prefer religious shows live in the South or Midwest, and nine of the ten top syndicated television ministries draw at least half their audiences from twelve southern states, plus Texas, Oklahoma, New York City, and Los Angeles. Only Robert Schuller enjoys a more evenly spread distribution. Residents of rural areas and small towns under 2,500 are eight times more likely to watch such programs than are dwellers in cities with a population of more than a million, and 58 percent of the audience is found in cities with less than 25,000 inhabitants.[9]

It is surely more than coincidence that the statistical profile of the evangelical movement bears a striking resemblance to that of the audience of religious radio and television. In 1977 George Gallup created considerable furor when he announced that nearly 50 million American adults claimed to be born-again Christians and accepted a literal interpretation of the Bible. Approximately two-thirds of these were women, nearly three out of five were over 50, half lived in the South, and 85 percent had no formal education beyond high school.[10]

The findings of Gallup's *Christianity Today* poll and its *Christian Marketplace* study strengthen the argument that the audience for the television preachers is composed largely of evangelical Christians. The first study reported that 98 percent of the viewers of religious television believe in God; 92 percent believe that Jesus is the Son of God; 92 percent attend church at least occasionally.[11] Many viewers of religious television, of course, watch denominational programs and local church services instead of or in addition to the programs of the nationally syndicated ministries. But since it is primarily these national ministries that have generated the current interest in the electronic church, the remainder of my discussion will focus specifically on them.

The weekly audience for these programs is small, with only Oral Roberts and Robert Schuller attracting viewers in as many as 2 percent of the households in the areas in which their programs are aired. Since each 100 viewer households contain approximately 150 viewers (130 adults), the viewing audience is significantly less than 2 percent of the total population. The total number of households containing television sets tuned during November, 1980, to one of the top ten programs produced by independent (nondenominational) ministries was less than 10 million. Even this figure may be quite high, since it assumes no overlap between audiences, an assumption no one familiar with the electronic church would make. The stars of the movement appear on the same programs, speak at the same rallies, and, increasingly, cooperate in various joint ventures, with clear confidence that they are appealing to the same people. Fund-raising organizations sell mailing lists of people known to contribute to more than one ministry. And Gallup's *Christianity Today* poll revealed that about half the "Orthodox Christians" who watch religious television watch at least two hours per week, indicating they watch more than one program.[12]

If the hypothesis of multiple program viewing is valid—and I have no doubt it is—the average weekly audience for the top ten programs is probably between 7 million and 10 million. Perhaps two to three times that many watch the programs on an occasional basis, an estimate that squares with a Harris Poll survey that places the audience for television preachers at approximately 23 million.

Whatever the true size of the total audience for the leading television preachers, that audience does not appear to be growing. On the contrary, it seems to have reached its peak and begun to shrink. In November, 1980, nine of the ten most popular television ministries were reaching fewer households than in February of the same year. Losses suffered by these nine ranged from Jerry Falwell's minimal 2.3 percent slippage, during a period of enormous publicity, to declines of 21 percent for Rex Humbard and Oral Roberts. In the case of the top six ministries, all had recorded larger household totals prior to 1980; thus, these figures are not an aberration, but part of a continuing decline. Oral Roberts, for example, has lost more than 40 percent of the audience he had in February, 1977.[13]

With these data as background, let us consider some of the major criticisms raised against the electronic church. Most of them fall into four broad categories: theological, ecclesiological, financial, and strategic.

The theological differences between the television preachers and their mainline critics are numerous, stemming in large measure from different understandings of the nature of scripture and the educational and other socializing experiences that have given rise to and resulted from these differences. The gospel of the electronic church, its critics say, is simplistic, amounting to little more than a proclamation that Jesus saves and a promise that accepting him as one's personal savior is not only painless but guaranteed to bring complete satisfaction in this life and the life to come. The charge is something of a caricature, but it is undeniably the case that the gospel according to evangelicals is less complex than that of the mainliners. Part of the reason is a pervasive evangelical conviction that the gospel was never intended to be an abstruse message comprehensible to only the intellectually sophisticated. On the contrary, it is explicitly "the simple gospel," the "old, old story," the "foolishness of God" that destroys the wisdom of the wise and thwarts the cleverness of the clever.

This predisposition to simplicity is exacerbated by the nature of radio and television, which specialize in messages that can be grasped easily by people giving less than full attention and that, if not grasped and accepted, can be tuned out in an instant. In their desire to attract and hold an audience, the critics charge, religious broadcasters have not just simplified the old, old story; they have changed its essential nature, offering cheap grace, salvation without sacrifice, the crown without the cross. Without question, the electronic church is vulnerable to these criticisms. The emphasis of many programs on success and celebrity stands in garish contrast to the portrayal and proclamations of the prophets, Jesus, and his apostles in the Bible. Oral Roberts repeatedly recalls that his mother told him to "be like Jesus," but can we expect to see Brother Roberts visit on-camera with a leper, a prostitute, or an undersized tax collector? Can we seriously imagine a charismatic talk show in which guests explain that faith in Christ has given their lives hope and meaning despite the fact they are still arthritic, blind, or dying of cancer? Will Robert Schuller ever showcase a believer who has truly sold all that he had and given it to the poor and now, like the Son of Man, has nowhere to lay his head? And if Jesus, who shunned fame and power as satanic traps and said rather more about self-denial than prosperity, came back today, would he again choose his envoys from the common people, or would he surround himself with beauty queens, running backs, militaristic politicians, pop and country singers, wealthy entrepreneurs, ventriloquists who speak in tongues, and born-again yo-yo champions? And instead of warning them to expect persecution and martyrdom, would he tell them, "Something *good* is going to happen to you! God has a wonderful plan for your life!"? The involvement of the television preachers in a medium designed primarily for entertainment has no doubt contributed significantly to their rush toward celebrity and consumer religion.

Television, however, is not solely to blame; nor are these men the first preachers to tickle the ears and delight the eyes of their congregations. Almost all major American evangelists have been skilled actors and showmen and have heeded Charles Grandison Finney's dictum that "the common sense people will be entertained." [14] They have drawn their crowds not simply with the preaching of the gospel but with stories that tingled the spine and tugged at the heart, with choristers who imitated locomotives and played the trombone, with prominent politicians and fabled tycoons, and, indeed, long before television, with entertainers and athletes and reformed scoundrels and heroes of every sort. If they have reflected long enough to ask how Jesus would react to such tactics, they have allayed misgiving with the conviction that he would delight in the crowds. The crowds, in turn, have delighted in the tangible evidence that it was possible both to enjoy the pleasures of the world and to move up with the Master.

Evangelicals, of course, are not the first Christians to have found a way to embrace the dominant culture. Many members of mainline churches have known the secret for years, and their disdain for the evangelicals' consumer religion is sometimes rooted as much in class and regional bias as in theology.

A second theological criticism raised against the television preachers is that they address themselves overwhelmingly to a narrow range of personal problems, displaying a lamentable lack of concern to apply the gospel to major social issues. This charge is perhaps most true of men like Oral Roberts, Ernest Angley, and other members of the healing-and-blessing fraternity who confine their attention to little more than the cure of physical and emotional problems and the promise of material abundance. It is of such limited truth when applied to numerous others that one wonders if the critics have paid much serious attention to what the objects of their criticism have been saying and doing for years. And, of course, though it was once raised against them, it is patently inapplicable to men like Jerry Falwell and James Robison and is no longer made against them.

Perhaps the most serious shortcoming of the charge that religious broadcasters, and evangelicals as a group, are overly concerned with personal needs and personal problems is an apparently insufficient realization that personal needs are real, often critical, and may have to be dealt with before individuals can begin to reflect on larger theological issues or address major social problems. Speaking to an audience composed largely of his critics, Pat Robertson observed that the Christian Broadcasting Network's counseling centers received about 1,397,000 calls in 1979. "Of these calls," he said, "not one person asked us about the theology of Barth, Tillich, or Reinhold Niebuhr, or about any . . . theological problem. They did say, 'My mother is a prostitute. What can I do?' 'My father committed incest with me when I was young. How do I avoid hating him?' 'My husband beats me up and has left me and the children. Can you help me?' and 3,955 said, 'We are getting ready to end our life. Is there some hope and answer?'"[15]

Furthermore, widespread personal problems are also social problems. When the television preachers or other evangelical Christians express deep concern over alcohol and drug abuse, nonmarital sex, pornography, homosexuality, abortion, divorce, and child abuse, they are dealing with problems that have enormous social consequences. And whether or not one agrees with the positions they are likely to take, it is obvious that neither their mainline critics nor the wicked "secular humanists" have been remarkably effective in providing the nation with clear solutions to these problems and issues.

Finally, one can hardly miss the irony of a situation in which, castigated for decades because of their inattention to major social issues, evangelical spokesmen have proved to be much more unsettling and alarming when they did address them. It may be, as Colin Williams has observed, that the growing concern with social issues among such men as Falwell and Robison is not the result of deep or thoughtful analysis but part of an attempt to draw on widespread feelings of estrangement from the political processes. Their promise of an "immediate fix," Williams said, is not essentially different from similar promises that have long been the stock-in-trade of revivalist preachers.[16] It is surely true that the effects of possible success are hard to predict. One who has been socialized to think in terms of peaceful coexistence, progressive education, extensive social welfare, rehabilitation of disadvantaged lawbreakers, and reliance on government as the great regulator and benefactor is apt to become uneasy at the thought of a further American turn to the right. But if the new conservatism leads to an unstable political and economic situation, problems with energy and other nonrenewable resources, high rates of unemployment, excessive crime and violence, misuse of alcohol and drugs, more broken families, and increased greed and selfishness, it would still be possible, barring all-out war, to go back to the old way of doing things.

Before moving to other criticisms, I would like to offer several observations based on unsystematic personal research. Those who have criticized the simplicity and consumer mentality of the electronic church often speak as if their own denominations offered a sharp contrast to it. This implication should not be accepted without reservation. It is unquestionably the case that, on the average, mainline ministers have a broader theological education than their evangelical counterparts. But that does not always translate into profound preaching. In the course of preparing a regular column for *Texas Monthly* magazine, I visit at least two churches each month. Although there are exceptions to the rule, the rule itself is clear: the thinnest, least theological preaching is in mainline churches, particularly in Episcopal, Methodist, and Roman Catholic churches. A discouraging number of pastors in these churches are given not to the discussion of basic biblical themes or key issues in contemporary theology or the application of the gospel to pressing social issues, but to anecdotal sermons with titles such as "Ten Top Tips for Tip-Top Christians." As for involvement of the church in social issues, it is true that the official leaders of the mainline denominations have consistently addressed themselves to key issues and have attempted to mobilize their members in support of positions that differed from those that appeared to be guiding the larger society. It is also true, unhappily, that they have been mightily resisted in these efforts and that their success in turning their denominations from their own, perhaps higher-class version of consumer Christianity has not been remarkable.

Ecclesiological criticisms of the electronic church cluster around two basic contentions. First, it is argued, an electronic church is no church at all, since it does not gather people into Christian community. By encouraging them to sit at home and listen to the radio or watch television instead of involving themselves in a real church, it deprives them of the spiritual and emotional growth that comes from engagement with live people and tangible problems and from the influence in society that believers can have only in community. It also leaves them without the succor and aid of the church when they are in need, since television preachers do not make house calls. Second, by keeping people at home, the electronic church is said to injure real churches by diminishing their numbers and, therefore, their capacity to function as effectively as they ought.

These charges have a surface plausibility, but available data offer scant justification for such fears. Gallup's *Profile of the Christian Marketplace* survey reported that 9.1 percent of the general public did indicate that their involvement in the church had lessened as a result of viewing religious television programs, but 12.1 percent said religious television had spurred them into greater involvement. Most (70 percent) said the programs had made no difference, almost half (40 percent) of those who say they are less involved because of religious television have never made a commitment to Christ in the first place, and a clear majority are not avid fans of religious programming.[17] Furthermore, evangelical theology quite explicitly prescribes involvement in a church as an essential aspect of Christian faith and practice, and no major television preacher indicates that watching his program and supporting his ministry constitute adequate Christian discipleship.

The mainliners' fear that the television preachers are inducing people to stay home from church stems in part from their concern over the precipitous decline in membership within their own churches. Perhaps those missing from the fold are staying home to watch Oral Roberts or Jerry Falwell, or perhaps they have been rustled by sheep-stealing, smooth-talking TV preachers who have transferred them into the several evangelical denominations whose membership is staying even with or even running ahead of population growth. Again, such suspicions have a surface plausibility, but recent research indicates that the decline in liberal churches is less a matter of members dropping out than of a failure to attract new members to replace those lost by death and other normal forms of attrition.[18] These churches are holding on to older members reasonably well, but they are not attracting—in anything like the numbers they once did—young adults under forty, especially those educated in secular colleges and universities and therefore fully exposed to the sweeping value shifts that surfaced in the 1960s. These young people, whose values include emphasis on personal freedom, acceptance of diversity, resistance to authority, and distance from traditional institutions, feel little need to belong to any church, much less to a conservative church espousing values so opposed to theirs. And they give little evidence that they pay much attention to religious broadcasters.[19]

The churches that have grown have been able to attract and hold

William Martin

their young people, most of whom live in the more culturally homogeneous South and Midwest and are less well-educated, less cosmopolitan, and of a lower socioeconomic status than their peers who have dropped out of the mainline churches. These characteristics have helped insulate them from the cultural shifts that have affected so many of their peers so profoundly and have enabled them to maintain loyalty to the values of their parents. It is possible, perhaps probable, that diffusion of the values that have weakened mainline churches will eventually have a comparable result in evangelical churches—indeed that is precisely what organizations like Moral Majority fear and fight so vehemently. For the time being, however, evangelicals are holding out and holding their own.[20]

The studies on membership decline also indicate that the claim that the television preachers are wooing large numbers of people away from liberal churches and funneling them into Fundamentalist churches is groundless. Members of the age group who constitute the largest segment of the audience for the broadcast ministries—people over 50—are the very ones who are staying with the mainline churches. Those who are leaving or failing to join these churches—well-educated, mobile, affluent young people—are the ones who have demonstrated the least inclination to listen and respond to the message of the media ministers or to accept the beliefs, discipline, and distinctive life-style of evangelical Christianity. Doubtless, some shifts in allegiance of the sort feared by mainline church leaders and claimed by the television preachers do occur. For the most part, however, both groups seem to have scored a clean miss.[21]

Finally, the specter of local churches decimated by the electronic church becomes even less credible when one recalls that the audience for these programs appears to be diminishing rather than growing.

Financial criticisms of the television preachers focus on the ways they raise and spend money and on their competition with the local church for the Christian dollar. The most important financial question about the electronic church is that of its direct effect on the finances of the local church.

It seems almost fatuous to suggest that the funneling of hundreds of millions of dollars into television ministries would not have an ad-

184

verse effect on local church budgets, especially since most of the money is given by church members. But that may in fact be the case. The key to making sense of such an apparently illogical assertion is to remember that this is not a zero-sum situation, in which a certain amount of money is set aside for contributions to various recipients and any amount given to one diminishes the amount available to another. Instead, there exists a donor pool comprising people known to be generous in their contributions to churches and related causes and willing to make cuts in other areas of their budgets to enable them to give more to these causes.

It is obviously true that money sent to a television ministry could have gone to a local church. But it is not clear that it would have. The money garnered by the media ministers does not just fall into their laps. It is cultivated and harvested with some of the most sophisticated fund-raising techniques in existence, and there is no overriding reason to believe it would go to local churches had these techniques not been used. Perhaps more important, what little evidence exists on the question does not provide much cause for panic on the part of the churches. According to Gallup's *Christian Marketplace* study, only 1.5 percent of the public named religious radio or television as their first choice for a charitable donation, in marked contrast to the 43.1 percent who named churches or mission efforts. In addition, only 2.3 percent said they contributed to religious radio or television more than once a year. It appears, then, that the bulk of the support for religious broadcasting comes from a dedicated corps of 2 to 3.5 million donors, some of whom doubtless give in a manner that is truly sacrificial.[22] It is even plausible that television ministries raise the level of awareness of the need for giving and thereby increase rather than decrease contributions to the local church. There are serious questions of ethics and stewardship that need to be asked of the electronic church, but it is not yet clear that it is a serious drain on church coffers.

A final type of complaint about the electronic church stems ultimately from a long-standing media strategy that has backfired on the mainline churches. Almost from the beginning of commercial radio, that strategy has had two major aspects. First, since the Federal Communications Commission requires radio and television stations to offer a certain amount of so-called public-interest programming and since it includes religious programming in the public interest category, the mainline churches, represented by the National Council of Churches, have insisted on the right to receive free airtime for religious programs. Second, utilizing its gatekeeper position with NBC and its influence with the other networks, the council not only managed to deny evangelicals access to most of the free time made available for religious programming but encouraged the networks' refusal or reluctance to sell time to those broadcasters willing to pay for it.

This two-pronged strategy gave mainliners a near monopoly over religious programming on network radio and television (particularly on NBC and CBS) and was doubtless a source of considerable satisfaction to those who believed the public was best served by non-Fundamentalist religious fare. It contained a serious flaw, however. It did not reckon with evangelical Christianity's unrelenting impulse to evangelize, to preach the gospel by whatever means available. Denied the favored treatment the mainline churches were receiving, evangelical broadcasters scrapped and scrounged and survived by setting up *ad hoc* networks, syndicating recorded broadcasts, and buying time on local radio and television outlets. But things began to turn their way in 1960. Station owners understandably liked being paid for time they might otherwise have given away free, and that year, when the FCC announced that paid religious broadcasts could satisfy its public-interest requirement as well as nonpaid programs, evangelicals suddenly found it even easier to buy time, while mainliners, if they were able to obtain free time at all, were given the least favorable slots. By 1980 over 90 percent of all religious broadcasts were paid broadcasts, and the vast majority of those were evangelical in nature.

Predictably, the mainline churches have been unhappy with these developments. They continue to maintain that broadcast licenses are a public trust and that those who receive them have an obligation to donate time to broadcasts that will serve the public. Certain religious and ethical views, they contend, need exposure in the public media but cannot be expected to attract financial support for production and airtime costs. Because broadcast licenses are a public trust, they insist, those who receive them have an obligation to facilitate such programming. If the present trends continue, they complain, groups holding unpopular views and those too poor to pay for broadcasts will not be able to get on the air, and the public will be denied the diversity of viewpoints it needs and deserves.

One can appreciate the official position of the National Council of Churches and the mainline groups it represents. The public is best served by a wide range of viewpoints, and I would like to see more religious programs that offer an alternative to the evangelical broadcasters. At the same time, my residual evangelical innards derive some satisfaction from watching mainline church leaders squirm over the outcome of their own policies, which arose from an effort to reduce the diversity of religious programming by shutting out those views they found unacceptable. For their part, evangelical broadcasters have made no apparently retaliatory effort to squeeze out liberal Protestant programming, but they are not meeting the needs of the people as well as are the evangelical churches. Pat Robertson observes that part of the success of evangelical broadcasts comes from the fact that these programs give people what they want instead of "just standing around wringing our hands about the success of the electronic church." Ben Armstrong, who has stood at the point in numerous confrontations with mainline critics, conceals his gloating delight less subtly: "We have won," he says. "People are much more willing to watch and listen to our kind of programs—and pay for them." [23]

Alarmed by declines in their own membership and impressed by the apparent success of the television preachers, mainline churches are beginning to show a willingness to pay for airtime, if necessary, and to utilize mass media in a more aggressive manner. The efficacy of such efforts is difficult to predict, but optimism should be guarded. Difficult as it may be to accept, there is considerable evidence that the electronic mass media are not particularly effective instruments of evangelization. Because the audience for evangelical broadcasts is not only modest but composed largely of active church members, and since less than 5 percent of the 61 million unchurched Americans discovered by a Gallup survey could recall ever having watched a television preacher other than Oral Roberts (12 percent) or Billy Graham (11 percent), the usefulness of the broadcasts as tools of evangelism—the primary justification used to raise money—must be seriously questioned. There is no compelling reason to believe that churches unable to hold people who have been reared in their midst (which is the case with most mainline churches) will be able to attract people by using a medium that has proved to have limited evangelistic value even for thriving denominations. Most people come into the church over natural bridges—at the urging and invitation of relatives and friends. Since that is the case, mainline denominations expecting television to halt their dispiriting decline might do well to heed Martin Marty's advice: "It's far better for churches to get their members off their butts and go out and bring people in than to go through the electronic media."[24]

To say that religious radio and television programming, as now utilized, are evangelistic tools of limited effectiveness for American audiences is not to say they bring no benefits at all to the evangelical community. In numerous ways they doubtless strengthen and deepen the faith of listeners by providing them with instruction, exhortation, inspiration, hope, encouragement, entertainment, example, and opportunity for service. They also serve a symbolic function of considerable importance. Evangelical Christianity has experienced real growth in recent years, to be sure, but a high proportion of those 47 million evangelicals were out there before the pollsters and the media discovered them. When the Jesus movement, the charismatic movement, and Jimmy Carter's announcement that he had been "born again" brought them more publicity than they had known since the dark days of the Scopes trial, they burst out of the closet with an energy and enthusiasm that surprised everyone, including themselves. The great growth of religious broadcasting not only reflects this aggressive spirit but helps maintain it. Evangelicals notice that virtually all the religion on radio and television is their kind of religion, that the secular media are fascinated with it, and that liberal Christians are panicked by it. The buoyant confidence produced by the realization that they are no longer a beleaguered backwater minority but a significant, thriving part of mainstream American Christianity has led to a greater willingness to share their faith with others and to increased efforts to strengthen and consolidate their gains by such means as the establishment of Christian schools to control the socialization of evangelical children, the publishing of Christian Yellow Pages to encourage evangelicals to support each other economically, and the formation of such organizations as Moral Majority and Christian Voice to influence elections and legislation. It would be difficult to determine precisely what effect the television preachers have on these processes, but the prominence of their participation in them is such that they surely deserve a significant share of the responsibility for them. Thus, even though they may produce few direct conversions, their role in the growth and apparent robust health of evangelical Christianity may be quite significant indeed. And that may well assure the electronic church a congregation sufficient to keep those cards and letters coming in.

NOTES

1. Ben Armstrong, *The Electric Church* (Nashville, 1979), 7.

2. Dudley Clendenin, "Christian New Right's Rush to Power," New York *Times,* August 18, 1980; Jonathan Kaufman, "Old-Time Religion," *Wall Street Journal,* July 11, 1980; "Preachers in Politics: Decisive Force in the 1980s?" *U.S. News and World Report,* September 15, 1980, p. 25; UPI, "Electric Church Stirs Less-Than-Holy Debate," Houston *Post,* December 8, 1979; Louis Gorfain, "Pray TV," *New York,* October 6, 1980, pp. 48, 56; "The Great Alternative," *Saturday Evening Post* (May–June, 1977), unpaginated offprint.

3. L. J. Davis, "Onward Christian Soldiers," *Penthouse* (February, 1981), 5, 59; Johnny Greene, "The Astonishing Wrongs of the New Moral Right," *Playboy* (January, 1981), 258; Jimmy Breslin, "Born-again Unease over Born-again Pols," Los Angeles *Times,* August 25, 1980; "Today," NBC-TV, May 5, 1980; "Campaign Report No. 3," *Bill Moyers' Journal,* WNET/Thirteen, September 26, 1980; Joseph F. Sullivan, "Fundamentalist at State House Warns Liberals," New York *Times,* November 11, 1980; Anthony Lewis, "Religion and Politics," New York *Times,* September 19, 1980; "A Tide of Born-again Politics," *Newsweek,* September 15, 1980, p. 28; "Falwell's Moral Majority— A Force to Be Reckoned With," Houston *Post,* September 27, 1980; Dudley Clendenin, "Rev. Falwell Inspires Evangelical Vote," New York *Times,* August 20, 1980.

4. William F. Fore, "There Is No Such Thing as a TV Pastor," *TV Guide,* July 19, 1980, pp. 15; James M. Wall, "The New Right Comes of Age," *Christian Century,* October 22, 1980, p. 56.

5. Allen Cowan and Frye Gaillard, "PTL Donations for Foreign Missions Used at Home," Charlotte *Observer,* January 8, 1979; Promotional literature of the Rex Humbard Foundation (Cuyahoga Falls, Ohio, June, 1979); Rex Humbard Foundation, "News for Release" (Akron, Ohio, 1980); Sullivan, "Fundamentalist at State House Warns Liberals"; *A Call to Arms . . . of Christian Love,* brochure of the James Robison Evangelistic Association (Fort Worth, n.d.); James Robison to supporters, December 5, 1980; Frances Swaggart to supporters, February 16, 1981; Bert Clendennen, various radio broadcasts, *ca.* 1972–74.

6. Gallup Organization, *Evangelical Christianity in the United States* (Princeton, 1978), 44.

7. Gallup Organization, *Profile of the Christian Marketplace, 1980* (Newport Beach, Calif., 1980), 22–30, with accompanying tables.

8. Gallup Organization, *Evangelical Christianity in the United States,* 43; Gallup Organization, *Profile of the Christian Marketplace, 1980,* pp. 22–30.

9. Gallup Organization, *Profile of the Christian Marketplace, 1980,* pp. 22–30; A. C. Nielsen Company, *Report on Syndicated Programs* (November, 1980); Arbitron, Inc., *Syndicated Program Analysis* (November, 1980).

10. Gallup Organization, *Religion in America: The Gallup Opinion Index, 1977–1978* (Princeton, 1978), Report No. 145.

11. Gallup Organization, *Evangelical Christianity in the United States.*

12. Nielsen Company, *Report on Syndicated Programs* (November, 1980); Gallup Organization, *Evangelical Christianity in the United States,* 43.

13. Nielsen Company, *Report on Syndicated Programs* (February, 1977–November, 1980).

14. Charles G. Finney, *Lectures on Revivals of Religion* (1835; rpr. Cambridge, 1960), 220.

15. M. G. "Pat" Robertson, address at National Council of Churches consultation on the Electronic Church (New York City, February, 1980).

16. Colin Williams, address at NCC consultation on the Electronic Church.

17. Gallup Organization, *Profile of the Christian Marketplace* (1980), 28.

18. See, for example, Dean R. Hoge and David A. Roozen (eds.), *Understanding Church Growth and Decline, 1950–1978* (New York, 1979). See also Carl S. Dudley, *Where Have All Our People Gone?* (New York, 1979).

19. Gallup Organization, *The Unchurched American* (Princeton, 1978), 58, 60.

20. Hoge and Roozen (eds.), *Understanding Church Growth and Decline;* Dudley, *Where Have All Our People Gone?*

21. Hoge and Roozen (eds.), *Understanding Church Growth and Decline;* Dudley, *Where Have All Our People Gone?*

22. Gallup Organization, *Profile of the Christian Marketplace* (1980), 47–58.

23. Robertson, address at NCC consultation on the Electronic Church; Ben Armstrong, quoted in Allan Sloan and Anne Bagamery, "The Electronic Pulpit," *Forbes* (July 7, 1980), p. 118.

24. Gallup Organization, *The Unchurched American,* 57–58; Martin Marty, quoted in Margaret Yao, "Big Pitch for God: More Churches Try Advertising in Media," *Wall Street Journal,* December 31, 1979, p. 10.

RELIGIOUS CHANGE IN THE AMERICAN SOUTH: THE CASE OF THE UNCHURCHED
Wade Clark Roof

Commentators over the years have spoken frequently of the distinctive features of southern religious life. "Almost every observer of the South has, sooner or later," according to Joseph Fichter and George Maddox, "recorded impressions about the pervasiveness and peculiarity of religious behavior and institutions in the region."[1] Views of religion in the South—not unlike those of the region generally—typically stress the theme of continuity. In scholarly as well as journalistic interpretation southern piety is portrayed as an enduring religiocultural complex seemingly impervious to change. Elsewhere in the modern world religious changes and secular trends may be rampant, but in Dixie the "old-time religion" supposedly persists and orthodoxy reigns supreme.

To be sure, there is much continuity. In the 1980s religion in Dixie is still characterized by high visibility, strong conservatism, and moral traditionalism. National polls and surveys document the South's continuing distinctive religiocultural features; despite mass cultural trends there is still a definite regional religious ethos and style.[2] Methodists and Baptists dominate the religious landscape, much as in the past. Although there have been some shifts in religious affiliations, these two historic bodies still exercise a disproportionate influence over the region. In addition, the "new evangelicalism," more polished and accommodating than the old, finds greater receptivity in the South than elsewhere in the nation.[3] What is truly remarkable about the South, and the Sun Belt generally, is that, though it welcomes new technologies and new migrants, regional ideologies and loyalties are not seriously undermined.

Yet, one should not be blind to the changes that do exist. Often the changes are subtle and pertain more to the relations between religion and culture than to institutional dynamics. Shifts in values and beliefs are less apparent than shifts in consumer behavior and lifestyles, but nonetheless they are crucial aspects of change. Especially in a setting such as the American South, the forces of modernity confront traditional norms and beliefs and in the process generate new and more pluralistic systems of meaning. Typically, religion becomes more privatized in modern life, more a matter of personal preference and choice and less bound by custom and convention.[4] Subtle shifts in values and outlook are likely to be overlooked in the polls and surveys. The simple fact is that though social scientists have gathered a substantial body of data on the "externals" of the southern religious establishment, on denominational bodies and church life, far less is known about the "internals," or the views of southerners toward religion, its role, and its significance in personal and social life, and it is the internals that have undergone the significant changes.

In this essay I shall explore some of these changes by examining the unchurched people of the South. Much attention recently has been given to the unchurched in America, especially their life-styles, values, beliefs, and moral attitudes.[5] The extent to which the churched and unchurched populations differ in their outlook is of growing interest in a highly pluralistic society and something that many commentators point to as a significant index of cultural and religious change. There is increasing concern about the rise of a more polarized culture, about an emerging cleavage between the two sectors—the traditional religious sector versus a more secular one. If nothing else, interest in the topic represents a new slant on the study of religion and promises to yield additional insights into the changing social location of traditional church-oriented religion in contemporary society.

To date there have been few studies of the unchurched in the South. In the past their numbers have been judged to be few. Religion has been so much a part of the culture that it was taken for granted; its visibility and presence were recognized as features of southern life. Many have observed the significance in the South of membership in a church and participation in religious activities. Francis Butler Simkins, for instance, observed that the region "forces religious conformity in a subtle and effective way, irritating the visitor by asking, 'To what church do you belong?' If the answer is 'no church whatever,' the southerner turns away bewildered. Unless he is widely read or widely traveled, he can scarcely conceive of a person who is decent in dress, manners, and morals, and who has no church inclinations."[6] Although bordering on caricature, this depiction is accurate enough. Virtually all the conventional religious indicators point to the South as a traditional, church-centered culture: high levels of institutional religious affiliation, large numbers of churches per unit of population, greater religious attendance than elsewhere in the nation, more positive attitudes toward churches, and strong belief that involvement within the institution is a prerequisite for being a good Christian.[7] Of all the regions of the country, the South best approximates a righteous empire.

The South's church-centered culture is all the more striking in view of the popular, low-church religious styles that have dominated the region. Popular southern Protestantism embraced southern culture, creating strong bonds linking the South's regional and religious identities. Because of their close alliance, pressures to affiliate with the religious establishment and to conform to church norms have been generated broadly in the culture. As Samuel Hill has argued in his perceptive essay "The South's Two Cultures," for a southerner not to line himself up with the church is to fail to ratify the churches' ultimate legitimation of the southern cultural heritage itself. Hill writes: "Cultural forces give the unchurched person the impression that he is somehow a threat to the entire society, a traitor to the cause, an inauthentic member of the regional community. Accordingly, the white southerner must belong to the church for the sake of establishing the solidarity and legitimacy of his culture."[8] Thus, the affinity between regionality and religiosity is of considerable significance in traditional southern life. So great are the bonds between them that it is impossible to understand one without the other.

For this very reason, then, the study of the unchurched takes on particular significance in the southern setting. In a time of rapid social change, the possibility of a breakdown of the South's cultural bonds between regionality and religiosity is very real. As regional self-consciousness declines, especially among the younger and more cosmopolitan groups in the South, there will likely be shifts in church-related behaviors and attitudes. Religious meanings once taken for granted as part of the fabric of regional life will likely lose some of their motivational and legitimizing force. Hill himself has pondered this possibility: "As Southernness becomes less important, uncritical subscription and loyalty to church religion is apt to follow a parallel course. This constitutes the crisis of the southern churches."[9] The implication is clear: regional change threatens to undermine the basis for membership in and loyalty to a church. Affinity between regionality and religiosity makes for religious vulnerability in a time of disjointedness. With the exposure of the regional cultural foundations of southern piety, the operative beliefs and norms of the South's religiosity are themselves threatened.

Given the likelihood that this is the case, I propose to look at the unchurched as character types embodying social and cultural change. Several questions about the southern unchurched are worth examining: 1) How do they compare with the unchurched elsewhere in relative size and social characteristics? 2) Are there differences in religious attitudes and styles between the southern and the non-southern unchurched? 3) Is there evidence of an increasing cultural gap between the churched and the unchurched in the South? Answers to these questions should shed some light on the religious changes occurring in the region. Moreover, the answers should lead to a better understanding of the social and cultural correlates of religious change, and the degree to which southern patterns are similar to and different from national trends.

The data on which the following analysis is based are taken from a special Gallup survey of unchurched Americans.[10] Administered in 1978, the survey was designed to gather information on the more than 40 percent of adult Americans who can be described as unchurched. It included a wide range of questions, thereby allowing detailed comparisons of the churched and the unchurched on matters of beliefs, values, and institutional affiliations. Interviews were carried out with 1,523 Americans selected from a probability sampling of the adult (eighteen years of age and older), civilian, noninstitutionalized population in the continental United States.

The religious profile of the sample was as follows: 60 percent Protestant, 27 percent Catholic, 2 percent Jewish, 1 percent Eastern Orthodox, 2 percent other religions, and 8 percent no religion. The regional breakdown was 27 percent southern and 73 percent non-southern. For the present analysis, nonwhites were eliminated, leaving a total sample of 1,371 persons. It seemed appropriate to limit the study to whites, since they make up the dominant culture.

In the original study, an *unchurched person* was operationally defined as one who was not a member of a church or synagogue or who was a member but had not attended church or synagogue in the previous six months, apart from weddings, funerals, or special holidays such as Christmas, Easter, or Yom Kippur. This definition combines notions both of institutional membership and religious participation, offering a more composite index of church involvement than the usual single indicators of religious commitment. Following common usage in Gallup research, the study defined the South as the eleven ex-Confederate states plus Kentucky and Oklahoma. Other regions are the East, Midwest, and West.

To begin with, there are fewer unchurched in the South than elsewhere. But regional differences are not large—certainly not as large as traditional stereotypes of the South might lead us to expect. The survey revealed the following general proportions of unchurched by region:

East	45%
Midwest	43%
West	53%
South	41%

Except for the West, differences among the regions are small. The South differs from the Midwest by two points, from the East by four points. Overall, the degree of similarity of southern and nonsouthern patterns is striking; there appears to be little demographic basis for believing that there are widespread differences between the southern and the nonsouthern unchurched. Perhaps differences were greater in the past, but they are no longer sizable.

If the unchurched are found in large numbers just about everywhere, are they also similar in social and demographic characteristics across regions? Dissimilarity would suggest a distinctive regional heritage; whereas similarity would point to broad national trends. The greater the convergence of regional patterns, the more likely it is that widespread secular changes are responsible for the large number of defectors from churches throughout the society. Table 1 illustrates various characteristics of the churched and the unchurched of the South and the rest of the nation.

Previous research on the unchurched has shown that gender and age are two of the best predictors of institutional religious defection. Males and young persons under thirty-five years of age are more

Table 1   Background Characteristics of the Churched and Unchurched in Percentages

	SOUTHERN		NONSOUTHERN	
	Churched (N = 210)	Unchurched (N = 132)	Churched (N = 553)	Unchurched (N = 450)
Age				
18–34	33	46	32	45
35–54	27	34	37	30
55 and over	40	20	31	25
Gender				
Male	44	55	42	56
Female	56	45	58	44
Education				
Grade school	28	27	20	16
High school	35	42	27	35
College	37	31	53	49
Years in present community				
1 year or less	12	20	10	17
2–5 years	16	30	17	17
6–19 years	27	18	29	32
20 or more	45	32	44	35
Number of relocations in past five years				
None	61	43	67	53
One	16	22	18	21
Two or more	23	35	15	26
Income				
Less than $7,000	26	26	18	20
$7,000–$15,000	32	34	26	27
$15,000–$20,000	20	17	21	23
$20,000 or more	22	23	35	30
Occupation				
Professional and managerial	17	12	18	19
Clerical and sales	8	7	13	11
Skilled trade	6	14	9	12
Semiskilled and laborers	10	13	6	15
Homemakers	26	15	27	19
Retired	20	14	14	12
Other	13	25	13	12

inclined to abandon religious affiliation. These patterns hold in almost identical proportion in the South and elsewhere: 55 percent of the southern unchurched are male, compared with 56 percent of the nonsouthern unchurched, and 46 percent of the southern unchurched are under thirty-five, compared with 45 percent of the nonsouthern unchurched. Noteworthy is the fact that regional differences increase with age; that is, among young respondents the percentage of those belonging to a church is quite similar across regions, whereas for older persons southern patterns are more distinctive. Generally, it seems that gender and age affect religious belonging about equally across the regions.

Another important correlate of the unchurched is geographic mobility. Data on number of years lived in the community and number of times relocated show the unchurched to be more mobile than the churched, and the southern unchurched even more so than the nonsouthern. A total of 35 percent of the southern unchurched have moved two or more times in the past five years; among the nonsouthern unchurched only 26 percent have done so. Wherever it occurs, geographic mobility disrupts community and institutional ties and thus undermines bonds linking individuals to stable social networks. In a region marked by an expanding rate of population movement, such as the South, there are, not surprisingly, high levels of religious defection associated with mobility. That this tendency shows up so clearly in the South is indicative of the broad sweep of changes now under way in the region.

Education is also important. Generally the churched have more education than the unchurched, since church membership in America has traditionally been more common for the higher-status, better educated groups. Although educational levels are lower on the average in the South, educational differences between the churched and the unchurched are much the same inside and outside the region. Whatever the secularizing potential of education, clearly its impact is not limited to any one part of the country.

Thus, there appears to be a common pattern of the unchurched across America. The southern unchurched differ only in minor respects. In terms of their social and demographic characteristics— their similarities to the unchurched in other regions are far more pronounced than their differences. However important belonging to a church may have been in the South in the past, there seems to be little basis for assuming a distinctive regional pattern at present. The evidence at hand suggests the presence of secular trends cutting across the regions, and common social experiences throughout America linked to religious disaffiliation.

How different are the unchurched from the churched in matters of belief and religious experience? Are there regional patterns of personal religiosity? To say that someone is unchurched does not necessarily imply a lack of personal belief or moral values or even a lack of religious seriousness and commitment. In modern America, where religious meanings are highly privatized and tailored to individual preferences, it is altogether possible for someone to abandon the institutional church and yet at the same time hold on to a strong personal faith. Evidence suggests that many Americans—probably growing numbers of them—have done just that: in effect, they are believers but not belongers. They still adhere to many traditional beliefs and practices without maintaining close institutional church ties.

Considering the broad sweep of cultural changes in the nation, there is every reason to believe that the privatization of religion occurs across regions. Fortunately, the data collected in the 1978 Gallup survey included various measures of religiosity, such as traditional beliefs, religious experiences, attitudes toward organized religion and privatized religious views and practices (see Tables 2–5). With so wide a range of religious indicators, it is possible to examine privatization in the culture broadly and to look closely at varying religious styles.

A comparison of the regions suggests there is less, not more, of a gap between the churched and the unchurched within the South on matters of traditional belief than elsewhere. That is, in beliefs about Jesus, the Resurrection, and life after death, there is somewhat greater homogeneity in the South; even the unchurched of the region are strong believers. But on one belief item, the gap between churched and unchurched is quite large, greater in the South than in either the East or the Midwest—belief in the literal interpretation of the Bible. Differences between the southern churched and unchurched on this issue amount to 24 percentage points. On this article of Fundamentalist faith, the spread is great enough to challenge any assumption that there is an orthodox consensus throughout the region. Only the

199

Table 2 Traditional Beliefs of the Churched and Unchurched by Region

	BELIEF THAT JESUS WAS GOD OR SON OF GOD		BELIEF IN RESURRECTION OF CHRIST		BELIEF IN LITERAL INTERPRETATION OF BIBLE		BELIEF IN LIFE AFTER DEATH	
	Percent	Difference	Percent	Difference	Percent	Difference	Percent	Difference
East								
Churched (N = 213)	84	27	90	31	30	12	77	30
Unchurched (N = 171)	57		59		18		47	
Midwest								
Churched (N = 237)	93	23	95	18	46	15	88	26
Unchurched (N = 180)	70		77		31		62	
West								
Churched (N = 103)	93	39	95	18	50	28	85	26
Unchurched (N = 114)	54		77		22		59	
South								
Churched (N = 210)	93	17	95	19	53	24	90	26
Unchurched (N = 143)	76		76		29		64	

Table 3 Religious Experiences of the Churched and Unchurched by Region

	REPORTING HAVING HAD RELIGIOUS EXPERIENCE		REPORTING HAVING HAD "BORN-AGAIN" EXPERIENCE		REPORTING HAVING MADE COMMITMENT TO JESUS	
	Percent	Difference	Percent	Difference	Percent	Difference
East						
Churched (N = 213)	33	15	24	10	66	37
Unchurched (N = 171)	18		14		29	
Midwest						
Churched (N = 237)	35	11	41	15	84	41
Unchurched (N = 180)	24		26		43	
West						
Churched (N = 103)	50	17	46	20	82	45
Unchurched (N = 114)	33		26		37	
South						
Churched (N = 210)	56	30	64	30	83	35
Unchurched (N = 143)	26		34		48	

Table 4 Attitudes of the Unchurched Toward Organized Religion

	PERCENTAGE OF SOUTHERNERS (N = 143)	PERCENTAGE OF NONSOUTHERNERS (N = 465)
Church or synagogue morality too restrictive	37	34
Church or synagogue not accepting toward outsiders	46	37
Church or synagogue too concerned with organizational as opposed to spiritual issues	58	57
Church or synagogue not enough concerned with social justice	41	38
Church or synagogue not effective in helping people find meaning	52	49

West, with its more polarized religious and secular cultures, has a wider gap on this point.

Concerning religious experiences, the gap becomes even greater for southerners. In self-reported religious and "born-again" experiences, differences between the churched and unchurched are greater in the South than anywhere else. A total of 64 percent of the southern churched, compared with the 34 percent of the unchurched, said they have been "born again." In the other regions, differences did not measure more than 20 percentage points. Despite high levels of experiential religion in the South generally, differences between the churched and the unchurched are quite apparent.

Perhaps the most striking findings are those concerning attitudes toward organized religion and privatized forms of religiosity. If southerners in the past were reluctant to be critical of religious institutions, this appears not to be so today. On a battery of items in the survey tapping attitudes of the unchurched toward churches and synagogues—on matters of morality, social justice, sprituality and meaning, and acceptance of outsiders—the responses of the southern unchurched are as critical, and in some instances more so, as

Table 5 Privatized Religious Attitudes and Practices of the Churched and Unchurched by Region

	BELIEVE INDIVIDUAL SHOULD ARRIVE AT OWN BELIEFS INDEPENDENT OF CHURCH OR SYNAGOGUE		BELIEVE PERSON CAN BE A GOOD CHRISTIAN OR JEW WITHOUT ATTENDING CHURCH OR SYNAGOGUE		PRACTICE SPECIFIC MEDITATION TECHNIQUES	
	Percent	Difference	Percent	Difference	Percent	Difference
East						
Churched (N = 213)	50		82		7	
Unchurched (N = 171)	63	13	92	10	6	1
Midwest						
Churched (N = 237)	48		73		6	
Unchurched (N = 180)	64	16	88	15	8	2
West						
Churched (N = 103)	52		65		7	
Unchurched (N = 114)	76	24	95	30	10	3
South						
Churched (N = 210)	47		59		4	
Unchurched (N = 143)	65	18	83	24	11	7

those of nonsoutherners. This tendency across so wide a range of institutional characteristics casts doubt on any assumption that southerners are less prone to find fault with religious organizations. Clearly, southerners speak out when they disagree with institutional programs and activities as much as Americans anywhere.

Items reflecting privatized religiosity are especially interesting. On matters of how much autonomy an individual should have in arriving at personal belief and whether or not one must attend church or synagogue to be a good Christian or Jew, the gap between the churched and the unchurched is considerable. The gap is greatest in the West and next greatest in the South. And with respect to the practice of meditation techniques, the gap is largest in the South. The differences between churched and unchurched in the West on these issues are not so surprising, considering the mix of cultures in that region, but that such differences are also evident in the South—even more so than in the East or Midwest—is revealing. Certainly the findings shatter any notion that the South is less privatized in religious styles than other areas of the country, and they lead one to question the extent to which southerners are more bound by the coercive force of custom on religious matters than are residents of other regions.

In sum, there seem to be consistent patterns of differences between the two constituencies across the regions. The patterns hold for a wide range of traditional and nontraditional beliefs and practices. There is considerable diversity in southern religious belief and practice, a diversity that defies simple generalizations and stereotypes. Whatever the homogeneity of the past, religious heterogeneity is very much a reality in the contemporary South.

Turning from religious to broad cultural styles, one is led to ask if there is a growing cultural gap today between the churched and unchurched. One theory that has commanded widespread attention in recent years suggests that there are two diverging cultures in contemporary America—the traditional, theistic, churched culture versus a more secular unchurched culture. The two populations appear to differ not only in social experience and location in society, but also in outlook, values, and life-styles.[11] To determine conclusively whether this is true, and if so, to what extent, would require more extensive data than are presently available. But the Gallup survey of unchurched Americans did include two sets of indicators pertinent to the question—data on patterns of friendship and of values. An examination of these yields some clues about the growing cultural divergence.

For any culture or subculture to persist, social interaction is critically important. Interaction within the group is essential to generating and transmitting a distinct way of life. The survey included three questions about the sources of the respondent's friendships (see Table 6). Not surprisingly, the churched and unchurched differ greatly in their attachments to their local communities and to their churches or synagogues. But the regional variations are surprising: in the West and South the divergences are large; in the Midwest and East they are somewhat less so. In the West and South the churched and unchurched apparently each have a greater tendency to limit their interaction with others to persons like themselves. In their friendships and close social networks, the two groups tend to travel in quite different circles. Hence it is altogether plausible that the differing social networks of the two groups help to sustain their distinct cultural styles.

The survey also examined several "New Morality" values, including attitudes toward abortion, sexual freedom, and drug usage (see Table 7). Again there were predictable differences between the two populations: the churched espoused more traditional views than the unchurched and were more opposed to the new values. Differences in values for the churched and unchurched were observed in all four regions, but they were greatest in the West, moderate in the East and South, and least in the Midwest. Generally, in attitudes toward morality, as in friendship networks, cultural differences between the churched and unchurched in the South are about equal to, if not greater than, those of the Midwest and East. The contrasting cultural styles are about as prominent in the South as anywhere else except the West.

Thus, there is evidence in support of a twin-culture hypothesis. Interactional and cultural differences are strongest in the West, but even elsewhere—including in the South—the gap between the churched and unchurched is substantial. Throughout America the two constituencies differ in social networks, value commitments, and life-styles. Differences between the two subcultures are probably

Table 6 Friendship Patterns of the Churched and Unchurched by Region

	ALL OR MOST CLOSE FRIENDS IN LOCAL COMMUNITY		ALL OR MOST CLOSE FRIENDS ATTEND A CHURCH OR SYNAGOGUE		ALL OR MOST CLOSE FRIENDS ATTEND OWN CHURCH OR SYNAGOGUE	
	Percent	Difference	Percent	Difference	Percent	Difference
East						
Churched (N = 213)	45		55		25	
Unchurched (N = 171)	46	1	14	41	11	14
Midwest						
Churched (N = 237)	60		62		25	
Unchurched (N = 180)	51	9	20	42	10	15
West						
Churched (N = 103)	57		65		34	
Unchurched (N = 114)	38	19	14	51	0	34
South						
Churched (N = 210)	54		70		38	
Unchurched (N = 143)	41	13	25	50	15	23

Table 7 "New Morality" Values of the Churched and Unchurched by Region

	PERCENTAGE APPROVING LEGAL ABORTION FOR MARRIED WOMEN	PERCENTAGE REGARDING EXTRAMARITAL SEX AS ALWAYS WRONG	PERCENTAGE THAT WOULD WELCOME MORE ACCEPTANCE OF SEXUAL FREEDOM	PERCENTAGE THAT WOULD WELCOME MORE ACCEPTANCE OF MARIJUANA USAGE	MEAN DIFFERENCE
East					
Churched (N = 213)	49	75	23	13	
Unchurched (N = 171)	73	49	42	29	21.3
Midwest					
Churched (N = 237)	45	80	14	7	
Unchurched (N = 180)	55	63	29	22	14.3
West					
Churched (N = 103)	36	85	16	5	
Unchurched (N = 114)	71	57	47	39	32.0
South					
Churched (N = 210)	31	80	13	9	
Unchurched (N = 143)	50	63	35	26	18.8

greater than those between the regions, which is itself interesting and provocative.

Taken as a whole, the results of the 1978 Gallup survey provide a profile of the southern unchurched similar in many crucial respects to the unchurched of the rest of the nation. Some distinctive southern features remain, but by and large the unchurched across the nation share much in common—religiously and culturally. Admittedly, this is only a single survey, and far more inquiry will be needed before one can speak definitively about the unchurched. And certainly there is not yet sufficient evidence to answer the fundamental question that inspired this essay, namely whether the cultural bonds between southerners and religion are breaking. Yet, the data at hand are suggestive and prompt some reflections about the study of southern religion.

Increasingly, religious developments within the region must be viewed in the context of the social and cultural changes occurring throughout the nation. This is not to deny the peculiarities and distinctive qualities of southern religion nor the fact that much of the heritage remains. Rather, it is to focus attention on those points at which regional religious trends parallel those elsewhere in the nation. There may be, as John Shelton Reed says, an "enduring South," but it is not static or unchanging.[12] Investigators are called upon to identify those features of southern religion now coming into line with national patterns and to put forward explanations for why some aspects of southern religion change and others lag far behind. No longer can an intact southern religious culture be simply assumed.

Whatever the continuities in southern religion, there are significant changes occurring as a result of broad cultural shifts in the nation as a whole. There is a growing cleavage between traditional values and more secular values, a cleavage that could be of increasing significance in American life. There are growing trends toward greater individualism, more personal freedom, and increased tolerance of diversity, especially among younger and more-educated Americans. Diffusion of these values into many sectors of society is occurring, as Daniel Yankelovich has pointed out.[13] Self-fulfillment and the achievement of a personal, satisfying life-style are major goals of Americans, goals in keeping with the trend toward greater privatization in religious commitment. At the same time, the rise of the new Christian Right and the deep involvement of such organizations as the Moral Majority in political and social issues suggest that traditional values and life-styles continue to have strong appeal. The results are a clash over moral and religious convictions and a greater cultural polarization. The cleavage is at the heart of American life, over matters of personal ethics and life-styles.

The religious future of the nation will likely be closely linked to this cultural clash. Unless the mainline religious institutions can forge a new synthesis of religiocultural meanings and thereby bridge the cultural gap emerging, even greater polarization may lie ahead. Too close identification of the churches with traditional values and life-styles may intensify the cleavage between the churched and the unchurched; possibly the churches will come to embody and symbolize the rift between two increasingly distinct cultures—one inside the churches and the other outside. Even if polarization does not intensify to this extent, it is hard to imagine a religious climate in America in the years ahead not characterized by greater diversity and personal choice. Privatization and pluralization are basic trends in the culture that are not likely to be reversed by the conservative religious resurgence so prominent in the America of the present day.

It may even be that diversity and choice will in time become more apparent in the South than in some other parts of the country. Already the region is undergoing rapid social change not unlike developments in the West in an earlier period. In both regions, religious change has been linked closely to broader cultural change. Furthermore, in the South, as in the West, churchgoers are considerably more conservative than elsewhere—a fact that helps explain the cultural divergences between the churched and unchurched in these regions. Nonchurchgoers are also much more liberal in the West, further widening the gap separating the two populations in that region. Although this phenomenon is not yet as evident in the South, it is not inconceivable that trends will move in this direction in the future. If so, the South may soon become the region most ideally situated for studying cultural and religious polarization in America, in which case there will be little doubt that the cultural bonds linking southerners and religion will have broken.

NOTES

1. Joseph Fichter and George Maddox, "Religion in the South, Old and New," in John C. McKinney and Edgar T. Thompson (eds.), *The South in Continuity and Change* (Durham, N.C., 1965), 359.

2. Roger W. Stump shows, for example, that contrary to the predictions of convergence, regional differences in religious affiliation have increased during the twentieth century. See Stump, "Regional Divergence in Religious Affiliation in the United States," *Sociological Analysis*, XLV (Winter, 1984), 283–99. See also William M. Newman and Peter L. Halvorson, *Patterns in Pluralism: A Portrait of American Religion* (Washington, D.C., 1980).

3. James Davison Hunter, *American Evangelicalism: Conservative Religion and the Quandary of Modernity* (New Brunswick, N.J., 1983).

4. The most systematic examination of religion and modernity is found in Peter Berger's writings. See *The Sacred Canopy* (New York, 1967) and *The Heretical Imperative* (New York, 1979).

5. Major studies include Russell J. Hale, *Who Are the Unchurched?* (Washington, D.C., 1977); David Caplovitz and Fred Sherrow, *The Religious Drop-Outs* (Beverly Hills, 1977); and the special issue of the *Review of Religious Research* (XXI [Supplement, 1980]) entitled *The Unchurched American: A Second Look.*

6. Francis Butler Simkins, "The Rising Tide of Faith," in Louis D. Rubin, Jr., and James Jackson Kilpatrick (eds.), *The Lasting South: Fourteen Southerners Look at Their Home* (Chicago, 1957), 87–88.

7. For a review of this literature, see Fichter and Maddox, "Religion in the South, Old and New," in McKinney and Thompson (eds.), *The South in Continuity and Change*, 359–83.

8. Samuel S. Hill, Jr., "The South's Two Cultures," in Hill (ed.), *Religion and the Solid South* (Nashville, 1972), 54.

9. *Ibid.,* 54.

10. Details of the survey and major findings are reported in Gallup Organization, *The Unchurched American* (Princeton, 1978).

11. For a general discussion of the cultural-divergence hypothesis and an analysis of the Gallup survey, see Wade Clark Roof and Dean R. Hoge, "Church Involvement in America: Social Factors Affecting Membership and Participation," *Review of Religious Research*, XXI (Supplement, 1980), 405–26.

12. John Shelton Reed, *The Enduring South: Sub-Cultural Persistence in a Mass Society* (Chapel Hill, 1986).

13. Daniel Yankelovich, *New Rules: Searching for Self-Fulfillment in a World Turned Upside Down* (New York, 1981).

CONCLUSION
Samuel S. Hill

The South has the reputation of being a distinctive subculture within America—in religion as notably as in any other dimension. In an interpretative conclusion one must ask if these essays support that view. What do we learn about the culture from the ten essays singly? And what do we learn from the whole collection, which ideally should transcend the sum of its parts? Do these works confirm and enlarge the general reputation or prevailing view of the region? Or do they refute it? Or do they shift the ground of our understanding?

To investigate these questions, it helps to look at what the received scholarly tradition and the conventional wisdom would have us believe about the role of religion in southern culture. The first assumption that greets us is the homogeneity of popular religion in the region. "Fundamentalist" is the label most often applied. But even if that excessive description is made more accurate by insisting on "evangelical," the supposition persists that a limited sampling of Christianity—conservative Protestantism—dominates the scene. Moreover, the presence of black people's religion alongside white people's religion is thought to strengthen that characterization, not dilute it.

Second, the biracial nature of historic southern society is universally acknowledged as a crucial factor in the society's religious life, as much so as in any other aspect. The Christianization of Afro-Americans is known to be one of the great stories in the antebellum society. Black religion has been documented as serving several purposes; it has been seen as a force controlling the slaves, as an inspiration to overturning their oppressed condition, and as the central institution in black society following emancipation and the war—an amplification of its place in their lives during slavery.

The persistence of religious forms and preferences over a lengthy period is the third standard theme. The establishment of the Church of England during the colonial period gave way to the new American nation's radical experiment in religious liberty, but it also fell before the aggressions of a revivalistic evangelical Protestantism, Methodist

211

and Baptist especially. By the 1830s a southern tradition had set in, with the evangelical community embracing, in addition to the two largest groups, the Presbyterians and the newcomer Disciples of Christ movement. A few other denominations were also present— the Episcopal, Lutheran, Catholic, and Moravian, for example.

It is often assumed that things have changed little over the past century and a half, notwithstanding the emergence of several sectarian bodies among white and black Christians early in the twentieth century. This view is predicated partly on the judgment that the lower-class position of these sects prevented them from wielding much influence. Also, the opinion that there is not a great deal of difference between the "major" evangelical bodies and these "minor" evangelical bodies is fairly widespread. Actually, the differences between the traditional evangelical denominations and the newer Holiness, Pentecostal, Adventist, and Fundamentalist bodies are real and significant. But their presence simply extends the southern spectrum toward the left (toward the individualistic or immediatist), the direction in which its momentum had been moving anyway. What really distinguishes southern religious patterns from "northern" is their span from center to left (that is from Presbyterian to Fundamentalist) and the slight influence from the traditional Christianity, especially Roman Catholicism, that, with its gravitational pull to the right, makes the North's span wider.

Insulation, that is, the isolation of southern religion from outside influences that might challenge and flavor its ordinary view of things, is the fourth quality in its reputation. Religion does seem different in the South, an opinion held with curiosity and occasional distaste by outsiders and one proudly taken for granted by the region's faithful. Separate regional denominational bodies have been around since the 1840s to show that, even in settings where schism did not occur or has been overcome, certain peculiar features and attitudes have been apparent. From the inside this has worked against commitment to ecumenism. From the outside it has slowed down a person's making the transition from, say, being a Methodist in Philadelphia to being one in Atlanta. The largest of the regionally independent bodies has often been described as being more regional than denominational, more "southern" than "Baptist."

The preoccupation of the regional churches with issues of personal morality, in contrast to social ethics, contributes a fifth theme to the reputation of southern religion. This shows up most prominently in the issue of alcohol—its use and sale. But it may extend also to gambling, playing cards, moviegoing, and conduct on the sabbath. At any rate, the churches' view of responsibility is seen as a spirit of abstinence from and squeamishness about, rather than as involvement in, general social concerns, most notably racial discrimination. There are exceptions to this rule, but they are swamped by the churches' convictions about personal moral purity, something they foster by their outspoken enthusiasm for their favorite causes.

A final aspect of the South's religious reputation is its pervasive evangelicalism. Usually referred to (incorrectly) as Fundamentalism, this feature gives it the appearance of being anti-intellectual, exclusively emotional, and party to regional customs whether admirable or not. But the southern center of religious gravity is much closer to radical Christianity than to traditional, and the strength of the sects is considerable in the region. What is perceived, however, runs deeper than those observations; it is, namely, that southern religion cares more about "holding fast" than adapting or being responsive. It emits signals of maintaining its purity, of serving its own internal ends more than keeping up with the changes in thought and policy suggested by the onset of the problems and positions associated with modernity. To put the point another way, southern religion appears to be more concerned with itself and its own preservation than with human need and the problems of contemporary society. It is thought to cling to an outmoded world view and to be an obstacle in the path of progress: quaint and charming, perhaps, but not a responsive, progressive force in a society beset by confounding novelties.

Glancing at the assumptions widely held about southern religion is instructive. But one needs to inquire whether the ten essays in this collection invite us to call those assumptions into question, perhaps even help us embark on new journeys into the field. Are there fresh angles of vision here? Are there novel emphases? Are there elements in the southern religious tradition held before us that we have not previously been disposed to see (owing perhaps to a myopia that accompanies its general reputation)? Are there perspectives not usually employed that will open up the subject for significant reappraisal?

Let me suggest a couple of fresh angles or new emphases that might be tested by way of loosening up preconceptions. One is that the history of southern religion is as much a series of new beginnings, even of revolutionary changes, as it is a continuity. Actually, the case is rather easily made, especially when the region's own history and culture are allowed to set the context rather than having general American historical patterns imposed upon it. This is surely a more equitable and accurate way of studying a culture, after all, than assessing it prescriptively.

To begin with, a change of far-reaching importance occurred between the 1740s and 1800, a period when European social values gave way to American ones. Not only was establishment outlawed, but the egalitarian aspirations of the plain people resulted in a preference for Methodist and Baptist forms, as aristocracy bowed to democracy.

This motion toward openness, ironically, came to squeeze out certain people and to enthrone a new dogmatic aristocracy by the 1830s. The same southern evangelical Christian community that had thrown off control seventy-five years earlier now insisted on controlling. Slavery and sectionalism crystallized into a firmness that society had never known before. Informally, the hold of conservative Protestant thought grew very tight, a fact made more impressive by the absence of any rival claimants.

A true social revolution took place in the months and years following emancipation and the war. The Afro-American sector of the population, given the chance to form independent, self-controlled churches, did so with incredible speed. And they did it in spite of white Christian pressure to perpetuate the arrangements fashioned under slavery, in particular to keep the freedmen inside the old denominational structures. But the occasion was ripe for a major transformation, not only with respect to autonomy, but also with respect to giving full expression to black worship, preaching, music, and sociability, which in the old regime had to some extent been limited to clandestine settings. Long before the 1950s and 1960s, when black religion was heard from by the entire American society, its emergence as a major cultural and religious form bespoke a revolution, a new creation, a fresh religious and social resource.

In both the black and white communities of southern society around 1900, another new departure erupted, to which David Edwin

Harrell's essay points. Before the 1890s the choices for denominational participation for the great majority were limited to Baptist, Methodist, and Presbyterian, with the Campbellite tradition (itself diverse) accessible in some areas. Two decades later, the latter had broken apart into the liberal Disciples of Christ denomination and the conservative Churches of Christ.

The Churches of Christ brotherhood acquired a life of its own and developed a regional strength from middle Tennessee and northern Alabama to sections of Arkansas, Oklahoma, and Texas. In its turn, the old Methodist tradition had given rise to several new sanctification-minded and spirit-endowed movements, those that came to be classified as Holiness and Pentecostal. These indigenous sectarian communities grew rapidly and spread widely, to a point where they number several million and are inclusive of black and white constituencies that range in social class from the poor to the substantial middle class.

It is somewhat novel to describe the history of religion in the South as dotted with discontinuities, new departures, and even revolutions. But such a description does fuller justice to the facts. Seeing things this way is partly a question of context. Compared with what took place in New England with the in-migration of Catholics from the 1830s on, or in western New York State upon the appearance of the Mormons, Adventists, revivalism, communitarianism, and the like, the South's shift seems quite undramatic. But compared with the remarkable equilibrium of nineteenth-century evangelical domination, the proliferation of options available in the South by 1910 or 1920 adds up to a transformation.

As if to underscore that point, the 1980s disclose a radically diverse regional evangelical community, with Fundamentalism having arrived at a position of strength, black Pentecostalism a major social force, and the Churches of Christ expanded into a fellowship with 1.25 million adherents.

A second fresh angle or new emphasis is the interaction between black and white in the South, both between people and between their respective forms of Christianity. Historically, interaction is simply a fact. At another level and on the current scene, this feature exists as a resource. White Christians and black Christians who are looking for means to revise or revitalize their religious life can look to each other. In other words, both blacks and whites have made basic contributions to the South's brand(s) of Christianity, and they continue to be present, potentially, to and for each other. One of the major revisions brought about by the civil rights revolution is often overlooked, namely, that while a brace of distinctive cultures persists in the region, each has friendlier access to the qualities of the other that it may wish to learn from or incorporate.

As more evidence is discovered, we are learning that the presence of blacks helped make, or even made, southern evangelicalism what is was. Donald G. Mathews has argued this interpretation forcefully. Even if he has gone somewhat too far in his conclusion, he has successfully drawn our attention to a rather obvious condition that has been easy to overlook.

In the antebellum South, blacks and whites were in church together, under the same roof, a part of the same congregation. When Baptists and Methodists met to worship, they sang. The kind of singing they did elicited hearty participation. When that happens, people cannot help but hear, even listen to, the sounds being made. Rhythm, inflection, and volume have their effects, and those qualities of black music-making contributed to the white-chosen, white-led, and white-"orchestrated" singing. A white worshiper may have been held back, been inspired, or been forced to note the contrast. He may even have wished those other people were not there. But he always knew they were.

Baptist and Methodist evangelicals listen to something else—sermons and prayers. Sometimes blacks preached or led the congregation in prayer. But at all times their articulated groanings and exclamations, their outspoken participation, were a feature of the service. Occasionally an owner would instruct his slave to keep silent during the service—but that very action highlighted the slave's audible presence.

Concerning the exclusion of blacks by whites in church services and activities, we have long known about segregated seating and separate entrances. The slaves came forward to the (Methodist) altar rail at a different time than the whites. Blacks were assigned different standards and grades of church membership, and occasionally these were rather lenient or expansive. In all, making provision for the membership and participation of blacks, whether and when to include and exclude, took considerable thought and planning.

Thus, in both negative and positive ways, black people, their vibrant presence and the servitude that defined their condition, contributed significantly to forging a southern evangelical tradition. By any fair account, blacks have done much to make southern evangelicalism what it is.

It follows that future studies of southern religion will need to see the two peoples as one, more often interactive than separated, in the context of the Old South. More work remains to be done on slave religion and on the religious life of the free blacks when slavery was the lot of most. However, we are still in the early stages of the study of the independent, separate black church movement that erupted following emancipation and ultimately claimed such a prominent place in southern society. Irrespective of period, acute historiography will need to concentrate more heavily on the common sources and interaction of white and black religion in the South.

The ten essays presented in this collection point to the surprises and challenges that greet investigators of the South's religious life, and thus they revise our agendas and perspectives somewhat. Specifically, they draw our attention to the significance of forces and factors we have heretofore either not known about or have pushed to the outskirts of our awareness. By seeing them all in their considerable diversity, we can find in each essay more than it intended to say by itself. Comparing them in clusters of two or three is especially illuminating.

The period around 1900 was, as noted before, a formative one in southern religious life. An equilibrium that had held for nearly a century was upset by new forces and the creation of new options. The rural and mountain poor took the initiative to ensure an indigenous church life for themselves. Harrell's essay outlines that development. However, two other, dramatically different movements were occurring at about the same time, as disclosed by Ralph E. Luker's work on an Episcopal theological enterprise and by J. Wayne Flynt's research into social gospel ministries being carried out by the churches.

Harrell concludes that the 1890s were a watershed in the evolution of plain-folk religion between 1835 and 1920. In the older denominations the Cumberland Presbyterians continued after 1906 but only after the loss of 51 percent of their membership to the southern Presbyterian body. In the same year the Churches of Christ, an informal network of like-minded independent congregations, went their own way, along a quite divergent path from their Disciples of Christ kinsmen. Among Baptists, the Landmark tradition resurged, basing its destiny on a direct succession of Baptist churches from the time of Christ and the apostles. Methodism spawned the Holiness movement, though not by intention, of course. But highlander Wesleyans rejected formalism, organization, and respectability in favor of vitality, perfectionism, and a setting in which they were at home. All these movements, plus Pentecostalism, siphoned off a sizable proportion of the membership of denominations that once had been home for the ordinary people but had grown large, centrally organized, and concerned with respectability. As Harrell reveals, the religious poor proceeded to take care of themselves. Inferior they might appear to others but certainly not to God. He had a haven and a calling for them, and they determined to find it.

That is how it was among a million or more of the southern plain folk—the poor and the dispossessed, blacks as well as whites. But on the top of a Tennessee mountain not far at all from Cleveland and Nashville, centers of plain-folk movements on the ascendancy, the Reverend Dr. William Porcher DuBose was formulating an Episcopal-style theology. His work at Sewanee brought to new heights a low-country tradition of South Carolina aristocracy begun by James Warley Miles, the Charleston Transcendentalist. Little is gained by seeing DuBose as uncaring toward the plain folk, just as reality is short-changed by sentimentalizing the achievements of the dispossessed. Yet, Sewanee is far removed from nearby Cleveland. DuBose worked out an interpretation of Christian meaning grounded in the Incarnation, in God's becoming flesh in Jesus of Nazareth, by way of contrast with the Atonement theology of most Protestants, who lifted up Christ's death as the heart of the message.

What is striking about the information Luker provides is the originality and exportability of DuBose's work. He fashioned a revised version of Anglican thought and a radical vision of Christianity that was, to say the least, different from the convictions of his various evangelical and sectarian neighbors. And it sold elsewhere. Anglicans and other Christians, as well as Episcopalians, read and studied the creative theological work of this son of the South—a man no more and no less its child than the Holiness, Pentecostal, and Churches of Christ leadership.

Wayne Flynt's combings of the religious life of Alabamians, only one hundred to three hundred miles south of Sewanee, during the same season reveals still another dimension. Social gospel ministries claimed the serious attention of a number of Christians. DuBose's confrere in Montgomery, the Reverend Edgar Gardner Murphy, was a major force in guiding the church to addressing social ills and human distress that appeared in the new industrial age. Baptists and Methodists, too, were engaging in direct social reform. All of these Christians saw and in various ways sought to ameliorate the conditions of poverty, urban and rural deprivation, child labor, the convict lease system, and much more. Exploitation and need were concerns their Christ asked them to share with him. They usually rooted all this in the evangelical message, but they identified many more social ills than did their later colleagues, who devoted nearly exclusive attention to a single cause, prohibition.

The years before and after 1900 were, thus, many-layered for southern religion. While it was a time of institutional maturation for the traditional denominations, novel developments such as liberal theology, plain-folk movements, and social gospel activities reflected the vigor of other sectors. All of them must be part of the picture of these decades between Reconstruction and the South's economic and political reintegration into the national culture during the eras of the New Deal and World War II.

The essays by Harrell, Luker, and Flynt suggest the role of geography in the study of southern religion. Although not determinative, it is a factor requiring far more detailed attention than it has usually received. For one thing, a kind of southern "burned-over district" appeared in the southern highlands, especially on the slopes of the western side. In his essay John Boles shows us that the Mississippi-Louisiana area differed somewhat from the states of the Atlantic seaboard and the Upper South. In particular, his research suggests that black and white members of biracial congregations in that area were often nearly equal in the eyes of the church. The Old Southwest seems to have permitted slaves more participation and more rights than other parts of the South. At any rate, mutual participation was often rather advanced. Slaves could count on reasonably fair treatment in church judicial matters and were even given the right to testify to the wrongdoings of their (white) fellow parishioners.

While noting that a moderate amount of intraregional diversity prevailed in the Old South (and has since that time as well), we must underscore how naturally our ten research scholars have written about "the South" as a single social and historical unit. The roots of that feature of regional life trace back, of course, to the southern sectionalism that had emerged by 1820 and the separate nation the South was from 1861 to 1865. These roots are all associated with slavery, the forcefully generative power of which is a subject of the essays by Clarence Goen, Randall Miller, and Richard Rubenstein. It infused far more aspects of regional culture than anyone intended, and resulted in more consequences than anyone could have imagined.

Goen's "Scenario for Secession" impresses the reader with (among other messages) the agenda-setting power of sectionalism and slavery for the three major denominations. Previously parts of national bodies, they divided along regional lines and over specifically regional issues. One wonders how much earlier than 1844 (for Methodists), 1845 (for Baptists), and 1861 (in the Presbyterian case) anyone would have predicted such severe sundering. As Goen notes, the revivalism that all used as technique for their expansion contained an associative impulse. Also, in the Methodist and Presbyterian cases especially, a strong sense of churchliness, of catholicity, might have been expected to hold congregations and judicatories together. In all three cases a common commitment to missions and educational tasks could have restrained any temptation to travel on separate paths. The fact of the matter is that such sentiments did not prevail. The formation of regional bodies accompanied regional causes, loyalties, friendships, networks, and traditions; chronologically, they came very early. Social, political, and economic factors overrode ecclesiastical convictions and recollections of cooperation. In other words, theology took a subordinate position to cultural identity.

Miller's essay dramatizes the generative power of sectionalism and slavery in quite a different way by telling the story of Catholics in the Old South. Like Methodists and Presbyterians, the South's Catholics opted for sectional values. Part and parcel of the society as the evangelical denominations were, their collapsing of Christian virtues and regional values into a single sacred-secular whole was, perhaps, somewhat natural. By contrast, one might suppose that Catholics would have been listening to a different drummer and have pursued a divergent course, maybe even quite resolutely.

In truth, the pressure on the South's small number of Catholics to conform was not less, only different. They longed for acceptance. Easily regarded as aliens and curiosities, and even as a dangerous force, they worked hard to adapt to their cultural environment. Their alignment with the regional cause lifted them from the fringe of regional society to a position of improved acceptability. In order to achieve this gain, they did not have to trade in Catholic faith for evangelical, but they did need to concede that slavery was a fact of life, an economic necessity, and on the whole a general benefit. The Catholic Church, hierarchy and laity alike, supported southern sectionalism. Energy that might have been invested in eradicating slavery was redirected to preserving Catholic identity. Such was the tenacious power of sectionalism and slavery over a minority community that belonged to an organization that far transcended the American South.

The grip of regional uniqueness outlasted the primary period—the antebellum era—and even its intense aftermath—Reconstruction—as well as the era of the New South and that of the Great Depression and beyond. It has in fact managed to inform the ongoing imagination and mythology of the southern people into our own time. Richard Rubenstein's interpretation of William Styron's novel *Sophie's Choice* points to the staying power of the image of slavery.

Rubenstein judges that, as in the case of *The Confessions of Nat Turner,* slavery, not the Holocaust, is the central theme of this novel of Styron's. At one level, Styron has the money inherited by his protagonist of the 1940s traceable to the sale of a slave in the 1840s. Deeper down, the novelist, a Tidewater Virginian, has to come to moral grips with the Holocaust of his own lifetime in some kind of connection with the system of slavery that permeated his society a century earlier. In coming to terms with it, he sees how much less severe slavery was than the Holocaust. He is thus constrained to deal justly with each of these enormities of the human enterprise. In doing so, he both discriminates between and correlates them. For Styron, so Rubenstein invites us to believe, the generative power of slavery persists as a mighty force of the imagination. It is probably the case that no other interpreter of the Holocaust has seen it by reference to his own American culture's history. In short, slavery lives.

As if to confirm U. B. Phillips' contention that the South's biracial character is the central theme of its history, another pair of essays, those by C. Eric Lincoln and John Boles, treat the religion of slaves and of southern blacks generally. The nature and the forcefulness of sectionalism and slavery created two distinctive forms of Christianity, both of which exemplify Protestant Christianity and, at that, evangelical Protestantism. The presence of blacks contributed heavily to making southern evangelicalism what it was. But the interaction between the two racial cultures went beyond that achievement. It gave rise to two religious cultures, so similar, yet so different. Lincoln and Boles endeavor to highlight the complexity of one of them, black religion, as an entity in its own right.

Boles's research guided him to the conclusion that blacks' religion was circumscribed by its very interaction with whites. Yet, the two races heard the same sermons, held membership in the same congregations, and participated in the same church business meetings. In the setting of Deep South church life, the slaves came as close to experiencing equality as they did in any part of their lives. Being a vital part of church provided a sense of purpose; it also implanted something of a revolutionary spark that occasionally was ignited.

Lincoln's approach takes him in other directions entirely. He places the historical development of black people in the service of interpreting their recent condition in American society. He sees their heritage as a much more nationally coherent, less regional force, especially in religion. Life in the northern states, not alone the storied lot of blacks in the South, is a vital ingredient. He discovers a kind of unity to the black church; at least, North and South are not dominant factors. With roots in the establishment of distinctiveness in the decades before the 1960s, the black church continued to be an important ethnic instrument. Once dominantly theological and spiritual in its impact, the black church has been partly taken over by sociological factors. How better can blackness be safeguarded from erosion and perpetuated intact than by ever-present black religious institutions?

This ironic twist to the black Christian heritage—there is more to it than its strictly religious self-understanding—is enlarged by what

Lincoln refers to as its replication of the white experience in ecclesiastical matters. While a force for unity in certain respects, the black church has been subdivided by schism. Black Baptists, Methodists, and Pentecostals come in a variety of shapes and sizes—National Baptists in at least three forms, Methodist Episcopal churches in three major bodies, and Pentecostals who are "by Faith," "in Christ," and the like. Lincoln believes that this fracturing of the black community in, of all places, the church, is not a function of theological concerns or even of political differences. Rather, he attributes the proliferation of black Christian bodies to "human and psychological" factors—to a replication of the white experience and to the fact of variety within the American black community. Most poignantly of all, the dearth of opportunities for leadership among American blacks has made quite a number of them ambitious to become leaders. Behavior driven by ambition helps account for the conflicts that have arisen within black Christian organizations and for the appearance of a number of powerful figures in the black church.

Perhaps Boles's analysis of the place of blacks in the biracial churches of the Old South tilts toward the sentimental and Lincoln's depiction of the lot of blacks in recent America is too grim. Or perhaps not. At any rate, these two perspectives demonstrate that black religion has a complex character. It is winsomely pure in certain aspects. It exhibits the typical human accommodation to external forces in other aspects. Withal, these two scholars provide quite different views of the meaning of black religion, a result that accords with the nature of black religion itself.

The interaction between religion and social change in the South—the impact of social change on the South's religion and vice versa—is the final theme of these essays that we will glance at. The Goen essay on the schisms that disrupted the major denominations along regional lines late in the antebellum period swings in both directions, clarifying the two-way interaction between religion and social change. Obviously, the vortex of forces active in the nation's political and economic life were being felt in religion. Disputes over the legality and legitimacy of slavery could hardly be kept outside the churches. Directly connected was the struggle over the relative positions of the federal and the state governments. Unmistakably, the secular was having an impact on the sacred in the religious life of the antebellum

South. But what is striking is the power with which forces also moved the other way. The decision by the Methodists and Baptists to form regionally separate organizations contributed to the establishment of the South as a separate nation in 1861. It was a harbinger of things to come; far more, it showed the South that having its own organization, accountable to no outsiders and thus its own to control, was both feasible and beneficial. This splintering of the major social organization of the South and the nation, as Goen puts it, weakened the Union and helped cause the final split between North and South.

In his essay on the electronic church—the television ministries of the past decade that have promoted conservative religion in league with conservative politics—William Martin shows how low are the walls that separate South and North in our own era, walls that were once very high. Evangelicals of the revivalist-moralist sort and Fundamentalists representing evangelical extremism have taken up the charge to transform the nation. Earlier, such people abstained from direct assaults on an evil society and on organized programs to revolutionize it, preferring to stay busy doing evangelism. Fundamentalism, largely a northern phenomenon, incidentally, viewed such involvements as contrary to their calling, as compromise with a wicked world. By partial contrast, southern revivalism was at home in its culture and provided both "good people" and moral influence for the public realm. It was not often politically activist, however.

The emergence of the Moral Majority, the Christian Broadcasting Network, Jimmy Swaggart's empire, and other television ministries reflects a veritable conversion. In these circles the church is regarded as an agent of change. Although by no means a predominantly southern movement in either leadership or following, the electronic church has strong ties and appeal to the South and some roots in it. To the degree that southern Christians are taking up this kind of religion and connecting it with untraditionally conservative politics, they have embarked on a national crusade. In any case Martin is writing about the church as agent of change.

How different, yet how similar, was the church as an agent of change in Wayne Flynt's South, specifically Alabama, between 1890 and 1920. The South's "industrial evolution" had wrought considerable havoc and dislocation in the formerly agrarian society. Episcopalians and Presbyterians, as well as Baptists and Methodists, heeded the call to reach out to stop human misery and exploitation. Through eleemosynary institutions, welfare capitalism, legislative reforms, health services, and much more, the churches determined to improve things in an unsettled society. And some of it was directed toward the structures of society, quite beyond the "personal ethics" approach that has so long typified southern evangelicalism.

Flynt's analysis also demonstrates the impact of "secular" changes on the "sacred" realm. The churches could not be blind to the new conditions that enveloped their members and others in their communities. A religious tradition that had preferred leaving secular matters to their own course or to other agencies was responsive to new employment patterns and to the clustering of people in towns and cities. Initially, it did not set the new agenda; however, looking about, it saw tasks crying out for attention and took them up.

Wade Clark Roof's essay on the unchurched in the South sets our sights on another way in which the church responds to change. Secular ways of thinking have made deep inroads into southern society. The elements within modernity that make traditional belief implausible or unattractive are part of the national scene, and the South is not excluded. In fact, Roof finds that two basic trends in the national culture, privatization and pluralization, are just that—national in scope. In the South, where the church is omnipresent and always an influence to be reckoned with, criticism of the church by the unchurched is quite vigorous. Even making allowances for the fact that the proportion of southerners without church membership has always been substantial, one can only conclude that the conditions prevailing in modern Western culture have crossed the boundary and made their mark on the most evangelical society in Christendom. The factors may differ somewhat between the South and the rest of the nation, but the resultant condition makes the two areas nearly indistinguishable. More than ever before in its history, the American South is a participant in the currents of thought that are informing Western civilization.

Thus, there seems to be a correlation between the theme of cultural unity in the midst of notable diversity and the fact that the whole of this volume transcends the sum of its parts. By having ten essays before us at once, we are granted more insight into southern religion than a simple addition of disparate pieces could have provided.

Southern culture is marked by religious momentum and has been since the 1870s and 1880s. Evangelical Protestantism, a movement characterized by great momentum, achieved dominance by 1830. Because it placed itself in the service of regional causes and crises, it was relatively inert for half a century. But ever since evangelicalism regained its momentum, it has been busy and aggressive, converting the lost, purifying an imperfect church, and going forth to transform the world.

The basic style of southern evangelicalism is indeed to rekindle, constantly rekindle, vital faith in every person and generation. We scholars of the tradition have begun to take southern religious people more at their own word with respect to what they think they are saying, believing, and doing, that is, with respect to what their intentions are. The scholarship of the immediate future must continue to honor them and their self-characterizations. Recognition of that will foster an enlarged and advanced effort toward understanding the religion of the American South.

The authors of this volume, singly and together, show us how truly diverse southern religion is. Their research also suggests that the South as a distinctive American culture has existed for a long time and that the cultural entity is larger than the parts of which it is the sum. Accordingly, the study of religion in the South, now such a promising enterprise, must operate dialectically—back and forth between "the South" and the numerous parts that make it up. One may presuppose the former but must never overlook the latter.

THE CONTRIBUTORS

JOHN B. BOLES is professor of history at Rice University in Houston.

J. WAYNE FLYNT is professor of history at Auburn University, Auburn, Alabama.

CLARENCE C. GOEN is professor of church history at the Wesley Theological Seminary in Washington, D.C.

DAVID EDWIN HARRELL, JR., is University Scholar and chairman of the Department of History at the University of Alabama in Birmingham.

SAMUEL S. HILL is professor of religion at the University of Florida in Gainesville.

C. ERIC LINCOLN is professor of religion at Duke University, Durham, North Carolina.

RALPH E. LUKER is assistant editor of the Martin Luther King, Jr., Papers at the Martin Luther King, Jr., Center in Atlanta.

WILLIAM C. MARTIN is professor of sociology at Rice University in Houston.

RANDALL M. MILLER is professor of history and American studies at St. Joseph's University in Philadelphia.

WADE CLARK ROOF is professor of sociology at the University of Massachusetts, Amherst.

RICHARD L. RUBENSTEIN is Robert O. Lawton Distinguished Professor of Religion at Florida State University in Tallahassee.

SELECTED BIBLIOGRAPHY

Baer, Hans A. *The Black Spiritual Movement: A Religious Response to Racism.* Knoxville, 1984.

Bailey, David T. *Shadow on the Church: Southwestern Evangelical Religion and the Issue of Slavery, 1783–1860.* Ithaca, N.Y., 1985.

Bailey, Kenneth K. "Protestantism and Afro-Americans in the Old South: Another Look." *Journal of Southern History,* XLI (November, 1975), 451–72.

———. *Southern White Protestantism in the Twentieth Century.* New York, 1964.

Baker, Tod A., Robert P. Steed, and Laurence W. Moreland, eds. *Religion and Politics in the South: Mass and Elite Perspectives.* New York, 1983.

Bode, Frederick A. *Protestantism and the New South: North Carolina Baptists and Methodists in Political Crisis, 1894–1903.* Charlottesville, 1975.

Boles, John B. *The Great Revival, 1787–1805: The Origins of the Southern Evangelical Mind.* Lexington, Ky., 1972.

———. *Religion in Antebellum Kentucky.* Lexington, Ky., 1976.

———. "Religion in the South: A Tradition Recovered." *Maryland Historical Magazine,* LXXVII (December, 1982), 388–401.

Bolton, S. Charles. *Southern Anglicanism: The Church of England in Colonial South Carolina.* Westport, Conn., 1982.

Bruce, Dickson D., Jr. *And They All Sang Hallelujah: Plain-Folk Camp-Meeting Religion, 1800–1845.* Knoxville, 1974.

———. "Religion, Society and Culture in the Old South: A Comparative View." *American Quarterly,* XXVI (October, 1974), 399–416.

Campbell, Will D., *Brother to a Dragonfly.* New York, 1977.

Cobb, Buell E., Jr., *The Sacred Harp: A Tradition and Its Music.* Athens, Ga., 1978.

Cone, James. *For My People: Black Theology and the Black Church.* Maryknoll, N.Y., 1984.

Connelly, Thomas L. *Will Campbell and the Soul of the South.* New York, 1982.

Daniel, W. Harrison. "The Effects of the Civil War on Southern Protestantism." *Maryland Historical Magazine,* LXIX (Spring, 1974), 44–63.

Dinnerstein, Leonard, and Mary Dale Palsson, eds. *Jews in the South.* Baton Rouge, 1973.

Earle, John R., Dean D. Knudsen, and Donald W. Shriver. *Spindles and Spires: A Re-Study of Religion and Social Change in Gastonia.* Atlanta, 1976.

Eighmy, John Lee. *Churches in Cultural Captivity: A History of the Social Attitudes of Southern Baptists.* Knoxville, 1972.

Evans, Eli. *The Provincials: A Personal History of Jews in the South.* New York, 1976.

Farish, Hunter D. *The Circuit-Rider Dismounts: A Social History of Southern Methodism, 1865–1900.* Richmond, 1938.

Flynt, J. Wayne. "Dissent in Zion: Alabama Baptists and Social Issues, 1900–1914." *Journal of Southern History,* XXV (November, 1969), 523–42.

Friedman, Jean E. *The Enclosed Garden: Women in the Evangelical South.* Chapel Hill, 1985.

Goen, Clarence C. *Broken Churches, Broken Nation: Denominational Schism and the Coming of the American Civil War.* Macon, Ga., 1985.

Harrell, David E., Jr. *All Things Are Possible: The Healing and Charismatic Revivals in Modern America.* Bloomington, 1975.

——. *Quest for a Christian America: The Disciples of Christ and American Society.* Nashville, 1966.

——. *The Social Sources of Division in the Disciples of Christ 1865–1900.* Atlanta, 1973.

——. *White Sects and Black Men in the Recent South.* Nashville, 1971.

——, ed. *Varieties of Southern Evangelicalism.* Macon, Ga., 1981.

Hill, Samuel S. *The South and the North in American Religion.* Athens, Ga., 1980.

——. *Southern Churches in Crisis.* New York, 1966.

——, ed. *Encyclopedia of Southern Religion.* Macon, Ga., 1971.

——, ed. *On Jordan's Stormy Banks.* Macon, Ga., 1983.

——, ed. *Religion in the Southern States.* Macon, Ga., 1983.

Hill, Samuel S. *et al. Religion and the Solid South.* Nashville, 1972.

Holifield, E. Brooks. *The Gentlemen Theologians: American Theology in Southern Culture, 1795–1860.* Durham, N.C., 1978.

Isaac, Rhys. *The Transformation of Virginia, 1740–1790.* Chapel Hill, 1982.

Kane, Steven M. "Holy Ghost People: The Snake-Handlers of Southern Appalachia." *Appalachian Journal,* I (Summer, 1974), 255–62.

Kurtz, Ernest. "The Tragedy of Southern Religion." *Georgia Historical Quarterly,* LXVI (Summer, 1982), 217–47.

Kuykendall, John W. *Southern Enterprize: The Work of National Evangelical Societies in the Antebellum South.* Westport, Conn., 1982.

Lincoln, C. Eric. *Race, Religion, and the Continuing American Dilemma.* New York, 1984.

———, ed. *The Black Experience in Religion.* Garden City, N.Y., 1974.

Lippy, Charles H., ed. *Bibliography of Religion in the South.* Macon, Ga., 1985.

Loveland, Anne C. *Southern Evangelicals and the Social Order, 1800–1860.* Baton Rouge, 1980.

Luker, Ralph E. *A Southern Tradition in Theology and Social Criticism: The Religious Liberalism and Social Conservatism of James Warley Miles, William Porcher DuBose, and Edgar Gardner Murphy.* New York, 1984.

Martin, Robert F. "Critique of Southern Society and Vision of a New Order: The Fellowship of Southern Churchmen, 1934–1957." *Church History,* LII (March, 1983), 66–80.

Mathews, Donald G. *Religion in the Old South.* Chicago, 1977.

———. *Slavery and Methodism: A Chapter in American Morality, 1780–1845.* Princeton, 1965.

Miller, Randall M., and Jon L. Wakelyn, eds. *Catholics in the Old South: Essays on Church and Culture.* Macon, Ga., 1984.

Peterson, Thomas V. *Ham and Japheth: The Mythic World of Whites in the Antebellum South.* Metuchen, N.J., 1978.

Photiadis, John D., ed. *Religion in Appalachia.* Morgantown, W. Va., 1978.

Pope, Liston. *Millhands and Preachers: A Study of Gastonia.* New Haven, 1942.

Posey, Walter B. *Frontier Mission: A History of Religion West of the*

Southern Appalachians to 1861. Lexington, Ky., 1966.

Proctor, Samuel, and Louis Schmier, with Malcolm Stern, eds. *Jews in the South: Selected Essays.* Macon, Ga., 1984.

Raboteau, Albert J. *Slave Religion: The "Invisible Institution" in the Antebellum South.* New York, 1978.

Reed, John Shelton. *The Enduring South: Sub-Cultural Persistence in a Mass Society.* Chapel Hill, 1986.

Scott, Anne Firor. *The Southern Lady: From Pedestal to Politics, 1830–1930.* Chicago, 1970.

Shortridge, James R. "A New Regionalization of American Religion." *Journal for the Scientific Study of Religion,* XVI (June, 1977), 143–53.

Smith, H. Shelton. *In His Image, But . . . : Racism in Southern Religion, 1780–1910.* Durham, N.C., 1972.

Spain, Rufus B. *At Ease in Zion: A Social History of Southern Baptists, 1865–1900.* Nashville, 1967.

Sutton, Brett. *Primitive Baptist Vision Narratives.* Perspectives on the American South, I. New York, 1981.

Synan, Vinson. *The Holiness-Pentecostal Movement in the United States.* Grand Rapids, 1971.

Tatum, Noreen Dunn. *A Crown of Service: A Story of Women's Work in the Methodist Episcopal Church, South, from 1878–1940.* Nashville, 1960.

Thompson, Ernest Trice. *Presbyterians in The South.* 3 vols. Richmond, 1963–73.

Thompson, James J., Jr. *"Tried as by Fire": Southern Baptists and the Religious Controversies of the 1920s.* Macon, Ga., 1982.

Walker, Clarence E. *A Rock in a Weary Land: The African Methodist Episcopal Church During the Civil War and Reconstruction.* Baton Rouge, 1982.

Washington, Joseph R., Jr. *Black Religion: The Negro and Christianity in the United States.* Boston, 1964.

Wheeler, Edward L. *Uplifting the Race: The Black Minister in the New South, 1865–1902.* Washington, D.C., 1986.

Wilson, Charles Reagan. *Baptized in Blood: The Religion of the Lost Cause, 1865–1920.* Athens, Ga., 1980.

———, ed. *Religion in the South.* Jackson, Miss. 1985.

INDEX

Adams, Samuel M., 138–39
Adventists, 212, 215
African culture: in slave culture and religion, 95, 110; West Africa, 95–96; transplanted to American South, 97, 107–108; oral tradition, 106–107
African diaspora: and African culture, 58, 67; in Caribbean and South America, 68; and black church, 71
African Methodist Episcopal Church, 55–56, 111–12
African Methodist Episcopal Zion Church, 54–57, 59–60, 67, 111–12
Afro-American Christianity: its interaction with whites' religion, 95, 101–102, 108; influences on, 97; fusion of African and Christian concepts, 97–99; style of worship, 104–105, 107, 108–109, 112; leadership, 104–106, 110–11, 112; underground church, 106–107; role of religion in survival of slaves, 109–11; formation of all-black churches, 111–13
Afro-American culture, 97, 107–108
Afro-Americans: Christianization, 211–12; importance of religion to, 214; interaction with whites, 216, 222; impact on evangelicalism, 215–17; their Christian heritage, 222–23; leadership, 222–23
Alabama: Disciples of Christ, 38–39; Churches of Christ, 38–39, 215; and Populism, 140; work of Home Mission Board in, 143; campaign against child labor in, 148; church work among mine workers in, 153–54
Alabama Baptist, 139, 148
Allen, Richard: expulsion from St. George's Methodist Church, 53–54, 63, 67–68; and Free African Society, 54, 63; as pastor of Bethel African Methodist Episcopal Church, 54–55; as deacon and elder, 55–56; as bishop of African Methodist Episcopal Church, 55–56; favors Methodist polity, 62–63, 65, 67, 68
American Baptist Association, 35–36
Anderson, Robert M., 43–44
Angley, Ernest, 180
Anglican church, 52, 64–65
Anglicanism, 218
Arendt, Hannah, 89
Arkansas: Disciples of Christ, 38–39; Churches of Christ, 38–39, 215; mentioned, 32
Arminianism, 28–29
Armstrong, Ben, 172, 187–88
Assemblies of God: membership and economic assets, 41–42; Baptist influence on, 50; mentioned, 40
Atonement theology, 8, 163–64, 218
Avondale Mills, 152
Azusa Street meeting, 40

Bakker, Jim, 173–74
Banner, Lois, 13
Baptist and Commoner, 35
Baptist Association of Savannah, 53–54
Baptist Congress, 148–49
Baptists: growth of churches, 13–16; influence before Civil